Interactional Justice

Interactional Justice explores how defence lawyers accomplish their role in interaction with others and highlights the ways in which they do loyalty work – constructing and conveying loyalty in emotionally and interactionally constraining situations.

By drawing on extensive ethnographic fieldnotes and interviews with lawyers, this sociological study brings their loyalty work to life and reveals to the reader the unwritten rules of emotional interactions. It presents how defence lawyers socially construct their duty of loyalty by negotiating informal and implicit professional and social expectations. This accomplishment demands emotion work and face work in order to perform a role which includes defending clients accused of heinous crimes and "losing" the majority of cases. As the defence team is central to this, the ways of doing teamwork are illustrated. Teamwork is also found to be essential between legal professionals to ensure that a criminal trial runs smoothly. All of this takes place within an overarching framework – the emotional regime of law – which aims to uphold the illusionary dichotomy between rationality and emotionality thus quietening the role of emotions.

Loyalty and teamwork are features of many professions, workplaces, and aspects of social life making this book an essential tool for understanding strategies for their accomplishment. Focusing on courtroom emotions and interactions, the book suggests how trials can be made more user-friendly and provides guidance for newly qualified legal professionals. The use of ethnographic fieldnotes and interviews provides scholars and students in the social sciences, teaching, law, and medicine with a colourful monograph which reveals and explains emotion and interaction rules. It also makes this book a useful tool for teaching and understanding qualitative research methods.

Lisa Flower is a researcher and senior lecturer in sociology and criminology at Lund University, Sweden. Her research interests include the hidden emotion and interaction rules in courtrooms and the legal profession.

Routledge Studies in the Sociology of Emotions

Mary Holmes is a senior lecturer at the University of Edinburgh, UK
Julie Brownlie is a senior lecturer at the University of Edinburgh, UK

The sociology of emotions has demonstrated the fundamental and pervasive relevance of emotions to all aspects of social life. It is not merely another specialized sub-discipline; rather it aims to reconfigure bases of mainstream sociology. This book series will not only be of interest for specialists in emotions but to sociology at large. It is a locus for developing enhanced understandings of core problems of sociology, such as power and politics, social interactions and everyday life, macro-micro binaries, social institutions, gender regimes, global social transformations, the state, inequality and social exclusion, identities, bodies, and much more.

Love and Society
Special Social Forms and the Master Emotion
Swen Seebach

The Emotional Market
Capitalism, Consumption and Authenticity
Edited by Eva Illouz

Emotions in Late Modernity
Edited by Roger Patulny; Alberto Bellochi; Sukhmani Khorana; Rebecca Olson; Jordan McKenzie and Michelle Peterie

Love as a Collective Action
Latin America, Emotions and Interstitial Practices
Adrian Scribano

Interactional Justice
The Role of Emotions in the Performance of Loyalty
Lisa Flower

For more information about this series, please visit: https://www.routledge.com/sociology/series/RSSE

Interactional Justice

The Role of Emotions in the Performance of Loyalty

Lisa Flower

Routledge
Taylor & Francis Group
LONDON AND NEW YORK

First published 2020 by Routledge

2 Park Square, Milton Park, Abingdon, Oxfordshire OX14 4RN
52 Vanderbilt Avenue, New York, NY 10017

Routledge is an imprint of the Taylor & Francis Group, an informa business

First issued in paperback 2020

British Library Cataloguing-in-Publication Data
A catalogue record for this book is available from the British Library

Library of Congress Cataloging-in-Publication Data
Names: Flower, Lisa, author.
Title: Interactional justice: the role of emotions in the performance of loyalty / Lisa Flower.
Description: First Edition. | New York: Routledge, 2019. |
Series: Routledge studies in the sociology of emotions | Based on author's thesis (doctoral – Lund University, 2018) issued under title: Loyalty work: emotional interactions of defence lawyers in Swedish courtrooms. | Includes bibliographical references and index.
Identifiers: LCCN 2019033714 (print) | LCCN 2019033715 (ebook) | ISBN 9780367248796 (hardback) | ISBN 9780429284854 (ebook)
Subjects: LCSH: Defense (Criminal procedure)–Sweden–Psychological aspects. | Criminal defense lawyers–Sweden–Psychology. |
Loyalty. | Emotions.
Classification: LCC KKV4630.D43 F572019 (print) | LCC KKV4630.D43 (ebook) | DDC 345/.07–dc23
LC record available at https://lccn.loc.gov/2019033714
LC ebook record available at https://lccn.loc.gov/2019033715

ISBN: 978-0-367-24879-6 (hbk)
ISBN: 978-0-367-64721-6 (pbk)

Typeset in Bembo
by Deanta Global Publishing Services, Chennai, India

MIX
Paper from responsible sources
FSC™ C013985
FSC www.fsc.org

Printed in the United Kingdom
by Henry Ling Limited

For Martin, Daisy and Harriet

In loving memory of Alex and Nanny Strawberry

Contents

Acknowledgements

First and foremost, I would like to acknowledge Malin Åkerström and David Wästerfors who supervised my doctoral thesis upon which this book is based and who have been my sources of inspiration throughout. My thanks also go to Åsa Wettergren, Stina Bergman Blix, Terry Maroney, Susan Bandes, Susie Scott, Helena Flam, Carl-Göran Heidegren and Ann-Mari Sellerberg for their support and expert enthusiasm, feedback and advice.

Thank you to my mum, dad and sister as well as Lena, Jan-Erik, Lucy, Lorna, Liz, Rachel, Rachel, Anna, and Esther who have always encouraged me in my study of various -ologies.

My eternal thanks go to Martin – whose unwavering support and promises to make cake helped me write this book. Still waiting for that cake though.

And finally, I would like to thank Daisy and Harriet who have shown me that it is possible to argue about anything, an accomplishment that is both impressive and exhausting, yet who are the best kids I could ever wish for.

Chapter 1

Lawyers and loyalty

> The prosecutor asks the defendant how he came to be in possession of the stolen items, and the defendant claims that he bumped into an acquaintance who gave them to him. When asked to describe the acquaintance, the defendant claims he does not remember what he looked like or what he was wearing. When asked what the acquaintance is called, the defendant thinks a while and says, "Hmmmm, Erving." Coincidentally, this also happens to be the (very unusual) name of the defence lawyer. The prosecutor points out to the accused that in his police statement he stated that the acquaintance he bumped into was called Danny Diamond,[1] which the arresting police officer has also testified to. When asked why he was wearing plastic gloves at the time of his arrest, he replies that it was because he thought that the items could possibly be stolen and he didn't want to get his fingerprints on them therefore "Erving" gave him his plastic gloves along with the items.
>
> Throughout all of this, the defence lawyer stares, almost without blinking, at the prosecutor. His facial features do not move: no raised eyebrows, no shake of the head. He is still: glasses in hand, body turned fully towards the prosecutor, not looking at his client. (Fieldnote)

Defence lawyers are often associated by many outside the profession with cases considered to be controversial or emotionally laden, such as rape, murder or terrorism. Cases where passions abound. Indeed, all of the defence lawyers I interviewed in this book tell me that they have been asked the question, "how can you defend a rapist?" However, the everyday work of defence lawyers in Sweden typically entails far more mundane scenes such as the "Danny Diamond" depiction here taken from my fieldnotes of a theft trial: the defendant claims innocence in the face of overwhelming evidence, a claim which his defence lawyer is expected to loyally represent. This defence work is further complicated by the unpredictability of a criminal trial where the unexpected should be expected and crises should be managed in the moment. In the pages to come, I explore how defence lawyers accomplish their role in such emotionally and interactionally demanding situations and show how loyalty is constructed and conveyed in these performances.

My starting point is that emotions abound in all criminal trials, even the mundane "Danny Diamond" ones, and that, consequently, the management of emotions is integral to the role of a defence lawyer: irritation when a client says something damaging in the court, surprise when a witness says something unexpected, disgust towards gruesome evidence, moral outrage at a crime, or even dislike towards an unpleasant client. I am thus interested in revealing how defence lawyers accomplish their professional role, a role which is rooted in the legal obligation of loyal representation and a role which plays a vital part in the accomplishment of justice, together with the "objectivity work" (Jacobsson, 2008) of prosecutors and judges.

This role accomplishment is made more problematic as, whilst there are clear guidelines that outline the defence lawyers' professional obligations, how they should actually perform this role is not explicitly set out; rather, it is guided by invisible rules – implicit expectations and shared understandings. What makes this all the more analytically demanding is that the overarching emotion norms in law are aimed at ensuring that it is "protected from emotion's pernicious influence" (Maroney & Gross, 2014, p. 143; see also Maroney, 2006). This means that emotions should be displayed subtly (Bergman Blix & Wettergren, 2015).

The particular context of Sweden also brings with it interactional and emotional challenges for defence lawyers not least because defence lawyers interact directly with clients before and during trials – which includes sitting next to them in the courtroom – unlike in other countries where there is less direct interaction. Teamwork is therefore vital in building and conveying the defence team. Furthermore, the relative informality of the Swedish courtroom, devoid of ceremonial robes and gowns, also places demands on defence lawyers in order to convey the professionalism integral to their role.

By analysing how defence lawyers talk about the expectations they face in order to present themselves in an emotionally appropriate and polite manner, I uncover the rules guiding their role construction and performance. Throughout this book, I show how defence lawyers accomplish their role in the specific context of the emotionally and interactionally constraining criminal trial and I reveal the overarching framework which guides them – the emotional regime of law. In particular, I show how defence lawyers' performances convey their role obligations, which are centred on the principle of loyalty and which require emotion work, facework, and teamwork, that is, loyalty work. I suggest that this loyalty is a legal loyalty – a professional obligation which shapes emotions, client relationships, and loyalty hierarchies. Although my focus is on defence lawyers in Sweden, as loyalty is an inherent aspect of adversarial systems, the findings of this book are of relevance to other jurisdictions and, indeed, other professions and situations where the conveyance of loyalty is required. Furthermore, because emotional regimes are in place in other organisations and professions, such as within politics, education, and social services, the framework depicted here can be applied to other spheres.

Emotions and law

Within certain academic disciplines such as law, sociology, and criminology, emotions have customarily been viewed with suspicion (Karstedt, Loader, & Strang, 2011; Weber, 1978). Emotions have been considered to interfere with rational judgement; hence, whilst the involvement of emotions in law "is so obvious as to make its articulation seem almost banal" (Maroney, 2006, p. 120), the centrality of emotions is often stifled, overlooked, or rejected in order to lift the rationality of law. This means that emotions are often neglected, distorted, downright ignored, or displayed subtly in order to create the appearance of rationality (Bergman Blix & Wettergren, 2015, p. 3).

This predominant reluctance to lift the role of emotions stems from the perceived risk that acknowledging their centrality may lead to the law being viewed as biased – not equal and universal, but partial and particular – especially when it comes to criminal law and criminal trials (Bandes, 1999b; Miller, 1997). We do not want judges making decisions based on their personal emotions, morals, or values; rather, judgements should be based on the morals and values communicated through the law (Bornstein & Wiener, 2009; Nussbaum & Kahan, 1996; Solomon, 1999). We do not want cases to be won based on the strength of a lawyer's acting abilities but on the strength of the evidence (Murphy, 2002, p. 112).

The law has thus traditionally been viewed as a peculiar paradox of unemotional emotionality. Consequently, although it solves conflicts, and any conflict, legal or otherwise, inherently entails some kind of emotional engagement, the role of emotions tends to only be openly accepted with regard to certain aspects of law such as family law (Abrams & Keren, 2010; Collins, 2008; Flower, 2014; Karstedt, 2002). Emotions are also more readily associated with sentencing and punishment or perceived as belonging to the lay participants of a trial (Braithwaite, 1989; Dahl et al., 2007; Feigenson, 1997, 2016; Kaufmann et al., 2003; Nussbaum, 2004; Sarat, 1999; Wessel et al., 2006). Likewise, legal professionals are often associated with objectivity, which, in turn, has earlier implied the absence of emotions which are now being revealed (Bandes, 1999a; Bergman Blix & Wettergren, 2015; Jacobsson, 2008; Maroney, 2011a, 2011b; Roach Anleu & Mack, 2017).

Over the past few decades different disciplines have therefore opened up to findings from other research fields such as neuroscience showing the inseparability of rationality and emotionality, which has led to a greater acceptance for emotions' constant, conscious, or unconscious, presence even in legal and sociological research (Barbalet, 2001, 2002; Damasio, Everitt, & Bishop, 1996).

The current turn towards the global "emotionalization of law" (Karstedt, 2002, p. 299; see also Lange, 2002; Laster & O'Malley, 1996) acknowledges the institutional space of criminal courts and procedures as a central mechanism for emotions in society and has begun to explore entrenched interactional and emotional performances in the courtroom, which are the focus of this book.

The contemporary scientific interest in emotions does not mean that emotions should become the focal point or root cause of all interactions, but their presence and value should be recognised, along with the demands that are placed upon them in order to render them appropriate to the situation (Sieben & Wettergren, 2010). My starting point is thus similar to that of other scholars of emotions in the courtroom, namely that "[e]motion is inherent in all human behavior and is embedded in social interaction, including in the courtroom" (Roach Anleu, Rottman, & Mack, 2016, p. 69).

My focus in this book is on one particular legal actor, namely the defence lawyer and, even more precisely, their performances in the criminal courtroom. Defence lawyers constitute a category of legal professionals who have received relatively little sociological attention, in contrast to judges, for instance, and thus warrant deeper theoretical and empirical understanding.

My work thus builds on the relevant research from other countries regarding this professional group in order to describe their role accomplishment and depict the performances of defence lawyers in Sweden. I also draw on dramaturgical studies of courtroom interactions and emotions, thus developing the dramaturgical and emotional understanding of the Swedish context, where emotions should be muted and interactions are ordered. The current state of the art will be presented in chapter three.

In this way, my study completes the trinity of legal principle performances in the Swedish courtroom by adding to the current literature describing the emotional labour of prosecutors and judges in Sweden (Bergman Blix & Wettergren, 2015; Jacobsson, 2008; Törnqvist, 2017; Wettergren & Bergman Blix, 2016). In England and Wales, a wider perspective of the emotional labour inherent in the criminal justice system has looked at lawyers (Westaby, 2010; Westaby & Jones, 2017), prison officers (Crawley, 2004), police officers (Van Stokkom, 2011), and probation officers (Fowler, Phillips, & Westaby, 2019) (for an overview, see Knight & Phillips, 2016); however, whilst such a view of the Swedish criminal justice system would be constructive, it is beyond the scope of this book.

Beyond focusing on defence lawyers, I also contrast the performances of different legal professionals, which I present as stemming from the legal principle each actor represents. This book thus presents justice as an interactional accomplishment. In particular, I focus on the fine detail of interactions and provide a unique insight into how the abstract principles are accomplished.

In order to show the ways in which defence lawyers' role is accomplished and the associated construction and performance of loyalty, I will address the following questions: How do defence lawyers present themselves, the defence team, and others? How are emotions talked about, managed, and performed by defence lawyers? How are loyalty and teamwork accomplished by defence lawyers and other legal professionals in the courtroom? And, finally, how is a criminal trial a team effort?

Why defence lawyers?

The choice of defence lawyers as my empirical focus stems from a number of factors. As I have already noted, the relative paucity of research regarding defence lawyers, particularly in comparison to the other legal professionals in a trial, makes them a novel group for research. Furthermore, a previous study I conducted on legal education in Sweden showed an academic focus on cultivating objectivity, which reproduced the false dichotomy between rationality and emotionality (Flower, 2014). This was prevalent in law students' emotion talk and in their implicitly learned emotion management strategies (Flower, 2014). I was thus interested in finding out more about how emotions are managed, talked about, and performed in law.

When I began gathering material, I found that defence lawyers are often talked about with some suspicion, perhaps even contempt. Remarks such as "do defence lawyers have feelings?" and "how can they defend rapists?" were common when I told people that I was writing about defence lawyers and emotions. Indeed, defence lawyers often get a raw deal, both in research and in the media, not only in Sweden but also in other countries such as England (McConville et al., 1994; Newman, 2012; Newman & Ugwudike, 2013; Travers, 1997). For example, Scheffer (2010, p. 96) writes that defence barristers are often met with reservation in England, the misconception being that lawyers "advise the client 'what he should not do,' 'what she should not say.'" The situation in Sweden is highlighted in a doctoral dissertation on Swedish prosecutors, who talk about defence lawyers as being driven by greed, dishonour, and personal gain and using dirty tricks to win points with their clients (Törnqvist, 2017, pp. 313–319). An article in *Dagens Nyheter*, one of Sweden's most-read daily newspapers, quotes the Director of Public Prosecution, Björn Blomqvist, as saying that it is becoming more common that defence lawyers in organised crime trials attempt to switch the focus of the case to procedural or peripheral questions, that they query the police's work methods, or that defence lawyers interrupt prosecutors, causing them to constantly answer questions (Andersson, 2015). Also, in an article in *Aftonbladet*, another of Sweden's major newspapers, regarding a major drug smuggling case, I read that lawyers love big words, so their rhetoric should not always be taken completely seriously (Cantwell, 2014). Additionally, a study of Swedish police working with youths describes certain defence lawyers as I-am-always-innocent-lawyers, thus constituting a hindrance for police work (Björk, 2011, p. 212).

These examples show that there can be a distrust of defence lawyers, a perception or bias which is rarely held about prosecutors or judges. Defence lawyers are, on the one hand, seen to be working in a high-status occupation, but, on the other hand, they are seen as performing something akin to a form of "dirty work" (Emerson & Pollner, 1975; Haller, 2003; Hughes, 1962; Tata, 2010), which pertains to working with moral, social, or physical taint. Their dirty work thus stems from defending rapists, terrorists, and paedophiles.

In contrast, some prosecutors, such as those working with sexual offences, are also considered to be involved in dirty work; however, they are seen to be attempting to clean such taint (Törnqvist, 2017), whilst defence lawyers are perceived as defending it.

As the way in which society perceives one's profession can be a source of stress, such assumptions are another element supporting the sociological need to study defence lawyers (Collings & Murray, 1996). In this book, I discuss how defence lawyers emotionally explain and justify their work – an approach that is novel for this occupational category. For instance, they talk with pride about the role they have, because, as one of the lawyers I interviewed told me, "even the biggest lowlife deserves to have the best defender."

All of this sparked my interest as to how defence lawyers view their work, which is a theme throughout the book, and how defence lawyers and prosecutors talk about each other, which I explore in chapter seven.

The role of the defence lawyer is to construct a "legal picture" (Sarat & Felstiner, 1986, p. 116) of the client, which requires that the lawyer put his or her personal emotional matters to one side in order to serve the interests of the client. This may be more problematic because, of the various legal actors in the courtroom, defence lawyers can have a great deal of direct contact with clients, unlike judges and prosecutors. I argue that this service-like role places higher demands on their emotional performances compared to other courtroom actors (cf. Hochschild, 2003). In other countries, there may be an intermediary between the defence lawyer and the client; for instance, paralegals in the U.S. protect attorneys from "emotionally draining client contact" (Lively, 2002, p. 215), whilst solicitors perform a similar role in England and Australia. Defence lawyers in Sweden, however, must regularly meet clients in emotional crisis, leading to demands on interpersonal skills. Such meetings find parallels with those between social workers and their clients – both constitute professionals meeting clients who may be in distress or who find themselves in vulnerable situations (Lloyd, King, & Chenoweth, 2002).

Furthermore, the nature of the lawyer-client relationship means that defence lawyers must manage the client's agenda and sense of justice, which may not necessarily be aligned with the defence lawyer's or the court's (Sarat & Felstiner, 1986, p. 125). This may make client meetings a complex social situation filled with conflict and which must be managed in a respectful and courteous manner.

The spotlight on defence lawyers also entails a special focus on loyalty as this is the guiding principle for their profession: to loyally defend their client, which was talked about by all of the lawyers I spoke to as the foundation of their role (Association, 2008). Whilst loyalty has gained sociological attention, its performance remains relatively unexplored and is therefore another theme running through this book (cf. Barbalet, 1996; Connor, 2007).

This brings me to another important aspect: defence lawyers are expected to manage competing loyalties – to the client, to the law, to the other participants of a trial, to the law firm, to the Bar Association, and perhaps even to their family and friends (see Mather & McEwen, 2001). How these loyalties are managed will be discussed in chapter four.

Another reason that defence lawyers make for an interesting point of empirical study is linked to their role in relation to their client – the defendant – who may be unfamiliar with a criminal trial and who may not know what is expected of him or her (Jacobson, Hunter, & Kirby, 2016). Furthermore, defendants are free to change their version of events during a trial. All of this places emotional and dramaturgical demands on the defence lawyer in the interaction with the client and, in particular, during the trial, and I present my fieldnotes to depict these situations.

And, finally, after I began to gather material for this book, I also discovered that the overwhelming majority of criminal trials – 93 per cent – led to conviction in Sweden (Nordén, 2015). Defence lawyers "lose" almost all the time. This sparked my interest as to how they talk about such losses, a theme I discuss in chapter six.

Before I continue, it is pertinent to address the claims that the defence lawyer's performance in a trial is irrelevant and that it is the facts of the case that are important. As the infamous O. J. Simpson's defence lawyer, Johnnie Cochran, pointed out to the jury at the highly publicised murder trial of Simpson's ex-wife and lover – if the glove doesn't fit, "you must acquit" (see also Shuy, 2005). Whilst exploring any link between performance and acquittal is beyond the scope of this book (although an interesting area for future study), my position is that the courtroom performances of defence lawyers are central to the joint accomplishment of justice and the smooth flow of a criminal trial. My focus is therefore not on conviction rates but rather on how the defence lawyer role is constructed and performed.

The methodology of studying loyalty

> When asked by the prosecutor why she asked the defendant if he owned a weapon, the witness replies that she thought the defendant seemed "unstable." The defence lawyer looks at the judge, then the prosecutor then back at the witness and looks at his fingernails again (…) Later on, during the closing argument, the prosecutor claims that the defendant could have fired a warning shot rather than shooting the victim. The defence lawyer shakes his head, rolls his eyes, and looks up at the ceiling. (Fieldnote)

A comment often made by those I have spoken to who have watched Swedish trials is that they are unexciting. Indeed, when I began gathering empirical material for this study in 2013, I wrote in my fieldnotes, "nothing is happening." A feeling of trepidation grew for the four years of fieldwork to come, which I began to fear would entail four years of boredom. However, after attending more trials, I began to see a glimpse of the cornucopia of emotional performances that were taking place. The more I observed, the more I actually saw. I began to see that, although the adversarialism of a criminal trial seems to be hidden behind the inquisitorial presentation of facts and under a veneer of restraint and control, gestures such as eye rolling, headshaking, and the checking of one's fingernails, as seen in the opening excerpts in this chapter from my fieldnotes of a murder trial, are all strategies for strategies for the role-appropriate display of antagonism fundamental to the adversarial trial in an emotionally appropriate way. I began to see the patterns in interactions and the construction and performance of legal principles, such as loyalty.

The interactionist starting point

My analytical starting point for this book is an interactionist one – that our actions are based on how we define a situation and how we interpret the actions and meanings of others (Blumer, 1959; Dellwing, 2012; Goffman, 1956). Situations are characterised by shared understandings and expectations as to what is going on and what each person should do. Our actions in the situation are then rooted in these expectations and grounded in the knowledge that other interactants have an opinion about our actions (Blumer, 1959; Cooley, 1922; Mead, 1934). The interactions that take place in these situations lead to the construction of symbols which are used to communicate and which have an underlying meaning (Berger & Luckmann, 1966; Francis, 1997; Goffman, 1956; S. Scott, 2015). A symbol thus represents something else – words are symbols, as are gestures. Both can be used as a way of communicating to others with whom we are interacting. We might understand that the situation we are interacting in is a date when the other person greets us with flowers and a hug. It is therefore via a process of shared meanings that we are able to understand and make sense of the actions of others and act in accordance. These shared understandings regarding the situation, including normative assumptions and expectations of what will occur, lead to an almost routine-like way of conducting oneself within the situation, which, as I will explain in more detail in chapter three, is captured by the interaction order (Goffman, 1956, 1983).

As loyalty is described by all of the defence lawyers as central to their role, I therefore use it as the base for their role performance. In this way, I am able to use the meaning conveyed as my starting point, namely loyalty, in order to discover the symbols or the ways in which this is communicated verbally and nonverbally in interactions (cf. Manning, 2001). My task is to connect the symbols with the underlying meanings being communicated; for instance, what does a blink communicate? The answer can be found in chapter four.

The social situation of a criminal trial is a particularly interesting site for sociological examination as, despite all the participants in a trial being in agreement that they are interacting in a criminal trial and that there are therefore associated expectations and obligations, within this overarching definition of the situation, there may be competing realities. For instance, the prosecutor may claim one version of events has taken place – that the defendant has committed an offence – which may contrast with the defendant's version – that he or she is innocent. Criminal trials are, thus, co-ordinated conflicts where face may be threatened in an institutionalised manner (Adelswärd, 1989; Goffman, 1952, 1956; May, 2005).

My analytical focus is thus centred on the defence lawyer's role accomplishment and the communication of the guiding principle of loyalty – how is it symbolised in defence lawyers' courtroom performances and how is it talked about? I show that it is the position of the legal professional that determines the guiding principle (i.e. loyal lawyer, objective prosecutor, or impartial judge), which, in turn, steers what the legal practitioner is symbolically representing in courtroom interactions. This, in turn, shapes the actual performance whilst simultaneously remaining within the boundaries of what is permitted in a criminal trial. I will conclude the book by showing how these performances work together in order for justice to be accomplished.

Additionally, following on from the social constructionist approach of symbolic interaction, I am interested in how facts are constructed in the courtroom. I therefore focus on the interactional aspect of fact construction and reveal the strategies used by defence lawyers to build up and undermine facts in the courtroom using verbal and nonverbal strategies which are particular to the social setting of the courtroom (cf. Potter, 1996, pp. 13, 102).

The empirical process

The empirical material for this book was gathered between September 2013 and April 2017 and consists of courtroom ethnography – writing fieldnotes during more than 50 criminal trials at four district courts in southern and western Sweden – as well as interviews with 18 lawyers.[2] Eight women (Vera, Siri, Sandra, Lydia, Lena, Lo, Kate, and Hilda) and ten men (Andrew, Martin, Charles, Peter, Perry, Harry, Daniel, Richard, Edward, and George) were interviewed, the ages ranging from early 30s to mid-60s, with the experience of working as a lawyer ranging from 1.5 years to over 40 years. I also attended several trials at an English Crown Court in order to see how adversarial trials can look in other jurisdictions.

In Sweden it is not permitted to film inside courtrooms; however, it is possible to obtain audio recordings of trials. After observing a trial for assault in which the defence lawyer was unusually aggressive, I obtained the trial's audio recording in order to combine it with my fieldnotes in the analysis, which I present in chapter seven. I have also included media coverage, autobiographies of defence lawyers, and other documents.

Trials are open to the public in Sweden, and therefore I was able to sit in the public gallery, which is often located at the back of the courtroom (occasionally to the side), affording the public (and the ethnographic researcher) a view of all of the actors involved and, in particular, frequently providing an unobstructed view of the interactions between the defence lawyer and the defendant. This includes not only the interactions in the full view of the court but also those taking place behind and underneath the desk – backstage – interactions which are not observable to the other legal professionals in the courtroom. Such hidden interactions will be revealed in my analysis, but, for the impatient souls out there, I can reveal that it can involve a calming hand on the knee or an occasional kick in the shins.

I became aware that it was the cross-examination that was the part of the trial where the action was at providing me with a great deal of my empirical material (Goffman, 1967). The closing speech also generated interesting fieldnotes, for example, showing that it was more acceptable to talk about and use emotions in a different way than in the remaining stages of the trial. The reading of charges and presentation of facts, however, often proved to be a relatively uneventful stage – perhaps attempts at stifling a yawn could be observed (which are nevertheless of analytical interest) but rarely anything more. My ethnographic eye thus homed in on certain phases of the trial, certain actors, and also, in particular, certain emotions such as anger and irritation: how they are displayed, who displays what, and so on. At the same time as this, my interviews with defence lawyers revealed that they talked about loyalty to the client being the central component of their role. This led me to focus in more detail on those instances where the defence lawyer is defending the client's version of events, thus symbolically communicating loyalty to the client, which, as I mentioned earlier, is most prevalent during cross-examination.

I also observed and wrote fieldnotes in the waiting rooms and hallways of courthouses, before trials began, during the breaks in proceedings, and afterwards as often defence lawyers, prosecutors, plaintiffs, and witnesses stand or sit in such areas adjacent to the courtrooms. This provided an opportunity for me to see some of the backstage work involved even though the main focus of this study is the defence lawyers' work in the courtroom.

Ethnographic studies such as this involve contemporaneously capturing interactions and then analysing them to find patterns. It is therefore important to maintain the context in which these interactions occur. Linked to this, the ethnographer is interested in finding out local meanings and interactions; therefore, it is also necessary to maintain an awareness and openness that what may be viewed as having one meaning outside of the courtroom may actually represent something else within the social context of the courtroom. For example, what may be seen as unawareness (unintentionally not observing something such as crying) outside of the courtroom may be a special instance of civil inattention (Goffman, 1956) in the courtroom – a way of drawing attention away from the facts that are being presented, as I show in chapters four, five, six, and seven.

Despite this you might still pose the question, is there a risk that I interpret everything I observe as instances of emotion management or performances of loyalty (see Merton, 1968, pp. 476–477)? I argue that the role of researchers is to look for underlying patterns and their own assumptions, attempting to uncover the former and override the latter (Anderson, 1999, p. 11). I have tried to avoid potential bias by using various sources and materials, thereby not solely drawing on my own notes. I can also add that, having presented the findings of this study to hundreds of defence lawyers, all of them have recognised the patterns described in this book.

I have also concentrated on avoiding other pitfalls associated with writing and analysing fieldnotes such as over-embellishing, over-interpreting, or simply describing a scene in order to fit my expectations (Fine, 1993). On occasions where an alternative interpretation seems possible, I have endeavoured to present this, in order for the reader to understand my analytical thinking. For example, in chapter four, I show that certain performances of loyalty could be seen as instances of doing disloyalty; however, by presenting how I have reasoned in drawing my analytical interpretations and by using other empirical material and cultural awareness, I hope to convince the reader that the picture I am painting is accurate. My goal is for the reader to more or less naturally draw the same conclusion as I have done based on my analytical argument.

After carrying out this courtroom ethnography and observing over 50 trials, I am able to select and present those instances of interaction which are representative but also those that deviate markedly from the usual. By highlighting the unusual, it is possible to see the norm because "[h]ow does the fish get to notice that it is surrounded by water (since it is all the time)? Only when it is hooked out on to dry land" (Strong, 1988, p. 236). For instance, in chapter four I use deviant displays of disloyalty to reveal the underlying rules for performing loyalty, and in chapter seven I show how anger should be appropriately displayed by presenting empirical material depicting an overly angry lawyer. Such depictions also serve to reveal the unwritten rules of the emotional framework at play.

As I conducted interviews and fieldwork over the same time span, I was able to pose questions in my interviews regarding something I had seen the day before in a trial or, in some cases, something that another defence lawyer had mentioned. For instance, as I discuss in chapter five, I observed that none of the defence lawyers stood up during a trial and I could then ask about this in the ensuing interviews. This means that the interview process became more of a guided conversation, ensuring that those areas of interest for the defence lawyers were also explored rather than merely mechanically following the same interview guide throughout. It also enabled the respondents to actively reflect, remember, and make connections, which I could then use to make further analytical connections (Wagner & Wodak, 2006). This meant that certain avenues were opened up and developed in later interviews, paths which I did not know would be available prior to the interview process, for example, the way in which defence lawyers talk about defending a person, not a crime, was not something that was in my interview guide but which I asked about in each interview after one of the respondents talked about it, as I discuss in chapter seven.

During the interview situation, I attempted to find the right balance of "playing dumb," whilst establishing rapport and giving the impression that I was comfortable in discussing the work of defence lawyers (see Rapley, 2011). I have only limited experience of studying the law, and therefore if there were terms I didn't understand I would ask for them to be explained. I also used follow-up questions whenever necessary in order to encourage the respondent to fully expand their answers – I was therefore conscious of not taking anything for granted. This led to surprises at times; for example, some of the lawyers said that they would defend a client as innocent even if the client has confessed his or her guilt, thus standing in direct contradiction to the guidelines of the Swedish Bar Association (2008).

The interview material consequently consists of defence lawyers' narratives regarding their identity construction – drawing attention to certain things and drawing attention away from other aspects that they would prefer to remain hidden (Baker, 2002; Dingwall, 1997, p. 58; see also Garfinkel, 1984; Silverman, 2013; Wright Mills, 1940, p. 904). Thus, I analyse how defence lawyers explain their role and the ways in which they make sense of their work (Czarniawska, 1997; Riessman, 1993).

The researcher's emotions are often relegated to a footnote, traditionally seen as an impediment; however, bringing the emotions of the researcher into the forefront is an important step in honing one's ethnographic eye (see Bitsch, 2018a, 2018b for an interesting and notable exception). I consider my role as a qualitative researcher to be an "emotional agent" (Kleinman & Copp, 1993, p. 54) using emotion work as part of my methodological toolkit, thereby increasing my sensitivity and reflexivity to the empirical material (see also Bergman Blix & Wettergren, 2014; Coffey, 1999, p. 57; Emerson, Fretz, & Shaw, 2011; Robinson & Schulz, 2009).

Outline of the book

Chapter two begins with a short presentation of legal systems and the characteristics of adversarial and inquisitorial systems before presenting an overview of criminal trials and the official guidelines for defence lawyers – in particular, the role of loyalty – in Sweden and other jurisdictions. The chapter ends with a short note on Sweden in order to orientate the reader. I then move on, in chapter three, to an overview of the state of the art combining my theoretical framework with a summary of the relevant literature.

This is followed by an exploration of loyalty and disloyalty in chapter four. The focus is upon the ways in which defence lawyers use loyalty, both as a guiding principle in their professional work and as a tool in order to get the job done: to represent clients. The competing loyalties that defence lawyers face are also discussed. The chapter ends with showing when cracks appear in performances, and disloyalty is conveyed using ethnographic fieldnotes to depict this.

In chapters five and six, I attempt to disentangle emotions and interactions for analytical ease. In chapter five, I focus on defence lawyers' facework – I emphasise the underlying meanings conveyed and show how the smooth flow of a criminal trial is a joint interactional accomplishment, demanding each social position to be dramaturgically performed appropriately. In chapter six, I explore the emotions and emotion work of defence lawyers, highlighting how proper and appropriate emotions are professionalised and thus rationalised and then performed. In these two chapters, I aim to show that a performance within a specific setting is shaped by an overarching framework, which, in turn, entails ensuring that one's emotions are in line with expectations and that one performs one's role appropriately.

The final chapter highlights the interactional and collective accomplishment of justice and lifts the other legal professionals involved in the construction of the defence lawyer's role by discussing the performances of impartiality and objectivity, comparing and contrasting to that of loyalty. Although this is touched upon in the rest of the book, this final chapter provides an overarching view of interactional justice[3] and the role of loyalty within. In particular, the way in which anger may be conveyed in a loyally appropriate way is depicted and used to illustrate the unwritten emotion and interaction rules in the courtroom. This chapter concludes with a closing argument, summing up the key findings and future directions.

Notes

1 This is a fictitious name but the name used in court was equally as fantastic.

2 Interviews were conducted in the lawyers' law offices and lasted between 50 minutes (as a legal emergency arose) and over 150 minutes. All but one of the lawyers I spoke to agreed to the interview being audio-recorded. During the interview that I was not permitted to record, I wrote copious notes, which I then wrote up directly after the interview. All other interviews were recorded and transcribed verbatim. One of the interviews was conducted in English after we chatted about how I came from England; however, the rest were in Swedish (which I am fluent in), which I first transcribed in Swedish and then translated the excerpts I wanted to use into English.

3 I use the term "interactional justice" to indicate my micro-sociological approach to studying interactions in the accomplishment of justice, in contrast to other uses of the term which focus on how courtroom users are treated and the information they receive (for example, see Bies and Moag 1986).

Chapter 2

Legal systems and loyalty

I will now introduce the study setting by giving a short overview of legal systems and criminal trials, with particular focus on adversarial systems. Criminal trials and the codes of conduct for defence lawyers in Sweden and other relevant jurisdictions will also be described with a special emphasis on loyalty. This is done because, as will soon be made clear, loyalty is a key component of adversarial systems. Whilst this book does not aim to have a comparative approach, similarities and differences will be highlighted between different jurisdictions when appropriate. This chapter concludes with a presentation of the societal context of Sweden and introduces the subtlety of the Swedish criminal courtroom.

Legal systems

All legal systems are different however they may be grouped together into families that have similar traits. For instance, civil law stems from Roman law and is used in many Western European countries such as France, Germany, Italy, Spain, and Portugal. Civil law systems have codified law which means that the law is set out in statutes and enacted by national parliament which arrange fields of law in orderly and comprehensive ways. In contrast, countries such as England, the U.S., Australia, Canada, Singapore, and Barbados have common law wherein laws are not found in acts of Parliament, but rather written and developed by judges when deciding particular cases, as seen in the use of "precedent" – that a judge is bound by what has already been decided. Juries may be a feature of common-law institutions but not civil law systems. There are also other systems of law such as sacred-law systems, for instance Islamic law.

Sweden is more difficult to place, with some scholars claiming it is a mixed system drawing on the Germanic model of law, unlike the other civil law systems mentioned earlier. Sweden also uses cases for guidance. I thus treat Sweden as belonging to a separate family of "Scandinavian law" or "Nordic continental law" (Friedman & Hayden, 2017; van Koppen & Penrod, 2003).

Adversarial, inquisitorial, and mixed system criminal trials

The criminal justice system is the system of law enforcement that is directly involved with apprehending, prosecuting, defending, sentencing, and punishing those who are suspected or convicted of criminal offences.

Although legal systems and criminal justice systems are often linked, with civil law tending to have an inquisitorial (also known as investigatory) system – such as in France and the Netherlands – and common law usually having an adversarial system – such as the U.S., England, and Australia – it is argued that the traditional division between the two systems has been worn down and no system is wholly adversarial or inquisitorial (Spencer, 2016). Furthermore, the system itself is unimportant – it is the fairness of the system, regardless of its theoretical or historical roots that is of consequence (Cainaniello, 2011).[1] A country may therefore have civil law but an adversarial system or a mixture of inquisitorial and adversarial features, such as Sweden which had an inquisitorial system until 1948 when a new code of criminal procedure was introduced (SFS, 1942:740).

Ambos (2003) argues that the difference between the two systems lies in how the truth is sought out and that the inquisitorial/adversarial divide only bears historical meaning because all modern criminal procedures are governed by the principles of orality and immediacy. Both systems share common characteristics: standard of proof, presumption of innocence, the right to counsel, and the right of confrontation (van Koppen & Penrod, 2003, p. 2). The main differences between the systems pertain to:

Establishment of facts: adversarial systems use open competition between prosecution and defence with the prosecution facing a burden of proof. Truth is established via contention thus placing the conflict between opposing parties in focus (May, 2005). It is essentially a contest between equivalent rivals where one is judged by one's peers (often, but not always, one's peers consists of a jury; however, a jury is not always necessary, for instance with plea bargaining in the U.S.). Inquisitorial systems in contrast, use investigation and the examination of all evidence – the form is more of an inquest aimed at establishing facts.

Judges: play a passive and neutral role in adversarial trials, pronouncing judgement based on the hearing. Inquisitorial trials have a judge who actively questions the parties directly.

Defence lawyers: play an active role in adversarial trials but less so in inquisitorial trials.

Prosecution: in an adversarial system, one citizen formally brings an accusation against another but in an inquisitorial system the prosecution is an organ of the state, building, and presenting a case.

Defendants: in adversarial systems guilt should be established objectively and by evidence exterior to the defendant whilst in inquisitorial systems the defendant has an active role in the discovery of truth, and the questioning of the defendant is central in proceedings. Furthermore, in adversarial systems the defence lawyer is client centred (largely based on the dependence of client fees based on services rendered). The defence lawyer understands that his or her opponent – the prosecution – is also client centred by instruction; therefore, the relationship between the two is oppositional. If the defence lawyer perceives his or her opponent to be more court based (and thus an advocate of the state) than client based then this becomes more like a mixed system or inquisitorial system where both sides assist the judge in reaching a just result (Lind, Thibaut, & Walker, 1973).

Witnesses: in adversarial systems each side may choose to call and question witnesses. In an inquisitorial system, witnesses may not be called or cross-examined and it is the judge who does the questioning. In common law systems, witnesses take an oath to tell the truth whilst in the U.S. as well as England and Wales the defendant also testifies under oath; however, this is not the case in other jurisdictions such as Sweden and Australia.

Weight of facts: in adversarial systems, the hearing, evidence, examination and cross-examination done by lawyers get priority unlike in inquisitorial systems where documents and information about the facts are prioritised.

Orality and openness: in adversarial systems, hearings take place orally and publicly, compared to inquisitorial trials which are closed and where written evidence is presented.

Cross-examination: in adversarial systems each party may examine witnesses, including one's own client. In inquisitorial systems, witnesses may not be cross-examined or even called (see Ambos, 2003; Spencer, 2016).

The inquisitorial aspects in the Swedish system can be seen in the judge holding order in the courtroom, the active role of the defendant, and the role of the prosecutor in preparing the case and representing the state. Depending upon the severity of the alleged crime, it is either the prosecutor or police (in minor cases) who decides on whether or not to initiate preliminary investigations and who then leads the investigation. The prosecutor has therefore an absolute duty to prosecute – he or she is obliged to initiate a prosecution if there is sufficient evidence to prove that a certain crime has been committed and that a certain person has committed it (Åklagarmyndighet, 2018).[2] The adversarial aspects are seen in the objectivity of the judges to whom the prosecutor should present evidence to in order to convince them of the case's credibility.

Although both judges and prosecutors have a duty of objectivity, I follow Bergman Blix and Wettergren's (2019) approach and analytically separate prosecutorial objectivity from judicial impartiality in order to highlight the differences in performances. Thus, although, strictly speaking, both are performing objectivity, I will treat them as two different principles being accomplished: objective prosecutor and impartial judge.

The adversarial system therefore brings with it a co-ordinated conflict where the truth can be established via contention and it is during the trial that adversarial aspects of the system are most prevalent (May, 2005; Wong, 2012). I argue that it is by observing this co-ordinated conflict that we can see justice being performed. It is here we can see the principle performances of objectivity, impartiality, and loyalty – of legal professionals "doing justice" (Wettergren & Bergman Blix, 2016). It is thus here that I have gathered much of the empirical material for this book.

In particular, it is during the cross-examination and final closing speech phases of the trial that the defence lawyer has the opportunity to perform, indeed, the cross-examination is a "dramatized argument (…) putting to the witness facts that can be proven otherwise for the purpose of having a dramatic 'face-to-face' presentation" (Park, 2003, p. 145, fn. 116), the aim being to draw attention to evidence (rather than producing new evidence). This is what makes the courtroom an interesting site for sociological enquiry. It holds a series of face-to-face encounters in an emotionally charged yet highly emotionally constrained situation as will be depicted in my analytical chapters.

Criminal trials in Sweden and other jurisdictions

Criminal cases in Sweden are handled in the first instance at District Court, of which there are 48 in Sweden but can also be heard at the Court of Appeal and later, the Supreme Court. In the English and Welsh criminal justice system, Magistrates Court deal with minor cases whilst Crown Court deal with more serious criminal trials held before a jury, and sentencing (Jacobson et al., 2016). In Australia, there are District Courts in the five most populated states which hear the majority of criminal cases triable by jury, akin to the Crown Courts in England and Wales (although in Victoria it is called the County Court) (Roach Anleu & Mack, 2017), whilst in the U.S. such cases are also heard at District Courts.

A trial is the main hearing where the court decides if a person suspected of a crime is guilty (Domstolar, 2018). In a Swedish criminal trial, the main actors are the judge, lay judges, prosecutor, and defence lawyer along with the plaintiff, defendant, witnesses and the clerk. The defence lawyer can either be a public defender – appointed and paid for by the court – or the defendant can choose to hire a different defence lawyer in which case the defendant must pay the defence lawyer's fees. If found guilty when represented by a public defender, the defendant may be required to pay all or part of the State's costs; however, if they are found not guilty then they are freed from these fees. Defence lawyers may be involved in trials regarding sexual offences, assault, unlawful deprivation of liberty, robbery, or any other crime which may result in a prison sentence.

The plaintiff[3] may have a legal advisor to help – counsel for the plaintiff. The counsel for the plaintiff is usually a member of the Bar Association, thus defence lawyers can also work as counsel for the plaintiff and are appointed in order to take care of the interests of the victim, for instance, when presenting the claim for damages. Counsel for the plaintiff is appointed by the court once the preliminary investigation is underway and is paid for by the State. If the defendant is convicted for the crime, he or she may have to pay the State for these costs incurred (Domstolar, 2019b). This role will be explored in more detail in chapter four.

In England and Wales, both barristers and solicitors can defend clients in criminal court; however, solicitors represent clients in Magistrates Court which handles minor cases whilst barristers work at the higher Crown Court level. In Crown Court cases, solicitors meet with clients and prepare the case before instructing a criminal barrister who presents the case at court (solicitor-advocates may also represent clients in Crown Court; however, this is more unusual). This is also the case in most states in Australia. Barristers thus represent solicitors as their "professional clients and defendants as their personal, identifiable lay clients" (Rock, 1993, p. 168). This "case" system has been criticised for shielding the barrister from the defendant, indeed the solicitor is considered to be the client according to Scheffer (2010, 97). In Sweden and in the U.S., this flow between client and lawyer (or "attorney" in the U.S.) is uninterrupted by case-files with clients meeting with their defence lawyer and sitting together in court. Consequently, I am able to observe this flow directly in the Swedish courtroom.

Barristers have limited contact with the defendant and only then in the presence of the instructing solicitor. The "cab-rank" rule means that barristers (in Australia, England, and Wales) are required to accept any case given by a solicitor. The majority of defendants at Crown Court in England and Wales, or District Court in Australia, are therefore represented by a member of the Bar – a barrister, a position akin to the Swedish advocate.[4] However, unlike Swedish advocates, barristers can switch sides, working some trials as the prosecution and others as the defence which, it has been argued, leads to "the embedded adversarial roles of the trial system becom[ing] detached from the selves of those who played them" (Rock, 1993, p. 39).

In Swedish District Court, there is one legally qualified judge (the presiding judge) and usually three lay judges who represent the general public (akin to a jury in Anglo-Saxon jurisdictions). The number of lay judges can change, for instance, if one lay judge is unable to attend, it is possible for proceedings to continue with only two. In cases with only a minor penalty or a maximum prison sentence of six months, the trial may take place without lay judges (Sangborn, 2016; SFS, 1942:740, RB, Kap 1, 3§). The presiding judge may be fairly active during proceedings, for instance asking clarifying questions (Aronsson, Jönsson, & Linell, 1987).

The lay judges are politically appointed – a process which has led to debate in Sweden. They have a mandate for four years, unlike many jury systems such as in the U.S. and England, which are randomly selected before each trial. Lay judges do not have legal training; however, there is an obligatory course they must take which, amongst other things, explains the legal system and their role within along with their obligation of secrecy and rules regarding incompetence (*jäv*). Lay judges are not permitted to ask questions during a trial, unlike the judge. I will return to lay judges in more detail in the final chapter.

Witnesses must promise to tell the truth; however, they are exempt from this if they are related to one of the parties in question, have a psychiatric disorder, or under 15 years of age (SFS, 1942:740 RB 36, 1§, 3§, 5§). The plaintiff and the defendant do not have such an obligation.

Following the trial, the judge and lay judges deliberate in seclusion – discussing the case and deciding how to rule. The decision can either be announced directly in the courtroom or as a written judgement at a later date (within three weeks). Most commonly, the judge begins deliberations by presenting how he or she has viewed the evidence, which laws it pertains to and also how the evidence should be interpreted. He or she then suggests an outcome. This is followed by a (usually short) discussion and the outcome is voted upon with a majority required. This means that lay judges in Sweden are not only able to decide on questions of guilt, but also on the punishment, unlike juries (comprised of laymen) in some Anglo-Saxon jurisdictions such as the U.S. who only decide on guilt. There is no separate sentencing hearing.

In a Swedish criminal trial, the judge, lay judges, and clerk sit in a row at the front of the courtroom whilst the defence lawyer sits on one side of the room at a table with the defendant sitting next to them. The prosecution sits on the opposite side of the courtroom to the defence, with the plaintiff (if there is one) sitting next to them. Witnesses sit in the middle of the courtroom when they give evidence and the public gallery where spectators, including journalists, can sit, is at the back of the courtroom.[5]

The positioning of the prosecutor and defence lawyer opposite each other indicates the adversarial nature of the trial. However, it should be noted that in other adversarial systems such as England and the U.S., lawyers stand side-by-side in the centre of the courtroom, positioned behind desks facing the judge. Barristers in England are regarded as less combative than their American counterparts who stand further away from each other (McMahon, 2006). In an English Crown Court hearing, the defendant stands at the back of the courtroom, in the "dock" whilst in the U.S., he or she tends to sit next to their lawyer. Close client relationships are accepted in the U.S. – a "strategic alignment" (McMahon, 2006, p. 852) aimed at conveying trust and teamwork, for instance, touching the client during proceedings may underscore this relationship. The layouts of criminal courts can differ in Australian District Courts, but the defendant does not tend to sit together with his or her barrister.

In Sweden, the defence lawyer is free to move around the courtroom although this is seldom done as I will explore in more detail later on in this book. Counsel in England and Wales always stand when addressing the court and American lawyers have the freedom to move around the courtroom (LeVan, 1984; Wolfe, 1994).

Trials in Sweden should follow the principles of immediacy (only evidence presented at trial is considered in the judgement), orality (all evidence should be introduced orally), and concentration (the trial should be concentrated in time) (Dahlberg, 2008; Wong, 2012). After the presiding judge checks who is present, the trial is divided into four main phases: (1) reading of charges by the prosecution after which the defendant is able to respond guilty or not guilty (usually it is the defence lawyer who responds); (2) the prosecution presents the facts of the case; (3) examination and cross-examination (questioning by the opposing counsel), starting with the plaintiff then defendant and lastly witnesses (the party that has called the witnesses begins); and finally (4) closing speeches. Only the third phase is dialogical (Aronsson et al., 1987, p. 103). Before the closing speeches the defendant's personal circumstances are dealt with, for instance, their criminal record and financial situation. There are short breaks in proceedings as and when needed. During these breaks, the judge, lay judges, and clerk are the only ones who may remain in the courtroom, all others must leave.

Swedish proceedings are relatively informal and less obviously adversarial than the Anglo-Saxon system (Aronsson et al., 1987). There are no wigs or robes worn; however, it should be noted that "the absence of robes and wigs does not mean an absence of formality, but rather that the rituals are less distant from the practices in everyday life" (Dahlberg, 2009). Prosecutors and defence lawyers tend to wear suits – only once have I observed a prosecutor wearing something other than a suit (he was wearing cargo pants), a striking difference in comparison to, for example, the English courtroom as will be presented shortly. The presiding judge also wears a suit; however, the lay judges may be more casually dressed.

This contrasts with other jurisdictions, such as England where barristers wear a wig and a black gown in Crown Court (solicitors may wear a wig and solicitor's gown if they wish). The formal garb worn by English barristers is seen to help maintain the professional hierarchy and to convey a sense of solemnity and dignity (McMahon, 2006). Australian barristers began wearing gowns and wigs in the latter part of the 19th century, before this there were no such traditions of legal dress (McQueen, 1999). This contrasts American and Swedish lawyers who have more freedom in choice of attire. Most American courts have guidelines similar to those of the U.S. Supreme Court: "[c]onservative business dress in traditional dark colors (e.g. navy blue or charcoal gray)" (Court, 2017, p. 3).

I suggest that the informality of the Swedish courtroom, devoid of ceremonial robes and gowns places interactional demands on defence lawyers in order to perform the professionalism that is one of the goals of their performance.

This is explored more fully in the coming chapters; however, the following excerpt from my fieldnotes from a criminal trial at an English Crown Court highlights the contrast between Sweden and England as will be revealed in the pages to come:

> As I enter the courtroom I am immediately struck by the difference in tone and formality compared to Sweden. Robes and wigs are worn by all. The judge enters the courtroom last and all rise upon her entrance. The judge is bowed to by the legal actors when entering and leaving the courtroom and she sits slightly elevated from everyone else. The defendant sits at the back of the courtroom, in the dock. There is thus no interaction between the defendant and his barrister. Once or twice the defendant's barrister turns and gestures or points towards him when arguing the case but the defendant appears more as a prop than an actual actor involved in proceedings. (Fieldnote)

This excerpt also points to the difference in opportunities for teamwork between barristers and their client during proceedings, not least due to the positioning of the defendant in the dock (Rossner, Tait, McKimmie, & Sarre, 2017).

Finally, the Swedish criminal trial is often differentiated from other systems with regard to the absence of a jury. For instance, Krister Thelin (2001, p. 86), State Secretary for the Justice Department in Sweden and judge, says that the presence of a jury in the U.S. leads to legal professionals using "emotional ploys" in the courtroom which is not the case in Sweden. He claims further that "the Anglo-American criminal process offers a dramaturgy, largely due to the role of the jury, that Swedish trials cannot offer" (Thelin, 2001, p. 136). I disagree however and argue that such emotional tactics are also used in the Swedish courtroom, however, in a subtle manner, as is shown in my analysis.

As already mentioned in chapter one, the overwhelming majority of criminal trials – 93 per cent – lead to conviction in Sweden (Nordén, 2015). This is because of the way the legal system works: prosecutors do not bring a case to trial unless they determine that the evidence they have gathered will most likely lead to a guilty judgement, which is an inquisitorial aspect of the system. In England and Wales this figure is currently 87 per cent (M. o. Justice, 2019), in the U.S. 94 per cent of trials lead to a guilty verdict (D. o. Justice, 2018), whilst in Australia 98 per cent of trials lead to conviction (Statistics, 2019). In chapter six, I present how Swedish defence lawyers make sense of working in a role filled with losses.

Defence lawyers' codes of conduct

My focus is on Swedish defence lawyers' role accomplishment, in particular, their courtroom performances and emotion talk which I argue are based on the laws, guidelines, and rules they should follow and which centre on the construction and conveyance of loyalty. Even though they do not receive explicit advice regarding *how* these rules should be performed, there are nevertheless similarities and patterns to be revealed as I show in the pages to come. Boon and Levin (1999, p. 296) claim that most legal systems include an expectation on lawyers that justice will not be compromised as well as including loyalty to clients in some way (however there are differences in jurisdictions regarding what loyalty entails and its limits). I will now present an overview of defence lawyers' obligations, in particular, loyalty to the client, in Sweden and contrast this with that found in three other jurisdictions with adversarial systems: England and Wales, the U.S., and Australia.

The lawyering profession in England is over 300 years older than the U.S., Australian, and Swedish systems (Ebervall, 2002). The profession of barrister is thus a well-established, clearly defined and exclusive field, long regarded as elite. Despite this long history, it was not until 1960 that official guidelines for solicitors were released and nearly four decades later (in 1998), the General Council for the Bar of England and Wales established the code of conduct of the Bar of England and Wales. This belatedness in the establishment of official rules is largely seen to be a reflection of the high societal and moral status enjoyed by barristers who were thus deemed capable of regulating themselves (Ebervall, 2002). This contrasts with the U.S. which had guidelines in place in nearly every State by the turn of the nineteenth century, with the American Bar Association's (ABA) rules formed in 1905 (Ebervall, 2002, p. 50). The Swedish Bar Association's code of conduct were first codified in 1971.

The official framework for Swedish defence lawyers is as follows. Defence lawyers must follow the law: the Swedish Judicial Code of Procedure (*Rättegångsbalken*) which states that defence lawyers may not be dishonest, imprudent, or unsuitable (SFS, 1942:740, Kap 8, 7§). The defence lawyer is also bound by law to protect the defendant's rights with zeal (*nit*) and care and, with that purpose in mind, expeditiously work together with the defendant to prepare the defence with the purpose of presenting the matters of the case in the proper light (SFS, 1942:740, Kap 21, 7§). Furthermore, a lawyer is duty bound to not disclose any information obtained in his or her professional capacity – that is, he or she has a duty of confidentiality (SFS, 1942:740, Kap 8, 4§).

In order to call oneself a lawyer (*advokat*),[6] one must be a member of the Swedish Bar Association which requires that the code of conduct is followed (Association, 2008). The law also states that as a member of the Bar Association, one is expected to follow their code of conduct (SFS, 1942:740, Kap 8, 4§). This means that the Bar Association has the mandate to decide and regulate what constitutes good lawyering conduct (Ebervall, 2008). The main purpose of this code of conduct is to protect the public from unqualified practitioners (although even non-members are also permitted to represent defendants at a criminal trial), the secondary purpose is to act as a professional guide for lawyers (Ebervall, 2002, p. 47).[7] The code of conduct states that lawyers hold a significant position in society as the protector of freedoms and rights and that:

> The principal responsibility of an Advocate is to show fidelity and loyalty[8] towards the client. As an independent adviser, the Advocate is obliged to represent and act in the client's best interests within the established framework of the law and good professional conduct. The Advocate must not be influenced by possible personal gain or inconvenience or by any other irrelevant circumstances.
>
> (Association, 2008, p. 4)

Furthermore, a lawyer should not make statements they know to be untrue nor should they scandalise or threaten an opposing party, make degrading comments regarding the opposing party, or introduce disparaging evidence or information regarding the opposing party "unless, in the circumstances, this appears justifiable in order to act in the best interests of the client" (Association, 2008, p. 28). Also, although a lawyer may not suppress or distort evidence, he or she "is not obliged to produce or invoke evidence or adduce facts detrimental to the client unless required to do so by law" (Association, 2008, p. 33).[9]

As the courtroom can constitute a scene for strong emotions even in Sweden, defence lawyers are expected to have strategies available for an appropriate performance within the performative and emotional constraints (Adelswärd, 1989; Bergman Blix & Wettergren, 2015; Dahlberg, 2009; Törnqvist, 2017). The guiding rule for defence lawyers is *foriteter in re, suaviter in modo*, "resolutely in fashion, gently in manner" (Blomkvist, 1987). For instance, those appearing before a judge considered to be difficult are advised to react to the judge's peculiarities *only* if it is in the client's interests and indeed then, only subtly: "with cool dignity, perhaps accentuated with raised eyebrows" (Blomkvist, 1987, p. 83). Violating these boundaries or using aggressive examination techniques may antagonise other legal parties in the courtroom, which may lead to the court being negatively positioned towards the defence lawyer (Blomkvist, 1987; Borgström, 2011; Mellqvist, 1994).

Although there is no mention of the word "loyalty" in the Bar Standards Board Handbook for England and Wales (2019), the code of conduct nevertheless outlines a defence lawyers' core duties as encompassing three principles: to rigorously represent the defendant; regardless of the crime or the person accused; and to ensure the confidentiality of information given by the client (Board, 2019). Lawyers are expected to "promote fearlessly and by all proper and lawful means the client's best interests" (Board, 2019, p. 33). Lawyers are characterised by partisanship, detachment, confidentiality, procedural justice, truth-seeking, and fairness and have duties to the client, the court, and the public (Smith, 2013). These principles, or similar, are also followed in the

Swedish, American, and Australian systems.[10] However, in comparison to the U.S., the partisanship of English and Welsh barristers, and indeed Swedish lawyers, falls short of pursuing the client's unlawful interests (Boon & Levin, 1999, p. 29).

Traditionally, loyalty to the client has been paramount in England and Wales, following the "zealous advocate" model, with loyalty to the public lowest ranked (Smith, 2013). However, there has been a shift over the past 20 years, deprioritising loyalty to the client in favour of loyalty to the court and the public to ensure procedural justice and to seek the truth (Smith, 2013). An example of this is when a mistake takes place during a trial. The barrister has a duty to immediately point out the mistake rather than saving it in order to make an appeal (Ebervall, 2002). The barrister is thus expected to place loyalty to the law over loyalty to the client. Such layers of loyalty will be explored in chapter four.

The "standard conception" (Boon & Levin, 1999) of the lawyer's role was developed and is used in the U.S. but is also used by lawyers in England and Wales, Sweden, and Australia. It comprises two overarching principles – neutrality and partisanship. Neutrality refers to lawyers taking all cases, partisanship demands that lawyers follow their client's instructions to the bounds of the law. There is a third principle which supports these first two, namely non-accountability which suggests that, so long as the first two principles are followed, the lawyer is "absolved of personal moral responsibility for the consequence of actions on behalf of clients. This is on the grounds that the role they perform is itself good" (Boon & Levin, 1999, p. 24). The neutrality of the barristers in England is seen in the "cab rank rule" they follow which means that they must take the next client in line. However, this does not necessarily imply moral neutrality, merely that all cases should be accepted.

Members of the American Bar Association are expected to follow the ABA Model Rules of Professional Conduct (ABA, 2018). Traditionally these rules have described, not only a duty of loyalty but also zealous advocacy as being central in the defence lawyer's work. Whilst the current ABA Model Code continues to include the duty of loyalty, it does not refer to "zeal" – apart from in the preamble which states that "[a]s advocate, a lawyer zealously asserts the client's position under the rules of the adversary system" (American Bar Association ABA, 2018, Preamble). Also, in the Criminal Justice Section of the ABA, there is a Standard stating that lawyers serve "both as officers of the court and as loyal and zealous advocates for their clients" (ABA, 2016, Standard 4-1.2b).

The most defining characteristic of the American defence lawyer is their role as partisans, zealously representing their clients within the boundaries of the law. Indeed, the "professional zeal (…) found in the United States [is] in a form that, for vigor, has no rival anywhere" (Wolfram, 1986, p. 581).[11] The loyalty of defence lawyers in the U.S. has been the subject of critique – loyalty to one's client demands time, passion, and resources that may be not be conducive to the greatest good of the greatest number and it demands that the lawyer is partisan (Fried, 1976). As with Swedish lawyers, the loyalty of the American defence lawyer goes beyond the loyalty seen in other areas of society. For instance, the defence lawyers have an obligation of confidentiality even after a short meeting which ends with the client choosing another lawyer. In the U.S., a lawyer can decide to work pro bono, without taking out a fee, yet still be bound by loyalty, confidentiality, and demands of competency (Ebervall, 2002). This is explored in more detail later on in this book.

The neutral partisanship of American lawyers is based on the idea that justice is achieved by the "competitive clash of two zealous adversaries, and that their effectiveness depends on trusting relationships with clients" (Rhode, 2003, p. 8). The primary duties of lawyers are to serve their clients with "courage and devotion," protect their constitutional rights and "provide effective and high-quality legal representation with integrity" (ABA, 2016, Standard 4-1.2b).

Similar to the other jurisdictions presented here, American defence lawyers have duties to the client including confidentiality, avoiding conflict of interest, due diligence, and efficacy along with duties towards the court such as the disclosure of perjury and finally duties to the profession such as reporting misconduct (ABA, 2016). Unlike in Sweden, the code of conduct differs slightly across the country as the court in each State decides which of the ABA's rules it will promulgate (Ebervall, 2002). Infringement of these rules can lead to lawyers losing their licence to practice meaning that they are no longer able to practise as a lawyer.

Australia has a similar barrister system to England and Wales; however, whilst the role of barrister is the same across Australia, the administration of the profession differs – in some states and territories the role of barrister and solicitor is split (as in England and Wales), but in others the two roles are fused. There is an independent bar maintained for those wishing to practise solely as barristers (Australian Bar Association ABA, 2019). All barristers follow the same code of conduct – Legal Profession Uniform Conduct (Barristers) Rules, outlining that barristers have a "paramount duty to the administration of justice" and are expected to maintain high standards of professional conduct, acting honestly, fairly, skilfully, competently, and diligently (Australian Bar Association ABA, 2010).

Members of the Swedish Bar Association risk being reported to the disciplinary committee if they are suspected of having broken the Swedish Bar Association's code of conduct (Association, 2008). This may lead to sanctions ranging from reminders, warnings, fines of up to €5300 and, in the most serious of cases, expulsion from the Bar. A compilation of decisions by the Board of the Swedish Bar Association and the disciplinary committee between 1987 and 1997 show that disciplinary action tends to target the neglect of official tasks, rather than behaviour in court (Bentelius & Agneklev, 1998; Wenne, 1988).

Swedish defence lawyers have been presented as have one of two approaches: "the hired gun" or "the moral agent" (Ebervall, 2002). The first of these defines their role as carrying out the client's objectives within the bounds of the law, client autonomy is thus central, indeed, "[l]awyers exist because clients do not know the law" (Ebervall, 2002, p. 403). The hired gun has a clear division between his or her personal moral position and professional role, thus subjective views regarding guilt or innocence are inappropriate. The basis for the hired gun's professional ideal can be traced back to the 1760s to the English jurist, William Blackstone, who wrote, "the law holds that it is better that ten guilty persons escape, than that one innocent suffer" (Blackstone, 1844). Ebervall (2002) claims that Swedish and American lawyers tend to follow the ideal of the hired gun.

In contrast, lawyers who see themselves as moral agents do not maintain a clear division between their personal feelings and their client, thus, unlike the hired gun, they may decline clients because of moralistic reasons. For moral agents, the interests of society, the courts, and the law weigh equally as heavy as the interests of the client, which play a more central role for hired guns (Ebervall, 2002, p. 403).

The defence lawyer is therefore an essential component of the criminal justice system, ensuring due process, equality of arms, and enforcing the prosecution's burden of proof (Smith, 2013). The role of the defence lawyers is to look after the client's interests and act accordingly, striving for the best possible result within what is legally and ethically permissible (Munukka, 2007, p. 315; Wiklund, 1973, p. 248; Wägeus, 2014). It entails not having any personal opinion regarding the client's guilt and focusing on critically evaluating the value of the evidence presented by the prosecutor (Borgström, 2011; Vinge, 1944, p. 44).

A short overview of Sweden

In order to orientate the reader to the particular societal context, I will now give a short description of Sweden. Sweden has been presented as a socially engineered country with a political culture of decentralisation, participation, and openness and with a pragmatic and non-ideological approach to societal problems, combined with a tendency for dialogue and negotiation enabling political and social compromise and solutions (Lundgren, 2016; Musial, 1998; Simon & Yaras, 2000). It is portrayed as a country of compromise: *landet lagom* meaning, not too much and not too little. Some even say that conflict may only arise in Sweden in order to reach a compromise (Simon & Yaras, 2000; Österberg, 1989). There is also a high level of trust in the political system and between citizens (Welzel, 2016).

It has been claimed that body language and emotional displays are seldom used in Sweden (Simon & Yaras, 2000). People in Sweden have been depicted as having a tendency to avoid strong emotional expressions, partly in order to avoid conflict but also because such robust and spontaneous emotional expressions are associated with childish and rash behaviour (Daun, 1998; Simon & Yaras, 2000, pp. 133, 147). However, I claim that body language and emotional displays are used, but that subtlety is called for. These aspects have also been discussed regarding legal professionals as the former State Secretary for the Justice Department in Sweden and judge, Krister Thelin (2001, p. 54) writes that Swedes are generally careful and reticent, factors which may influence courtroom performances. I have thus endeavoured to remember that "cultural variability requires cultural competence" (Maroney, 2015, p. 3) in order to see the comparatively subtle emotions in the Swedish courtroom.

In Scandinavian, there is a well-known yet implicit rule known as "Jantelagen" (Sandemose, 1934/1968). This is a concept that was first introduced by a Danish novelist in the 1930s, to describe the notion that one should not think that one is better than anyone else, a cultural understanding that is widely referenced even today (Sandemose, 1934/1968; S. Scott, 2016; Simon & Yaras, 2000). There is therefore an assumption that defence lawyers in the Swedish courtroom do not give emotionally dramatic, theatrical performances as they do not wish to break the cultural understanding that one must follow "Jantelagen." My position is that the performances I have observed may partly be in compliance with informal societal conventions; however, they are far more nuanced, convoluted and agency driven, than mere adherence to this cultural understanding.

The subtle theatre of the awfully modest Swedish courtroom

In the pages to come, I will show that interactional accomplishments in Swedish criminal trials require appropriate adversarialism and subtlety. They require professional performances and implicit expectations, excluding raised voices and large emotional displays. This is summed up by one of the defence lawyers I interviewed – Peter – who likens the courtroom to a "living theatre," however, he has one important caveat, that the drama or acting – the theatre – is not overstated. He tells me that "obvious theatre" should be avoided because "you're there to represent your client, as a lawyer. You're not his or her twin." Obvious theatre is therefore associated with being "too personally involved" as Peter goes on to say and as many of the other lawyers I interviewed also talk about. Indeed, such obvious theatre is perceived as "uncivilised" and "bad manners" – breaking the etiquette of the courtroom as I will explore in more detail later on.

Performances should consequently be subtly dramatic performances: understated and muted. For Peter and other lawyers I spoke with, overstated emotional displays are not only associated with too much emotional engagement, but also with insincerity and falseness, leading to the perception that one has placed loyalty to one's client over loyalty to the legal system, another theme to be explored more fully throughout this book.

Such performances are also considered to break the *landet lagom* rule of not sticking out, as Lena who is another of the defence lawyers I interviewed says "Swedes are perhaps a bit more timid" in comparison to their U.S. counterparts, a contrast also drawn by many of the other lawyers I interviewed. There are thus unprompted comparisons drawn between Sweden and the U.S. by many of the lawyers I interviewed, indicating that the U.S. adversarial system is a natural point of comparison for them. For instance, one of the defence lawyers I interviewed, Daniel, says of American lawyers:

> Their ability to express themselves is much better than ours here, I mean, the arguments I have heard here in relation to those I have heard in the U.S. – it's more of a drama, we are awfully modest in everything we do here somehow. (Daniel)

Also Hilda, a lawyer I interviewed with first-hand experience of American trials, describes them as more accomplished performers in the courtroom. She tells me:

> Americans are so incredibly better than us. They have to convince a jury in another way (…) I have attended trials at the Superior Court and there you have the kinds of things, like, I mean, if you notice that a witness is making a bad impression, then you should get up and walk around because then the jury follows you the whole time and they don't look at the witness, but if it's a credible witness, then you should establish credibility and expertise – confidence for the witness – by asking lots of personal questions: what do you do? Where do you live? Things like that. Then the 12 jury men and women gain confidence for what the witness is going to say (…) I mean we aren't so skilled I would say. We are a little bit more cousins from the countryside (…) I mean, they are much more capable in the U.S. I think. (Hilda)

Vera is another defence lawyer I interviewed who talks about the difference in the two legal cultures, describing performances in Swedish trials as less dramatic:

> That is the legal culture we have – we don't go to theatre lessons, because we, I don't know, perhaps it has roots in the fact that we don't have a jury? So, we don't have anyone to gesticulate for and like, win points via feelings by doing that. Instead, we have a more, kind of, strict legal culture. The facts should be presented – it should be grounded in fact. (Vera)

Vera presents the strict Swedish legal culture as relying on the quality of the facts that are presented, not on how they are presented. This is also mentioned by another defence lawyer working with criminal cases, Perry, who uses more disparaging terms to depict the performances of defence lawyers in jury trials.

Perry says, "if you compare how they carry on in other countries, the Swedish trial doesn't work like that." However, my argument in this book is that there are still dramatic performances – acting – at large in the Swedish courtroom, but that there is often resistance to acknowledging this. The lawyers I spoke to thus fall into two categories.

The first category of defence lawyers acknowledges that a courtroom can be like a theatre and use dramaturgical terms to describe their role, for instance, defence lawyer Martin tells me in our interview that he likes "acting in trials."

In contrast, Harry, another criminal lawyer I interviewed, falls into the second category, refuting comparisons to the theatre, telling me that a trial "is not a theatre show." Similarly, defence lawyer Lydia, tells me that there "isn't so much theatre in Swedish courts" which she describes as sitting in court making faces. Lydia therefore associates "theatre" with theatricality which is, per definition, insincere, overly extreme and intended to attract attention. Perry shares this understanding and describes such performances as "silly," telling me that defence lawyers who have "very active facial expressions in court [are] a bit ridiculous actually."

The difference in these two contrasting accounts of a trial can be explained by their understandings as we see earlier. Perry and Lydia associated terms such as "acting" and "theatre" to melodramatic theatricalism – acting is linked with over-acting – whilst for others, such as Martin and Peter, it is an accepted part of their role performance. It is a professional expectation. For Martin and Peter, even the absence of overt emotional expression involves acting in order to appear professional, similar to the non-overtly emotional, business-like demeanour used by judicial officers (Barbalet, 2001; Hochschild, 1983; Roach Anleu & Mack, 2017).

My analysis in the pages to come therefore focuses on the subtle drama of Swedish criminal trials. Although you will not read about lawyers jumping up shouting "objection!," a furrowed brow can still be dramatic and still convey the same meaning. A dramatic performance is thus a central part of the defence lawyer's role in Sweden too. This subtle, mundane drama combines the factual and inquisitorial nature of a documentary presenting the facts, with the drama of the adversarial trial system whilst remaining appropriate to the courtroom.

Concluding comments

By now the scene is set for the subtle legal drama to come. In this chapter, my aim has been to give an overview of legal systems and criminal trials and the role of legal professionals within. The scope has been broadened beyond the specific setting of the book to show that whilst the empirical focus is on the work of defence lawyers in Sweden, the loyalty they are guided by is a central aspect of adversarial systems in other jurisdictions thus opening up the pages ahead to a wider audience.

Notes

1 Indeed, the term "inquisitorial" may have derogatory connotations with links to persecution, however, such connotations are out-dated and inaccurate (Ambos, 2003)

2 In Sweden as well as England and Wales, the police have a duty to investigate any criminal offence reported to them. When a suspect is apprehended, it is the police or the Crown Prosecution Service (CPS) in England and Wales or the Swedish Prosecution Authority (SPA) who will then decide whether to press charges. If charges are brought in England and Wales, the case moves to Magistrate's Court in the first instance and subsequently to the Crown Court in more serious cases. In Sweden, cases are handled at District Court at the first instance. The court then decides on the type of criminal offence committed, whether or not a criminal offence has been committed, and the punishment (see Jacobson et al., 2016). This means that there is no option for "plea bargaining" – negotiations between the prosecution and defence that may lead to a conviction, based on a confession – as found in other jurisdictions, such as the U.S.

3 By definition, the plaintiff is the party who initiates a criminal proceeding, a role that is taken by the prosecutor in Sweden. However, in order to make for easier accessibility for the reader, I use the term "plaintiff" rather than the more correct term "injured party." Furthermore, as my interest is not in who brings the case to court, rather on courtroom interactions, I consider it to be an acceptable usage of the term.

4 The Swedish equivalent of a solicitor would be a "jurist" – a person with a law degree.

5 In Sweden, trials are usually open to the public although spectators are rare. Direct-sent TV is not allowed, although live-reporting in the form of live-blogging and tweets along with radio coverage is permitted with the permission of the presiding judge. See Thelin (2001, p. 136) for a discussion on the impact that the introduction of courtroom TV could have on the Swedish courtroom. Thelin (2001, p. 142) argues for the increased transparency that can arise from a more open courtroom leading to fewer misconceptions and misunderstandings of the principles of rule of law and criminal procedure.

6 Although the correct translation is "advocate," I have chosen to use the term "defence lawyer" which I believe will be easier for the reader to use.

7 Although other jurisdictions, such as the U.S., has an established research field of legal ethics, in Sweden it is mostly discussed amongst lawyers (Ebervall, 2002, p. 47).

8 I use "loyalty" to encompass both fidelity and loyalty.

9 In addition to these Swedish rules, defence lawyers should also follow the European code of conduct which states that a client should be represented without regard to the defence lawyer's own interests, and that a "lawyer shall while maintaining due respect and courtesy towards the court defend the interests of the client honourably and fearlessly" (Europe, 1988, p. 13). They must also follow Article 6 of the European Convention of Human Rights (ECHR, 1950) which states that everyone has the right to a fair trial.

10 T. Smith (2013, p. 131) claims however that the English system may be moving towards a more inquisitorial system with increased power given to judges and increased reliance on written information in criminal proceedings yet still maintaining adversarial aspects such as a two-party structure, live evidence and the separation of fact-finder and arbiter of the law. Some argue that this indicates the move to a "managerialist" (McEwan, 2011) system or indeed, a mixed system as in Sweden.

11 Moreover, every American citizen has a constitutional right to a defence attorney if he or she is suspected of a crime: "[i]n all criminal prosecutions, the accused shall enjoy the right to a speedy and public trial, by an impartial jury of the State (…) and to have Assistance of Counsel for his defence" (States, 1791).

Chapter 3

The emotional courtroom

The conceptual and theoretical underpinnings see the emotional regime of law as guiding and shaping the emotions, emotion work, and facework of those working within its remit. These performances thus sustain and reproduce the emotional regime which is aimed at silencing emotions and smoothing interactions. In this chapter, I develop Reddy's (2001) concept of "emotional regimes" by combining Goffman's (1983) "interaction order" and "ceremonial order" (1957) with an "emotional order" – a term I use to refer to Hochschild's (1983) "feeling rules." I use the term emotional order rather than Hochschild's (1983) original concept to underscore that there are different rules to be followed in courtroom interactions. The aim is to show that the emotional regime ensures interactional flow – order in the courtroom – and which requires interaction, ceremonial, and emotion rules to be followed, all of which overlap each other. The defence lawyer's role accomplishment and conveyance of loyalty should therefore remain within the boundaries or what is permitted by this framework.

As I am interested in defence lawyers' performances in Swedish criminal trials which are adversarial in nature with regard to the courtroom roles of legal professionals (and indeed, lay participants), the majority of the research I present here focuses on Anglo-American adversarial systems (Wong, 2012).

The emotional world of the criminal trial

The interest in exploring emotions in law – a field which had traditionally been viewed as shielded from emotion's influence – led to the emergence of a new area of research, namely law and emotion which was kickstarted with the book *The Passions of Law* (Bandes, 1999b) in the late 1990s. This is a collection of multidisciplinary essays[1] exploring how emotions permeate the law. It marks the starting point for the demolition of the illusion of unemotional legal rationality and unemotional legal actors and sparked several streams of research exploring how emotions are reflected in law, how specific emotions are experienced and understood as well as how specific theories of emotion are embedded in law (Maroney, 2006). For instance, research has looked at the role of disgust as a basis for law-making (Miller, 1997; Nussbaum & Kahan, 1996), the function of shame in the sanctioning and reintegration process (Braithwaite, 1989) and the bearing of compassion and remorse in sentencing (Bandes, 2015b, 2017).

Emotional regimes

A major stream of law and emotion research explores the emotions of legal actors. This body of research finds its roots in studies showing that although emotions are universally recognised when they are spontaneously expressed, we are socialised into socially and culturally acceptable emotional experiences and expressions (Ekman, 1992; Ekman & Friesman, 1969).[2] This means that social structures, norms, and values shape the rules which guide our daily interactions, including our emotions. Hochschild (1983) developed this approach by studying the emotions of flight attendants and debt collectors in order to understand the expectations such workers face regarding their emotions, and how they work with their emotions in order to meet said expectations.

These rules for our emotional participation in society are known as an "emotional regime" (Reddy, 2001), reproducing and enforcing emotion rules and setting the limits for what is emotionally possible (Hochschild, 1983). Certain emotions are therefore permitted in an emotional regime, others are not. Prescribed emotions are representative emotions linked to overarching goals and self-image whilst proscribed emotions are non-representative emotions seen as obstacles to the realisation of the guiding principles or rules (Flam, 1990a, 1990b, p. 231; 2000). Indeed research shows that there is a suspicion towards strong emotions in parts of Western society, with coolness and detachment preferred (Stearns, 1994; Wettergren, 2009).

The concept of emotional regimes can be used to explain the emotion rules on a societal or organisational level, or regarding a particular social setting. It can therefore be used in a variety of social situations. The focus in this book is on the emotional regime of law which pervades in Western law and which continues to reproduce the illusion of a strict division between emotionality and rationality. My attention will also be on how this manifests in the particular context of Sweden, with a specific focus on showing how defence lawyers accomplish their role in the criminal trial (cf. Bergman Blix & Wettergren, 2018; Bladini, 2013). I am thus interested in showing the emotional regime of the criminal trial and contributing towards a deeper understanding of:

> How emotions are used and expressed in a regime that officially denies their influence (…) The subtle exchange of emotions between court professionals is a fundamental element in the joint effort to create the appearance of a rational (unemotional) procedure.
>
> (Bergman Blix & Wettergren, 2015, p. 5)

There are two concepts which are similar to that of emotional regimes and here I will briefly explain the differences and why I have opted for my chosen concept.

The concept of emotional regimes is similar to that of "emotional communities" (Rosenwein, 2002, 2010, 2015) which are bonded together by shared emotional valuations and emotional expressions rather than the social system as is the case with social communities. A society may have several emotional communities outlining which emotions are considered to be valuable or harmful, how the social bond between community members is affected by said emotion, and the rules for emotional expression (Rosenwein, 2010). The main difference between the concepts of emotional regimes and emotional communities is that emotional communities do not have "a set of overarching emotional norms from which people seek relief" (Rosenwein, 2002, p. 842 fn. 76) but rather are a gathering of similar emotional styles or emotional norms (Rosenwein, 2010, p. 258). This implies that there is no ruling body or community formulating and presiding over sanctions, unlike in Reddy's (2001) concept of emotional regimes. I argue that the law, and in my particular case, the criminal trial, has a clear sanctioning body, both in the form of the judge but also in the form of disciplinary boards. Reddy's (2001) concept is therefore more appropriate.

Rosenwein (2010, p. 255) also distinguishes emotional communities from emotional regimes as she states that the latter "suggests that one set of emotional norms is true for all" – that there is one emotional regime. However, Reddy (2010, p. 243) states that it is possible to talk about emotional regimes in the plural as an emotional style within an overarching emotion norm system that can be enforced and sanctioned, thus constituting an emotional regime within the emotional regime.

Another related concept is that of "emotionology" (Stearns & Stearns, 1985) which originally referred to the ways in which emotions should be experienced, expressed, and directed and the ways in which institutions "reflect and encourage these attitudes in human conduct" (Stearns & Stearns, 1985, p. 813). Emotionology can also include a positioning (morally, prudentially, and aesthetically) within social encounters; however, similarly to the concept of "emotional communities," there lacks a sanctioning aspect (see Bamberg, 1997, pp. 311–312).

Emotion work

As we have already seen, we should ensure that our emotions remain in line with cultural, situational, and interactional expectations. I will use the term "emotional order" to refer to these expectations, and I present the emotional order as one of the mechanisms upholding the emotional regime of the criminal trial, along with the rules for interactions and civility as will be detailed later on in this chapter.

In order to follow the emotional order, we should manage our emotions or as Hochschild (1983, p. 7) writes, we use "emotion work" to "induce or suppress feeling in order to sustain the outward countenance that produces the proper state of mind in others." Emotion work entails managing the range, intensity, duration, and target of our emotions to ensure they are appropriate to the situation and associated role. When our emotions are bought and sold for a wage, they become commodities – emotion work becomes "emotional labour" (Hochschild, 1983; see also Wright Mills, 1951, pp. 182–183). Emotional labour is likely in jobs where there is personal interaction with the public, where workers should produce emotional states in others and, where the emotional labour of workers is monitored by an "emotion supervisor" (Hochschild, 1983, p. 153). Hochschild (1983) thus concludes that professionals perform a different kind of emotional labour as they lack such a supervisor who is immediately on hand. Research has subsequently shown that professionals may therefore be "privileged emotion managers" (Orzechowicz, 2008, p. 154) and could face even greater demands on emotion management than service workers who have traditionally been linked with emotional labour (Wouters, 1989).

Research on emotional labour initially explored the service industry but has consequently looked at the emotional labour of professions such as doctors, teachers, clergy members, and police officers (Kinman, McFall, & Rodriguez, 2011; Pogrebin & Poole, 1991; Smith & Kleinman, 1989; Stenross & Kleinman, 1989; Zembylas, 2004).

It is also worthy to note that although many professions, particularly high-status professions such as law, medicine, and theology, may have formalised codes of conduct or practice, there are often no explicit rules as to how these codes of conduct should be performed. This also applies to legal professionals – whilst there are explicit codes of conduct outlining one's professional role, including obligations and expectations, how this role should actually be performed remains unsaid.

If we break an emotion rule, we risk being explicitly or implicitly sanctioned for our transgression and thus reminded of the underlying rule that we have deviated from. This practice of sanctioning is part of the emotional socialisation process taking place on a daily basis in repeated interactions and in a variety of contexts and situations with the goal of fitting our emotions to cultural and contextual norms. When it comes to defence lawyers, and indeed legal professionals generally, this is often an implicit process rather than an explicit part of formal education (see Flower, 2014). Professional emotions are therefore a taken-for-granted aspect of one's role as a legal profession much in the same way that medical professionals are expected to learn appropriate emotions (Smith & Kleinman, 1989).

Legal professionals

It is therefore here that we find the roots of much of the research on legal actors' emotions. This research began by focusing on judges, not least due to their central role in proceedings but also, as I have already noted, because the judicial ideal has traditionally depicted judges as objective and impartial, capable of making decisions unaffected by emotions. Scholars have thus unpicked the myth of judges as emotionless entities – robots devoid of feelings that might influence decision-making (Maroney, 2006, 2011a, 2011b; Maroney & Gross, 2014). Robot judges are therefore replaced by emotionally aware judges – able to regulate their emotions in order to make them appropriate to their judicial role, a role centring on the performance of impartiality (Bergman Blix & Wettergren, 2018; Fielding, 2011; Maroney, 2016; Roach Anleu & Mack, 2005, 2017; Tata, 2007).

The emotions of prosecutors have also been explored. In Sweden, this work has shone a light on how prosecutors talk about balancing conflicting emotional ideals such as gut feeling/rationality, receptiveness/scepticism, and intimacy/distance in order to construct a professional identity (Törnqvist, 2017; see also Asp, 2012; Jacobsson, 2008). This professional prosecutorial identity is grounded in the principle of objectivity – the legal position of the Swedish prosecutor. Other studies have shown how prosecutors use empathy as a professional tool, in order to prevent cynicism amongst other things (Wettergren & Bergman Blix, 2016, pp. 11–12). Similarly in the U.S., prosecutors perceive themselves as having to fulfil demands of objectivity and thus professionalism (seen as being honest, dependable, respectful, and trustworthy) by ensuring a balance of emotions: suppressing inappropriate emotions by putting up emotional "walls" or becoming emotionally detached whilst maintaining the emotional involvement required to spur motivation (Bevis, 2009, p. 14). Objectivity is therefore transformed from a symbolic construction into legal beliefs, acts, and performances, a process which has been presented in Australian prosecutors as balancing objectively defined legal evidence, with a subjective interpretation of which evidence is necessary for a conviction (Rogers & Erez, 1999).

When it comes to defence lawyers' emotions, the research is less developed. In England and Wales, Harris' (2002) study differentiates between different types of emotional labour done by barristers used either in private interactions with other legal professionals or in public interactions with laypeople and legal professionals, and which may entail not only the display but also the suppression of inappropriate emotions. The vulnerability of criminal barristers stemming from austerity cut-backs preventing barristers from executing their role as well as they would like has also been shown (Dehaghani & Newman, 2017). Research on solicitors has shown that asylum law solicitors are expected to work with their emotional displays in order to develop trust and show empathy, skills which are vocationally learned (see also Boon, 2005; McConville et al., 1994; Westaby, 2010).

In the U.S., Pierce (1995) shows the emotional elements of lawyering by comparing the emotional labour of litigators with paralegals. She finds that a criminal trial entails not only legal argumentation but also the "emotional presentation of self as intimidating or strategically friendly" (Pierce, 1995, p. 8) in order to achieve the desired result of winning. Litigators may therefore perform as "Rambo litigators" (Pierce, 1995) using aggression, anger, and intimidation for strategic purposes. Other ploys include "strategic friendliness" (Pierce, 1995) which includes politeness, tact, courteousness, friendliness, and sometimes, playing dumb (see also Levenson, 2007; Maroney, 2012; Turrow, 1987). Rambo litigators are contrasted with "mothering paralegals" (Pierce, 1995) who were more nurturing and caring. Both roles were strongly linked to gendered expectations and doing gender thereby reproducing gendered hierarchical and occupational structures (Lively, 2000; Pierce, 1995).

In comparison, the emotion work of defence lawyers in (adversarial) Norwegian rape trials shows that defence lawyers' courtroom performances are adjusted in line with expression rules as well as "changing cultural narratives and political conditions" (Bitsch, 2018, p. 118). Accordingly, defence lawyers may choose an "instrumentally decent" (Bitsch, 2018, p. 118) lawyering, as a Rambo approach in rape trials is deemed inappropriate. I find that Swedish defence lawyers may also eschew a Rambo performance with lawyers finding an appropriate way to perform anger and aggression which I will depict in detail in chapter seven.

Moving back to the U.S., Waldron (2000) shows that defence lawyers' emotional displays are adjusted depending on whether they are in the courtroom or behind the scenes. Defence lawyers thus:

> Recognize the emotional cues of judges and defendants and each other. They 'play off', their co-workers' emotional displays, coordinate their use of emotional 'props', signal each other with emotional key words. Emotional teamwork is essential if they are to achieve their jointly desired task goals.
>
> (Waldron, 2000, p. 80)

On the surface, the atmosphere of a Swedish criminal trial is less dramatic than that portrayed on TV and films, portrayals which, even in Sweden, are often of American trials. Expectations of a trial can thus be associated with such medialised depictions (see also Adelswärd, 1989; Fielding, 2006; Greenfield & Osborn, 1995; Machura & Ulbrich, 2001; Thelin, 2001).

Dahlberg (2009) agrees with Adelswärd (1989) that emotions should remain controlled and regulated in the Swedish trial system to a greater extent than is the case in the Anglo-American adversarial system which he writes is "based on a dramatic confrontation between prosecution and defence in front of a jury of lay people" (Dahlberg, 2009, p.129). I argue, however, that there is still a dramatic confrontation in the Swedish courtroom, but that it is subtly dramatic (cf. Bergman Blix & Wettergren, 2015).

This brings me to another aspect of the defence lawyers' role which will be explored in this book, namely the strategies used by defence lawyers to present themselves and others in the courtroom and how these performances can be seen as a joint accomplishment together with others. Empirically, this book is novel in providing detailed insight into how defence lawyers interactionally defend their clients in the courtroom. My focus is not on juridical representation, but interactional representation. In particular, I show the subtlety of defence lawyers' work. It thus also opens up for deeper understanding of how, not only legal roles, but also other professional roles, are accomplished. Before embarking on this, I wish to present how the criminal trial can be seen as an ordered interaction (cf. Rock, 1993).

The social world of the criminal trial

Goffman's (1983) dramaturgical approach to understanding the social world sees us all as actors performing roles and following unwritten rules which he calls the "interaction order." The interaction order decides why we do what we do based on who we are in relation to others in any given social situation where two or more people are present and able to perceive the other's response. It ensures orderliness in all social situations and enables interactions to be predictable – we know what is expected of us and we know what to expect of others (Misztal, 2001, p. 314). Moreover, interactions are not only ordered regarding *what* we are expected to do, but also *how* we are expected to do it, which Goffman (1957) refers to as the "ceremonial order." Here, we find the rules of conduct or etiquette, politeness, and courtesy. The interaction order thus frames what we should do in any given occasion; the ceremonial order gives us the rules for how to do it civilly. Additionally, as already mentioned, I have chosen to call the aspect of the emotional regime that pertains to emotions the "emotional order" as not only does it order our emotions but it also ensures order is upheld in the courtroom (and indeed, society), by ensuring that roles are appropriately performed and expectations are met. Because emotions are interactional phenomena – an emotional regime must also encompass interactions. Accordingly, the emotional regime of a criminal trial shapes emotions and simultaneously guides how the roles within are dramaturgically conveyed.

The interaction order consists of norms, rules, and expectations of how we should behave in the presence of others in order for us to convey the courtesy and respect appropriate to the situation and our roles within (S. Scott, 2015). A role such as defence lawyer is thus linked with certain rights and obligations and is constructed in interaction with others. This leads to norms being created regarding the defence lawyer role, in that we come to expect certain things about defence lawyers. This does not mean that the defence lawyer's role is set in stone or that they lack agency, but rather that the defence lawyer role is a "loose template for action" (S. Scott, 2015, p. 74) enabling individual interpretation and meaning-making. My interest is thus in how defence lawyers make their role – how do they perform and convey it to others?

The answer to this is found in their presentation of self and impression management strategies – rules surrounding how defence lawyers present themselves to others (Goffman, 1959). Goffman (1959) writes that whenever a person comes into our presence, we attempt to glean information about that individual regarding structural characteristics such as socioeconomic background and occupation, as well as personal characteristics, such as trustworthiness. This "social information" (Goffman, 1959) is intentionally or unintentionally expressed by the individual and is, in turn, impressed on others. In this way, we are both the senders and receivers of information, attempting to portray a certain picture of ourselves to others whilst also forming impressions of others based on the signals they have conveyed. As Goffman (1956b, p. 3) writes:

> When an individual appears in the presence of others, there will usually be some reason for him [or her] to mobilize activity so that it will convey an impression to others which it is in his [or her] interests to convey.

In this book, I will show that in order for the trial to run smoothly each cast member should perform his or her role appropriately – loyal lawyer, objective prosecutor, and impartial judge. These principle performances should follow the interaction order, ceremonial order, and emotional order which I present as the three supporting pillars of the emotional regime of the courtroom. This means that the lawyer should defend, the prosecutor should prosecute, and the judge should decide. Hence, prosecutors and judges have a duty of objectivity, in contrast with lawyers who should subjectively defend their clients (Ebervall, 2008). Although each of these teams is working towards the common goal of justice, there are underlying tensions which threaten to disrupt performances.

All of the lawyers I interviewed talk about the importance of each actor staying in character, indeed, failure to stick to one's role can lead to irritations and delays and can even, as defence lawyer Siri tells me, lead to the whole system collapsing. Each role differs and is linked to an associated legal principle and thus duty and also, performance. This role differentiation and divergence is talked about by legal professionals as being a vital part of the justice process. For instance, Martin talks about the role-uniqueness, telling me:

> The [prosecutor's] role of course, is to prove the claim that my client has done something [illegal] and to call for punishment. I should question this evidence as much as possible and the judges, they sit there and somehow objectively consider the evidence. So, it's these three roles which all have different tasks. (Martin)

Criminal defence lawyer George also tells me that these differences are "so distinct that you have no problem falling into that role." Lo also describes how each performer tends to stay in character thereby helping the trial to run smoothly:

> The prosecution has their role, I have my role and the court has their role. For the most part [the trial] runs along smoothly, it's actually quite unusual that there are big annoyances between lawyers and prosecutors. It happens, but it's quite rare, because both sides are aware that they have their role in the courtroom. (Lo)

We therefore see that role differentiation is an inherent part of a criminal trial. We see too that all of these legal professionals share a commonality in that they are expected to display loyalty to the law by performing their legal principle appropriately. This, in turn, sustains the social situation of the criminal trial. I will return to this throughout the book but particularly in the final chapter.

Integral to this process is the collective understanding of the situation at hand, for instance, a criminal trial. According to Goffman (1959), it is via a process of shared meanings that we are able to understand and make sense of the actions of others and define the situation: what is it going on here? Is it a date, a lecture, or a criminal trial? This includes normative assumptions and expectations and leads to an almost routine-like way of conducting oneself within the situation – the criminal trial.

The definition of the situation is sustained by following rules as to what should be attended to and what should be systematically ignored in order to protect against threats to this definition of reality (Goffman, 1961b, p. 19; Strong, 1988). In the case of a criminal trial, the social situation may centre on competing claims to reality: the defendant claims innocence, the prosecutor claims guilt. However, even in such instances where versions of reality clash, there is still agreement on the overarching definition of the situation – a criminal trial. What makes this situation more interactionally and therefore sociologically interesting, is that not all participants are initiated into the interactional framework of the criminal trial thus leading to possible disruptions (Goffman, 1956b, p. 21).

A number of ethnographic studies of the English Crown Court have explored the social world of the courtroom, several of which have either had an explicit dramaturgical perspective or which may be read through a dramaturgical lens as I will now present (see also Carlen, 1976; McBarnet, 1981; Travers, 1997). For instance, Rock (1993, pp. 2, 56–57) finds the criminal trial to be "ceremonial, disciplined and staged," filled with "understated acting" and "professional emotionality." Professional emotions are not something to be explicitly discussed and learned, but rather a form of tacit knowledge drawing on one's "emotional capital" (Cahill, 1999). The socialisation process of legal professionals is aimed at ensuring that their motivations, expectations, and values are aligned with the legal profession (Boon, 2005; Flower, 2014).

Building on Rock's (1993) work, Scheffer (2010) describes solicitors and barristers' awareness of the restrictions and possibilities they face regarding their performances. He highlights the predictability that the interaction order provides, guiding performances as well as forming how these performances are received (see also Dahlberg, 2009; Rossner et al., 2017). Other research has shown that, despite the highly formalised and ritualised nature of a criminal trial, it can still be "structured mayhem" (Jacobson et al., 2016) involving delays, disruptions, and adjournments. This is explored in more detail in this book, in particular, the unpredictable nature of a criminal trial is seen as a central contributing factor to this ordered disorder.

Facework and defence lawyers

A dramaturgical approach to understanding how we interact with one another can also be used to show the different strategies that defence lawyers use to convey a specific impression or "face" to their audience, an audience which may consist of their client, legal professionals, other lay participants of a trial, or indeed spectators (Goffman, 1959). Goffman (1967) defines face as the public image that we claim for ourselves in certain situations and which is in accordance with the norms and values of the group, setting, or local culture. For defence lawyers, it entails upholding lawyer face. A criminal trial can be seen as constituting an inherent face threat for the defendant with the prosecutor questioning the impression – of innocence – the defendant is attempting to convey (Adelswärd, 1989, pp. 743–748; see also Törnqvist, 2017). Indeed defendants interviewed after a trial often spontaneously talk about feelings of loneliness and degradation (Adelswärd, Aronsson, & Linell, 1988).

Face is upheld by using "facework" to ensure that the impression we are conveying is in line with expectations (Goffman, 1959). This means that if we perceive that our face has been threatened or that we have conveyed the wrong face, we attempt to correct the attack, misperception, or deviation, or prevent any future mishaps so that we can continue to present ourselves in accordance with expectations.

We convey a certain impression using both verbal expressions but also non-verbally using clothing, bearing, facial expressions, voice, and props all of which Goffman (1959) calls the performance on the "personal front" (see also Freund, 1998; Waldron, 2000 for a discussion on emotional props).

Studies in England and Wales have looked at how legal professionals use performances on the personal front as part of their daily work. For instance, Scheffer (2010) describes how barristers may use props such as wigs, white collars, and black robes to convey the gravity along with the formalised and ceremonial aspects of a trial. The use of such props is seen as a deliberate strategy to convey authority, particularly for those unaccustomed to the courtroom (Jacobson et al., 2016, p. 201; Rock, 1993). In contrast, defence lawyers in Sweden must find other strategies to do this, without the ceremonial aid of wigs and robes as I will show later on in this book.

Another way in which we show alignment to a role and convey a particular something to a particular other is by using "dramatic productions"

(Goffman, 1972, p. 125). These can be gestures and facial expressions aimed at highlighting and portraying facts which might otherwise have been missed (Goffman, 1956a, p. 19). I have further developed this concept to show how we may also want to draw attention away from facts by using "dramatic reductions" and in this book, I show such dramatic reductions to be an integral part of the defence lawyers' professional toolbox. These strategies use the body as a tool when verbal communication is not possible; therefore, I have termed them "bodywork." The importance of such bodywork should not be understated as when non-verbal and verbal communication are in conflict, the verbal message is virtually ignored and, furthermore, the dissonance between the two forms of communication leads to the performance being perceived as unstable, insincere, and confusing (Argyle, 1974; Argyle, Alkema, & Gilmour, 1971; Burns, 1992).

Facework is used by defence lawyers to stay in face, to threaten the face of others, and to save face when threatened. Facework is thus used in an attempt to control the conduct of others, particularly the responsive treatment we receive from them. Defence lawyers may wish the other – for instance, the prosecutor or the client – to think something in particular about them, or instil a sense of harmony in order for interactions to be sustained, or indeed, they may attempt to trick or dupe the other.

If we inadvertently present an inconsistent identity to the impression we wish to project, we have given the 'wrong face' which may lead to us 'losing face' by being discredited, losing dignity, and feeling shame. In such episodes, we are 'out of face' as we have failed in upholding the intended impression. If we 'give face' to someone else in such situations by offering an escape from their embarrassment, then we help by 'saving' their face (see S. Scott, 2015, p. 96). We perform face-saving strategies in order to save the face of others out of our respect and consideration for them, and ourselves and we do this whenever we are in the immediate presence of others. In the majority of interactions, we want to help someone who has done something out of character by disregarding it – we look the other way when someone trips, we pretend not to notice when they mix up their words. If we were to draw attention to such embarrassments, we leave ourselves exposed for being viewed as rude or mean.

There are several studies of the U.S. courtroom trial exploring the multiple uses of facework in adversarial courtrooms, for instance as a way of requesting information, clarification, or confirmation; making an accusation; and controlling the interaction (Archer, 2011b; Penman, 1990). Archer's (2011a, 2011b) work on im/politeness in legal contexts explores lawyers' use of facework during cross-examination. She develops Goffman's (1967) types of face threat (intentional, incidental, and accidental) to include a new zone of "strategic ambivalence" (Archer, 2011a) which combines intentional impoliteness and incidental face threat. It describes how lawyers may intentionally threaten another's face but that such face threats lack malice, thus the resulting face damage is incidental, arising as a by-product of the lawyer's quest to bring forth evidence (cf. Goffman, 1967).

Facework has also been shown to be a strategic part of presenting evidence and may even entail damaging the face of one's own client in order to prove his or her innocence (Harris, 2011a, 2011b). It can also involve threatening a witness' face by reacting with disbelief at their testimony in order to protect one's own and one's client's face (Penman, 1990).

While outside of the courtroom such strategies might lead to the receiver of the face damage feeling aggrieved, in the courtroom they are "legally sanctioned by courtroom conventions and norms" (Archer, 2011b, p. 6; cf. Goffman, 1967; Harris, 2011b). This is not to say that those on the receiving end of the questioning do not perceive it as impolite or malicious, indeed, lay participants' lack of knowledge regarding this facework can lead to the exacerbation of face damage – that lay participants experience being subjected to face attacks despite a lack of intention on the behalf "attacker" who may see such aggressive face threats as a part of their professional role (Archer, 2011a, p. 3222, 2011b). Defence lawyers can therefore claim that they are not attacking the witness or plaintiff, rather performing their role of searching for evidence (Lakoff, 1990; Tracy & Tracy, 1998).

Behaviour that would otherwise be considered as rude outside the courtroom context may be an acceptable part of the criminal trial's ceremonial order and thus, of the emotional regime of the criminal trial, providing that it remains polite and is aimed at the appropriate target. This supports the argument I am making, that preparing the defendant for what to expect in a trial is an important part of teamwork as it reduces the risk that cross-examination (or questioning) is experienced as a face threat. Cross-examination is the point during a trial when face threats are most likely to arise – it provides an opportunity to deconstruct evidence, make impressions, and convey emotions (Archer, 2011a).

Other studies looking at courtroom facework show how lawyers in jury systems may create a persona (Hobbs, 2003, p. 276) in order to affiliate themselves with the jury. This is achieved by constructing a shared identity with jurors using different rhetorical styles – adjusting speech patterns to more closely identify with jurors. Although Sweden does not have a jury system, Hobbs' (2003) study is of relevance as it discusses situationally adjusted, interactional strategies for presenting oneself in court which I explore from a non-verbal perspective.

So facework can be used to save our own face by using defensive strategies, or we can attempt to save the face of others by using protective strategies (Goffman, 1959). There is also a third form of facework, namely "collective facework" (Rossing & S. Scott, 2014, p. 167) which is used when the shared identity of a group is threatened. The concept of teams will be introduced in more detail shortly; however, here I will introduce the concept by explaining that each team member has responsibility for upholding the team impression and that the effects of such collective facework will be felt by all in the team

(Goffman, 1959; Rossing & S. Scott, 2014). Collective facework strategies are therefore used to save the face of the group as a whole, rather than just individual members (Rossing & S. Scott, 2014). I will argue that collective facework strategies are used by the defence lawyer in order to sustain the face of the defence team (client and lawyer) which I refer to as team face.

The frontstage and backstage of the courtroom

Performances are given in the front region – frontstage – and are adjusted in relation to the audience (Goffman, 1963a). There are associated expectations for the performance when one is frontstage, expectations that are based on the interaction order and the identity values of the society (Goffman, 1963a). Performances are prepared in the back region – backstage – away from the audience's eyes (Goffman, 1963a). This is also where we can relax. The border between frontstage and backstage is determined by the performance and based on the function that the region should have at the time of the performance. If we do not live up to the audience's expectations as to how we are supposed to be, behave, look, and act when we are performing frontstage, we risk being labelled as deviant and being disqualified from social acceptance (Goffman, 1963b; A. Persson, 2012, p. 22).

By linking Goffman's (1963a) theory to Reddy's (2001, p. 324), we can see that an "emotional refuge" constitutes a "backstage region" (Goffman, 1963a) – a place where the rules of social interaction and, I argue, the rules of emotional interaction, are loosened and where frontstage performances are prepared and subsequently scrutinised and discussed. Accordingly, an emotional regime encompasses both the frontstage where emotion rules should be strictly followed and the backstage where rules are relaxed. My focus is on the performances in the courtroom which will be discussed as frontstage performances, contrasting with backstage areas such as the waiting room with regard to the courthouse, but also other areas such as the law office. To these may be added other backstage areas where the lawyer is no longer in his or her role of defence lawyer, such as when they are at home. However, my interest is in the performance when in one's professional role.

One study in the U.S. which looked at the performances of defence lawyers found that jurors paid attention to the backstage performances of legal and non-legal actors and used such "offstage observations" such as that seen in the waiting room, to bolster opinions based on front stage observations, for instance, what had actually been presented in the case (M. R. Rose, Seidman Diamond, & Baker, 2010).

I am therefore interested in seeing the criminal trial as a theatre with a frontstage and a backstage. The courtroom itself is frontstage whilst other areas such as the waiting room and chambers for the prosecution are backstage areas for preparation and relaxation (Goffman, 1956b). Once the light turns green on the display outside the courtroom signalling that proceedings are underway, defence lawyers, prosecutors, lay participants in the trial, and the public are welcomed into the courtroom and the trial begins (see Mattsson, 2014).

The following excerpt from my fieldnotes written when I was waiting to go into the courtroom to observe a highly publicised murder trial, shows the difference in interactions and emotional performances in the courtroom and those that take place in the waiting room outside. This excerpt can be used to highlight the difference in backstage preparations and the frontstage performances:

> There are around 30–40 people standing near the entrance to the courtroom. I was one of the first to arrive and I am standing opposite the door. People are chatting with each other in normal tones of voice. Next to me are three reporters who are talking about various cases they have covered and what they think will happen during the day's proceedings. The trial is due to begin at 9am and at 8:59am the chatting dies out and there is quiet in the waiting room. People stand a little stiffer, many facing towards the door. It is eerily quiet, everyone waiting for the announcement over the loudspeaker that the trial is going to begin and that we are permitted in to the courtroom. When the announcement is made at 9am people push each other slightly to get through the door and I feel like I have to push back in order to enter. Although I was one of the first to arrive, I end up in the midst of the crowd of people jostling to get in. (Fieldnote)

We see here that those waiting outside the courtroom converse normally until just before the trial is due to begin. We then see a shift from the relaxed backstage emotion rules of the waiting room where laughing and joking are permitted, to the stricter emotion rules of the courtroom. This expectation of the shift in emotion rules can be seen in the minute leading up to the start of the trial. Differences in the ceremonial order are also glimpsed with pushing and jostling outside the courtroom, in comparison to the stricter rules of propriety inside.

I observed laughing and joking in the waiting room on many occasions not just between members of the public, but also between defence lawyer and client. Bodily contact between defence lawyer and client – an arm around the shoulder for instance – is also more common in the waiting room in comparison to the courtroom. These differences reveal shifts in emotion rules and interaction rules pertaining to frontstage and backstage areas (Goffman, 1956b; Hochschild, 1983; Reddy, 2001).

Teamwork

Up until now I have focused on individual performances; however, performances may require co-operation between two or more performers in a team. Indeed, Goffman (1956b) writes that within many social establishments there is a form of two-team interplay underway. In the case of the trial, it is a three-team interplay: the defence, the prosecution, and the judges each working towards sustaining the criminal trial (Goffman, 1956b, p. 57).

A team performance is nevertheless made up of individual performances which may be similar or dissimilar but they should still fit together to present a team impression – a "single routine" (Goffman, 1956b, p. 48; see also Gathings & Parrotta, 2013). Each of the players must present themselves in the associated social definition of the role they are performing. For instance, the client who is a defendant in a trial must direct at himself or herself the associated social definition – defendant face – whilst the defence lawyer must foster, by appearance and manner, the social definition of someone who will defend the client – lawyer face. Together they make the defence team – team face. Team performances also entail uniting behind a shared reality; this means that the client's version of events becomes the defence lawyers' reality upon which the defence is based. When the team's cooperation fails or breaks down, reprimands will not be given frontstage, rather they will occur behind the scenes, backstage so as to not disturb the flow of interaction or the definition of the situation (Goffman, 1959, p. 64). A teammate is therefore someone:

> [W]hose dramaturgical co-operation one is dependent upon in fostering a given definition of the situation; if such a person comes to be beyond the pale of informal sanctions and insists on giving the show away or forcing it to take a particular turn, he is none the less part of the team.
>
> (Goffman, 1956b, p. 51)

Whilst teamwork entails a degree of social responsibility, mutuality should not be assumed (Goffman, 1972). In the case of defence lawyers, there is a unilateral degree of social responsibility as the client has no obligations to the defence lawyer.

One of the team members becomes the director of the performance which I present as the defence lawyer. It is the director who allocates the parts and the performance on the personal front that both lawyer and client employ (Goffman, 1956b, p. 61). Teamwork also involves "staging talk" (Goffman, 1959, p. 173) which refers to the discussions teammates have backstage regarding how they are going to conduct their performance. It is a dress rehearsal aimed at predicting or anticipating possible problems or disruptions and finding ways of managing them in order to reduce the risk of embarrassment arising during the performance.

I argue that the lawyer and defendant are expected to act as a team "with" each other, as evidenced by "tie-signs" which symbolise a link between them – a relationship (Goffman, 1972). Tie-signs symbolising the lawyer-defendant team can take the form of objects, acts, or expressions but it is their conduct that reveals evidence about the relationship (Goffman, 1972, p. 194).

In the Swedish courtroom, an obvious tie-sign is the spatial positioning of the defence lawyer and defendant in the courtroom: sitting next to each other, immediately declaring that they are a team. In some courtrooms, the lawyer and defendant sit on the right-hand side whilst the prosecutor and plaintiff sit opposite but in other courtrooms the seating is mirrored, with the prosecutor and plaintiff sitting on the right-hand side and the lawyer and defendant sitting across from them on the left-hand side of the courtroom. This means that sometimes when I have entered the courtroom, it is not immediately obvious who is the prosecutor and who is the defence lawyer. I can observe the tie-signs: that there appear to be two opposing relationships in the courtroom but in order to pinpoint which team is which, I have to move beyond the tie-sign to study how the relationship is communicated.

On several occasions I observed a prosecutor and defence lawyer laughing together or chatting in the backstage of the waiting room, but usually only when the defendant was not present (for instance, if the defendant was in custody or had gone outside to smoke). Discussions could range from the case itself, to gossiping about other colleagues or mundane talk regarding daily life. This chatting can be seen as a "tie-sign" signalling a link between the defence and the prosecution – that both are involved in the overarching team performance of a criminal trial, despite each of them playing different and antagonistic roles (Goffman, 1956b, 1972). It signals an institutionally "anchored relationship" (Goffman, 1972, p. 205) between them such as friendship or professional collegiality (cf. Scheffer, 2010).

However, upon entering the courtroom this tie-sign disappears, pointing to the immediacy of such signs signalling the current relationship (Goffman, 1972). This shift also shows the role obligations and expectations associated with the role of defence lawyer. Chatting with the prosecutor, who is seen as the opposition in the adversarial aspects of this mixed system, may give the wrong impression, conveying loyalty to the legal system over loyalty to the client. A criminal defence lawyer I interviewed, Kate, tells me regarding her relationship to the prosecutor that her clients "shouldn't think that we are friends and that I therefore don't represent [the client] completely." The "impression of opposition" (Goffman, 1956b, p. 125) between teams should be maintained at all times and thus the loyalty line upheld. This impression could be discredited by appearing friendly and chatting even if this informality occurs backstage as the defence lawyer is still in character – the backstage can still be frontstage depending on the relationship (Goffman, 1963a).

The emotional and dramaturgical mechanisms at play in the performance of teamwork will therefore be shown in the pages to follow – how teams are constructed, directed, and managed – thus filling another crack in the research field. Exploring the strategies and the ways in which teamwork is interactionally accomplished in the courtroom, and in other situations, is previously undeveloped and my findings have implications for an array of other professions and everyday situations where teamwork is required.

Concluding comments

By now it is clear that this book draws on dramaturgical theory and emotion sociological theories as analytical tools using Goffman's (1983) concept of the interaction order to show the rules of interaction and the associated concept of the ceremonial order to highlight the etiquette of a criminal trial. To this I add a new concept of the "emotional order" to capture the appropriate emotions within, drawing on the work of Hochschild (1983). The emotional order shapes what you should feel, how you should show it, and who should feel what, whilst the interaction order shapes what you should do, how you should do it, and who should do what and, finally, the ceremonial order shapes how this should all be done courteously. These orders are integrated and serve to uphold the emotional regime of a criminal trial and I explore the emotion work and facework within. My goal is to show that the purpose of the emotional regime of a criminal trial is not only to stifle emotions' influence but also to provide the frame for the smooth flow of interaction. Loyalty should therefore be performed in accordance with the emotional, interaction, and ceremonial orders.

Even if emotions and interactions are ultimately intertwined, I attempt to disentangle them for analytical ease. In the chapter on defence lawyers' facework, I emphasise how the smooth flow of a criminal trial is a joint interactional accomplishment, demanding each social position to be dramaturgically performed appropriately, focusing on the defence lawyer's role. This will be developed more in the final chapter. In chapter six, I explore the emotions and emotion work of defence lawyers, highlighting how proper and appropriate emotions are professionalised and thus rationalised and then performed. I aim to show that a performance within a specific setting shaped by a specific overarching framework entails ensuring that one's emotions are in line with expectations, but also that one performs one's role appropriately. The latter is not necessarily only about producing an emotion in others, rather it is also about conveying information to others which is in one's interests to convey – such as loyalty.

Notes

1 Although Maroney (2006) notes that social sciences and life sciences are notably absent in the book.

2 For analytical ease, I make the distinction between emotional engagement and emotional expressions or displays (Ashforth & Humphrey, 1993; Morris & Feldman, 1996; Vince, 2006). An emotional display may therefore be the communication of an emotional experience; however, an emotional display may also occur without the concomitant emotional experience (cf. Burkitt, 2002).

Chapter 4

Loyalty and disloyalty

This book is about the defence lawyer's role accomplishment which includes the construction and performance of loyalty. This chapter will therefore present different ways of understanding loyalty: as an emotion, as a form of interaction, and as a legal duty. I conclude this part of the chapter by offering the duty of loyalty as a role obligation for defence lawyers, forming their interactions and emotional performances. The role of loyalty in the lawyer/client relationship is then depicted before showing their loyalty talk, in particular how they make sense of their professional loyalty by using emotional accounting. The competing loyalties that they face will be considered at the end of the first half of this chapter. In the second half of this chapter, I discuss deviant performances – performances of disloyalty which I use to reveal the underlying rule for how loyalty should be conveyed. The two central themes to be explored are defence lawyers' legal loyalty and disloyalty.

What is loyalty?

The word "loyalty" stems from the Old French "loialaté," which, in turn, stems from the word "loyal" rooted in the French "loial" and Latin "lex" and "legalis" (concerned with the law) (Oxford, 2015). It has been used in Western civilisation since written records began to refer to faithfulness or adherence to one's promise such as an oath or word of honour, and later, faithfulness to the sovereign or government. Loyalty has thus traditionally been towards one's own values, family, religion, the monarchy, and/or the nation. The concept as we use it now, is often aimed at denoting a special relationship and is therefore seen as arising in relation to someone or something else – a person, a cause, a product, or an ideology – in a particular context (Arvidson & Axelsson, 2014, 2017; Boszormenyi-Nagy & Spark, 1984; Connor, 2007; Hirschman, 1970).

Loyalty can thus be seen as an interactional process, but is it an emotion? This question deserves some attention before I move on to show how defence lawyers talk about loyalty, not least due to the relative lack of academic consensus regarding loyalty.

Loyalty as an emotion

Part of the definitional problem, not only pertaining to loyalty but also to the definition of emotions in general, stems from the various levels on which emotions operate, for instance cultural, social, cognitive, and biological, with each of these aspects differing in relevance for different fields of research (Turner, 2009). There is nonetheless an overarching agreement that emotions have situational cues, physiological changes, emotion labels, and expressive gestures, as defined by Thoits (1989). This leads to questions such as: if emotions can be physiologically experienced and if emotions can be expressed, what does loyalty feel like and what does it look like? Before I can answer these, I have to first tackle the question of whether or not loyalty is an emotion.

This is difficult to pin down. For instance, Solomon first claims that loyalty is an emotion (Solomon, 1990), then writes that "loyalty (...) presumes certain emotions (even if loyalty is not itself an emotion)" (Solomon, 1997a, p. 492) and claims instead that it is a phenomenon (Solomon, 1997b) or a virtue (Solomon, 2004). This lack of clarity is interesting as Solomon's original claim that loyalty is an emotion has been used by subsequent scholars as support for the loyalty-as-emotion argument.

One such scholar is Barbalet (1996) who writes that emotions operate on both a conscious and non-conscious level but that they are most commonly associated with "high feeling states relating to subjective and individual behaviour" (Barbalet, 1996, p. 81; see also Jasper, 2011). That is, we tend to view emotions as something that we are consciously aware of and which we act upon. He draws on Solomon and describes loyalty as an emotion consisting of a low feeling state, high cognitive aspects, and one that is socially rather than individually manifested. Barbalet (1996) thus presents loyalty as a background emotion – we rarely feel overwhelmed by loyalty. This gains support from Rosenwein (2015, p. 7) who writes that most things can be defined as an emotion because an emotion is anything with an affective valence (as decided by the culture and the emotional community). Thus, even a low valence counts as an emotion.

Barbalet's (1996, pp. 79–80) argument for loyalty as an emotion also centres on the idea that loyalty maintains relationships, even when confidence in the relationship is gone, and even when trust in the other part is absent. Loyalty can therefore exist, even when trust fails as loyalty brings with it the confidence that trust will return (Tenhouten, 1996). There is thus a temporal aspect to loyalty – it is a future-oriented emotion that is a source of motivation and justification for action. It provides us with a guideline for how to act in regard to an unpredictable future, providing us with expectations and reducing uncertainty (Barbalet, 1996). I will return to this shortly.[1]

Connor (2007, p.142) also supports loyalty as an emotion, "because our loyalties conjure up affect-laden responses. Some of these responses are intermingled with other emotional states such as pride, joy, anger and even sadness."

Connor's argument is that loyalty is an emotion as it invokes a physiological response – it triggers a mixture of emotions. Similarly, Barbalet (2002, p. 1) argues that emotions are not only a physiological response, but also a mental response – an emotion is us registering that something matters, as is the case with loyalty.

To sum all of this up, loyalty is not necessarily one, specific emotion, but rather an amalgamation of emotions that are triggered by something we consider to be important. We feel loyalty when we feel fondness and pride, for example.

The cognitive aspects of loyalty as an emotion are seen in it stemming from a deep and stable attachment to something or someone we care about, motivating action and defining identity, thereby linking us to social groups (Connor, 2007). Similarly, loyalty can also steer us towards "inaction" (Barbalet, 2002; Connor, 2007) – we avoid engaging in certain actions in order to avoid engaging in disloyalty.

The social basis of loyalty is thus mirrored not only in it requiring commitment to someone, or indeed, something (for instance, a cause, on object, or a product) but also because there is a strong likelihood that others are also devoted to that same thing or person. Loyalty ties us to other things and other people and involves shared understandings with those others who share our loyalties, giving us a sense of belonging and gratification (Grodzins, 1956; Royce, 1995/1908). It is consequently central for social processes and has been presented as one of the bases of social life (Barbalet, 1996).

The social and relational nature of loyalty is also shown in its reciprocity; however, one is not necessarily re-paid in terms of mutual loyalty, rather, the giving of loyalty can be repaid with a sense of belonging, identity, or financial rewards (Barbalet, 1996; cf. Clark, 1987, 1997; Connor, 2007; Fletcher, 1995). When it comes to defence lawyers, the object of the defence lawyers' loyalty may also lead not only to feelings of belongingness, for instance, to the Swedish Bar Association, but also, in contrast, to feelings of moral suspicion from outsiders as I have already previously discussed – how can you defend a rapist? Implicit in this is that a (suspected) rapist is not a person worthy of loyalty.

We now have some of the answers to the questions posed at the beginning of this section. Loyalty is an emotion as it has physiological, cognitive, and social aspects. For instance, the social aspects of loyalty are seen in the way that it motivates us and gives us a sense of belonging and in the way that it arises in interaction with something or someone else. The apparent absence of physiological aspects can be explained by treating loyalty as a background emotion that can spark foreground emotions which we reflect over, such as pride in our loyalty to a cause, a football team or indeed, the legal system or anger if we experience disloyalty. It can therefore also be seen as a complex emotion, consisting of other emotions arising in social interactions (Kahneman, 1992; Larsen et al., 2004; Plutchik, 2001).

Loyalty as a form of social interaction

Following on from the aspects of temporality that I have just presented, loyalty as an emotion has been explored by Simmel (1950, p. 385). He argues that society is made up of patterns of interaction or "social forms" – specific ways of interacting with each other in a similar manner. For instance, a conflict or, indeed, a co-operation always has the same form, no matter time, place, participants, or starting point. Simmel (1950) argues that without such "sociations," society would collapse. I therefore discern parallels to Goffman's (1983) "interaction order" as each social form has specific features making it easily recognisable for interactants, thus reducing uncertainty regarding expectations of the interaction and acting as a blueprint for future interactions.

For Simmel (1908/2009, p. 517), these interactions are initiated by emotions such as aggression or erotic impulses. Furthermore, the specific type of social form that one engages in also shapes "the inner state of feeling that corresponds to it" (Simmel, 1950, p. 383). Entering into a social form thus produces the appropriate emotional experience. Entering into a conflict, for instance, may bring with it feelings of anger, a response which is based on emotional memories arising from previous encounters (see also Cantó-Milà, 2013).

This, in turn, leads to "second order forms" stemming from interactants orienting towards each other (Simmel, 1950; see also Gerhards, 1986; Shilling, 2002). Simmel writes that faithfulness – which he also refers to as loyalty and which is also sometimes translated from the original German as loyalty – is one such second-order form, using emotional experiences from previous encounters to guide us and engage us in future encounters. That is, we engage in a co-operation (social form) which links the interactants together and cements the interaction and the social bond that arises, thus leading to a sort of emotional investment – the second-order social form. These second-order social forms thus extend momentary social bonds into the future by coupling a social form with emotional engagement (Simmel, 1950). Again, we see that loyalty is presented as future oriented.

Simmelian loyalty is therefore aimed at maintaining a relationship to other – ensuring that the relation continues, independent of personal feelings that might arise (Simmel, 1950, p. 381). Simmel writes further that a formal contract can be entered, such as with marriage, to ensure that this form remains constant despite changes in our lives but loyalty can, by itself, act as a bridge between the fluidity of life with its ever-changing circumstances, motivations, and drives that touch us and whatever it is one is loyal towards. One's inner feelings and outer relationships are aligned: loyalty forms our feelings and our feelings constitute loyalty.

Whilst Simmel sees loyalty as a second-order social form arising from a social interaction, Arvidson and Axelsson (2014) argue that loyalty is a first-order social form – a blueprint for interaction. I find myself agreeing with this latter perspective – if a social form is one whose basic elements are the same no matter the contents, we can see that this is how loyalty works: the same basic ingredients of loyalty are in place regarding each loyalty one has. Ergo, it is a social form.

However, I also consider loyalty to be an emotion, as presented in the previous section. Hence, although we can enter into a social form that has the ingredients of a loyal interaction, the emotion of loyalty is also constructed and reproduced in such loyal interactions.

The duty of loyalty is therefore a social form providing the blueprint for interactions. It is also a role obligation inherent in the defence lawyer's legal position. Accordingly, defence lawyers are expected to convey loyalty in interactions (both backstage and frontstage), a performance which requires the management of inappropriate emotions. Therefore I argue that, just as Swedish prosecutors accomplish objectivity by doing "objectivity work" (Jacobsson, 2008), defence lawyers do loyalty work. I therefore see loyalty as an interactional and emotional accomplishment – it is something that is actively done, constructed, performed.

Before I move on to present how defence lawyers talk about this, it is also necessary to make a further distinction – that between personal and professional loyalty.

Defence lawyers' professional loyalty

Personal loyalty is contextual, developing in particular relationships and growing from previous ties such as the loyalty found with family and friendships (Connor, 2007; Fletcher, 1995). Personal loyalty is therefore something that can be progressively built up over time and something that one has autonomy over. This contrasts with contractual loyalty which stems from an explicit commitment and which begins and ends with entering and leaving the agreement (Connor, 2007). For instance, a business contract may entail a company choosing a certain supplier of products. Loyalty is consequently shown to the supplier, however, once the contract ends, the company is free to switch to another supplier.

Which category does the loyalty of defence lawyers fall into? Is it a loyalty that develops gradually in a lawyer/client relationship? In short, no. It is an immediate loyalty. It is a loyalty that binds the lawyer to the client and one that risks sanctions if it is deviated from. Their duty of loyalty is an institutionalised loyalty – an established part of the legal system and one's role within.

Defence lawyers' loyalty to the client is presented by the lawyers I interviewed, as "not personal loyalty, but a professional loyalty" as Peter words it. He goes on to describe the difference between personal and professional loyalty saying, "you should still be independent from the [client] – you cannot make yourself dependent on [him or her]. You should not be bound by what a client says, but you should listen to it." Professional loyalty thus means independency from the client. Kate reiterates this in our interview, saying:

> We should always see the case based on the client's interests, but you should not be so emotionally engaged to a client, for instance, that you can't see the case objectively and advise the client in a good way (…) and above all else you should not be dependent on your client, you have to be independent. (Kate)

Sandra also talks about this, telling me:

> You don't have an equals sign in the courtroom, rather you have a loyalty – you look after your client's interests. It's not about me as a person at all – who I am has no meaning in the courtroom. It's not about me at all. (Sandra)

We see than that for Peter, Kate, Sandra, and indeed many of the other defence lawyers I interviewed, professional loyalty means the lawyer as a person becomes insignificant – they are a tool for channelling their client's legal voice whilst remaining distinct and independent from said client. This emphasises the contextuality and role specificity of the defence lawyer's professional loyalty which is also developed by Peter in the following excerpt:

> You are not acting as a human, a fellow human being in the courtroom. You are not. You have a role to play. Outside the court, you can act as a fellow human being, you can give a helping hand. You can really feel sorry for someone or you can address them in a much more personal way but in the courtroom, you have a job to do. (Peter)

Peter implies that there are assumptions and rules regarding how one should react as a private person – a normal actor who would help others, which differ to how one should perform in one's professionally loyal role (cf. Maroney, 2011b; Roach Anleu & Mack, 2017).

Theirs is therefore a form of contractual loyalty which I have called professional loyalty. The contractual nature of this loyalty stems from a number of factors. If a lawyer becomes a member of the Bar Association then he or she should follow its code of conduct which requires loyalty to one's client and loyalty to the law (and thus intrinsically – loyalty to the Bar Association's code of conduct). The contractual nature of this agreement is reflected in the fact that the defence lawyer has agreed to be a member but can choose to leave the Bar Association, or indeed be disbarred, thus freeing him or her from this duty of loyalty. So, whilst on the one hand this professional loyalty is a compulsory loyalty, it is also possible to end one's professional loyalty, in the same way that personal loyalties can be finished; however, choosing to disregard professional loyalty would have professional consequences (Arvidson & Axelsson, 2014; Fletcher, 1995).

This also means that when a defendant hires a defence lawyer, the defence lawyer gains power of attorney and has the authority to represent the defendant in a court of law. The defence lawyer is therefore entering into another agreement, this time with the defendant – an agreement to loyally represent him or her. However, here the timeframe differs from personal loyalties. Even after the lawyer/client relationship has ended and even if such a relationship is never fully established but the lawyer has given legal advice – the defence lawyer still has a duty to not reveal information discussed in confidence. This can also be seen as a form of loyalty to the client, even when the client is no longer a client.

I therefore suggest that the temporality of a defence lawyers' professional loyalty is also somewhat different to many other forms as loyalty to the client continues after their working relationship has finished. If the lawyer decides to leave the Bar Association or is disbarred, then he or she is no longer bound by the duty of loyalty and may choose to reveal information disclosed by clients, although such instances are unusual. Similarly, defence lawyers' ability to disregard this loyalty is also limited as many of them present themselves as taking on all cases and, although lawyers in Sweden do not use the cab-rank rule of English and Welsh barristers, both have limited opportunity to protest dissatisfaction regarding client allocation (cf. Hirschman, 1970).

Professional loyalty for criminal lawyers entails not only independence from the client as previously mentioned, but it also brings an expectation that one's own loyalty to the client may not necessarily be repaid by the client in terms of reciprocal loyalty. For instance, Andrew, one of the defence lawyers I interviewed tells me, "I have 100 percent duty of loyalty to [my clients] – they have zero duty of loyalty to me so it's really a state of opposition (*motsatsförhållande*)." Sandra also talks about this telling me that although the client does need to communicate with their lawyer, "they absolutely do not have to have any loyalty to their lawyer, in fact it is important that they do not feel loyal to their lawyer – they can switch lawyer or get a second opinion if they want to." Professional loyalty is thus a one-way street, or perhaps it is more accurate to say that professional loyalty is repaid with satisfied clients and, failing this, satisfaction in one's own performance. This brings me to a related aspect, namely the role of loyalty in the lawyer/client relationship.

Loyalty and the lawyer/client relationship

Lawyers' talk about the importance of client independency in professional loyalty raises questions regarding the type of lawyer/client relationship that is expected. For criminal defence lawyers, endeavouring to maintain a professional divide between oneself and one's clients is talked about as paramount;

for instance, George tells me regarding the clients he has in criminal cases, "you try and avoid personal relationships. You get close to many clients in a way and you notice sometimes that they want to take it a step further but I rarely want to do that." This form of professional loyalty talked about by criminal lawyers contrasts with some of the business lawyers I interviewed who talk about having a different kind of relationship with their clients. For them, professional loyalty can entail a closer connection. For instance, Richard tells me, "you get to know your client pretty well, there is a lot on the social side – in the end they become part of your circle of friends." I also asked Edward – a lawyer specialising in business law – about this and he tells me that his clients believe:

> It's that personal contact – that you slowly build up trust, that you have an ongoing dialogue, and that you check-in with each other – that part is very, very important, it's not just the competence. (Edward)

Edward is describing a mutual trust, in contrast to the trust talked about by criminal defence lawyers. For instance, although the client must trust that the criminal defence lawyer will fulfil his obligations, the defence lawyer can only hope that the client will not change his or her version of events, will show up for court and behave appropriately during the trial (Ebervall, 2002). Edward also touches on another important aspect here – the reciprocity of the relationship. The lawyer's loyalty in business law may be paid back, in turn, by clients choosing to retain the same law firm for many years, in contrast to the non-reciprocal repayment presented by criminal lawyers, not least because, unless the client is a repeat offender, legal representation may be a one-time deal. When I asked George about this – if he considers there to be any difference in relationships with business clients and criminal clients – he surprises me by saying:

> Both yes and no. I think it's easier to get close to a client when the playing rules are clear and for some reason that's more usual with business clients. They know they have come here for a service and they expect to get that service, and they know what to expect and as long as that works then you can have a good relationship on the side. But regarding clients in criminal cases [laughs] firstly, it's usually a relationship that exists whilst the case is going on and then it finishes. And, in many respects, that relationship is personal, because it's often a business relationships although they usually don't pay for it themselves and they tend to have other interests regarding contact with lawyers rather than getting out of this contract or getting a better deal – they simply want to get out [...] The relationship becomes more personal I think because the conditions aren't always as clear for people who are thrown into a client/lawyer relationships compared to a business relationship. (George)

George's comments support my argument presented previously in this book: that the client's lack of initiation into the interaction order of the criminal court and thus, the client's role within, leads to increased emotional and interactional demands on the defence lawyer to uphold a professional loyalty. Defendants may not only be unaware of what is expected of them in the courtroom, but they may also be unaware as to what to expect of the lawyer/client relationship. In other fields of law, this may be even harder to uphold, as Vera tells me:

> In cases where the lawsuit has been going on for two and a half years sometimes – in custody cases and visitation disputes – then the relationship easily becomes an important component in driving the case. (Vera)

Thus, it is inaccurate to talk about a one-size-fits-all lawyer/client relationship, rather the field of law and the nature of the case shapes the relationship and thus the form of the professional loyalty to be shown. By viewing the client relationship in terms of professional loyalty, rather than personal loyalty, defence lawyers are able to set the framework for how this relationship should be formed: not a friendship but a contractual obligation wherein both parts have different motivations for entering into the union (cf. Fried, 1976). Professional loyalty takes different forms depending on the field of law, and depending on the client. This brings me to another aspect of lawyers' work, namely that they can have one of two different roles during a trial – defence lawyer or counsel for the plaintiff. Whilst my focus in this book is on the role of the defence lawyer, it is nevertheless of interest to present how this role differs to another role that a lawyer may have – that of counsel for the plaintiff.

Loyalty and the lawyer role

In trials that may lead to a prison sentence, the plaintiff has the opportunity to be appointed counsel who will represent his or her interests in the trial, in contrast to the prosecutor who focuses on proving the defendant's guilt. The counsel for the plaintiff tends to be a member of the Bar Association and several of the defence lawyers I interviewed told me that they also sometimes work representing the plaintiff. This switch is, however, not seen as a switch of sides – from defending to prosecution as is the case with barristers – rather it is talked about in terms of working in two different roles, both of which entail placing the client first. We see therefore that lawyers can have multiple roles in their repertoire, each of which has different audience expectations and "normative codes of conduct" (S. Scott, 2015, p. 74) associated with it. This, in turn, means that the face presented as counsel for the plaintiff will differ to the face presented when sitting on the opposite side of the courtroom. However, the guiding principle and role duty remains loyalty and not a switch to prosecutorial objectivity. Indeed, when working as counsel for the plaintiff, it is possible to be even more dogged in one's representation, following a more expressive set of emotion rules according to several of the lawyers I interviewed. Sandra talks about the different emotional performances and thus emotion rules that pertain to her role as a defence lawyer in contrast to those when she works as counsel for the plaintiff:

> It's much easier for the lawyer's feelings to be moved, or however you want to put it because [as counsel for the plaintiff] it's more, that you are on that person's side and then perhaps you don't have the same, sometimes I think that, when you sit there in court and someone is talking about, the plaintiff is talking about what they have gone through and it can be something so terribly sad, it really can. And I am a very emotional person and can, like, when someone talks about how they have been completely devastated or been assaulted in front of their children and seen the terror in their children's eyes and so on, then of course it can show, that you actually are affected by it. And sometimes it can be the case that the whole courtroom is affected, and it would have been strange otherwise. But I think that you try and perhaps stay even more objective when you sit there and represent the person who is suspected of this crime precisely because it would be almost disloyal to show that you are affected. I think that you try and control yourself, or at least, I do. (Sandra)

We see that Sandra talks about different emotion rules for the two roles which she may have. As counsel for the plaintiff it is acceptable for her to display emotions such as sadness arising from her client's testimony, whereas displaying sadness in response to the plaintiff when working as the defence, could be interpreted as disloyal. There are thus rules outlining who is an acceptable emotional trigger for one's emotions in each particular role. Furthermore, although, as we will soon see, defence lawyers are able to show emotions in line with their client's testimony, they have greater expectations on them to keep these emotions under control in order to maintain the appearance of professionalism. This divide is not as strict for counsels for the plaintiff; however, there should still be clear boundaries regarding the lawyer/client relationship as Vera talks about here:

> When you are counsel for the plaintiff, for example, then there a number of curative conversations – the client talks about how it felt, or that they are really upset. And of course, my task in that role [as counsel for the plaintiff] is to listen to the client's vulnerability. How terrible they have felt afterwards, you know. That they have felt persecuted, that they have terrible pain and nightmares. That's part of our duty, at the same time as the client should also know that they are not sitting there and crying in front of a friend who is going to give them a pat on the shoulder. Rather, you are telling me this, it's part of my duty to listen and put together a damages claim and that's where my duty ends. Then the client can ring up

> later on and cry and think that [the situation] is really tough – we don't have that kind of relationship – we are not friends. It's really important that, irrespective of the context, the client always understands that this is my lawyer I have turned to and that you don't mix up those roles, so to speak, because we are not friends. That role should always be in place and that drawing of boundaries should always exist. (Vera)

As counsel for the plaintiff it is more acceptable to go "all-in," fighting for your client's right to damages. This, combined with the often sensitive or upsetting nature of the victim's experiences, risks relationship boundaries becoming unclear, as Vera talks about in the previous excerpt (adding another type of lawyer/client relationship as discussed in the previous section). Linked to this, Kate tells me that in her role as counsel for the plaintiff, she may also attempt to produce emotions in her client or witnesses that highlight the version of events being presented:

> Of course, when you are sitting there as counsel for the plaintiff and you have a client who is claiming damages because they have felt terrible for a really long time, if you have, for instance, a parent who is going to come in and witness about it, then it's really good if the mother can show how tough it's been for the daughter (…) you make sure you pose a few questions to the plaintiff, that is – the client, not just ask, "has it been tough?" and then be satisfied with a "yes," but instead, he or she can describe how [it has been tough]. (Kate)

Thus, in both roles – defence lawyer and counsel for the plaintiff – loyalty is the principle performance and there is an expectation that one should manage one's own emotions and the emotions of others. However, the emotion rules differ slightly regarding the source of the emotional trigger, and the zone of emotional display, that is – how much emotion can be shown. The lawyers I interviewed talk about more emotional displays being acceptable for counsels for the plaintiff, in contrast with the more restricted emotional displays of defence lawyers. Indeed, counsels for the plaintiff may also display less subtle emotions than prosecutors. As I will show in the Rambo-Bambi extract presented in the final chapter, the counsel for the plaintiff has the strongest display of disapproval regarding the defence lawyer's cross-examination of her client – the counsel for the plaintiff shakes her head more obviously and repeatedly, in comparison to the prosecutor's single head shake.

Loyalty talk

Although professional loyalty may entail various types of client relationship, there is one commonality for all lawyers I interviewed when it comes to loyalty, and that is that every one of them talk about loyalty as the building block upon which their role is based – "the most important" and "an absolute right" as two defence lawyers describe it. Indeed, Sandra, one of the defence lawyers I interviewed, tells me that:

> The only task that a lawyer has is to loyally take care of the client's interests. This permeates everything. You don't really have any other commitments. Of course, you have to follow the law etcetera, but you don't have to be considerate to anyone else. (Sandra)

Loyalty to the client is the form of loyalty that is most talked about in the interviews I conducted with lawyers and I will shortly return to this point, but before I do it is important to present a clearer picture of how defence lawyers talk about loyalty. We now know that they talk about professional loyalty as entailing a contractual independence from one's client, at least for criminal lawyers, but now I want to explain this professional loyalty in more detail by linking back to something I mentioned in the introduction of this book, namely the dirty work of defence lawyers and the moral suspicion they face from members of the public, the media, and indeed other legal professionals.

These perceptions stem, in part, from the specific nature of defence lawyers' work – showing that the prosecution's evidence is insufficient in proving their client's guilt. Defence lawyers have no obligation to lift evidence that goes against their client. This means that a guilty person could go free if the prosecution does not build and present a strong enough case for conviction. This leads to what many outside the lawyering profession may consider to be an ethical or moral grey-zone: if the role of the defence lawyer is to loyally represent clients and thus not present things to the court that may make the client look bad or indeed, guilty (to put it simply) – does this mean that there is a risk that guilty clients go free? To put it simply – yes. George talks about this in our interview, telling me:

> I don't defend that this person has committed a rape. It's a given that the prosecutor should prove something, and it's my job to try, perhaps in some cases, to put forwards evidence for the opposite and then it can be the case that a guilty person is freed because that's how the system is built. And then you can ask, have I worked for what is just and right in the eyes of the common man (*gemene man*)? But for me, it's right, because I see it from the context of the system, I don't see it as a layperson. For me it's obvious that even someone who has actually committed a rape should be freed if the evidence isn't solid and then it's not a problem for me to defend that person. We can imagine the opposite – that you fall into the trap of starting to judge what this person has done without knowing that he is actually guilty, then we would no longer have a society with rule of law. (George)

George lifts an important and contentious point that defence lawyers all talk about: one of the cornerstones of the Swedish legal system is the presumption of innocence – that guilt must be proven in a court of law and failure to do so could mean that a guilty person goes free. So, how do lawyers make sense of their role in this process and of their professional role in general?

Emotional accounts

In the previous extract, George uses his position in the legal system to explain, justify, create meaning, and make sense of his role – he gives an "account" (Baker, 2002; Ogletree, 1993; Rennstam & Wästerfors, 2015; M. B. Scott & Lyman, 1968; M. B. Scott & Lyman, 1970). Andrew also does this in the following excerpt, telling me,

> If you work as a defence lawyer then you have to be convinced that every individual who is suspected of a crime deserves to have their case heard, have a fair trial and they have the right to a defence. (Andrew)

Andrew and George are explaining their role based on their position in the legal system. All of the defence lawyers I interviewed gave similar accounts and also tell me that it is usual for them to explain their work at social occasions such as dinner parties or family events. This can also be seen in an interview with a well-known criminal defence lawyer in Sweden who explains that when he is faced with the inevitable how-can-you-defend-a-rapist question at a social occasion he usually tries to glide out of the situation by pointing out that no-one is guilty before he or she has been sentenced and pointing out that everyone, including the person asking the question, wants to have a defence lawyer if they get into trouble with the law, and then it's fortunate that someone is willing to do it (Olsson, 2017, p. 50).

The defence lawyers I interviewed thus used accounts to show their membership in a certain professional category – defence lawyer – as seen in the way that their actions and motivations are explained as stemming from their position in the legal system (Baker, 2002). This is necessary because, as Sandra tells me, people may initially have a sceptical attitude towards her role in defending someone accused of rape, "almost like I think that rape is good, that I put an 'equals sign' between them" (see Siemens, 2004). She is telling me that she is perceived by others as doing what sociologists have labelled "dirty work" (Emerson & Pollner, 1975; Hughes, 1962; Tata, 2010). Indeed, all of the defence lawyers I interviewed stated that they have faced such preconceptions which, many of them said, was not the case for prosecutors or judges (see also Bandes, 2006b). Defence lawyers therefore present, or account for, their role as defending the person not the crime, which is a "bloody cliché" as Andrew puts it, but accurate nonetheless. This is also highlighted by Harry who tells me that, as a defence lawyer:

> You might have to represent someone who is accused of beating their child to death. They should not be exposed to a harder punishment than necessary. There is a legal system: a judge, a prosecutor, a lawyer and a suspect. The accused should be able to be represented by the law. (Harry)

Another example of this is Geir Lippestad – one of the lawyers who represented Anders Behring Breivik accused and later convicted of murdering 76 people, the majority of whom were youngsters, on the Norwegian island of Utøya and in Oslo on 22 July 2011. Lippestad writes that he hesitated when he was first offered the case due to the enormity of Breivik's crime but his wife, Signe – a nurse – remarked that if Breivik had been injured, she would have provided care for him. She would not have asked who he was, what he had done or why he was there. Signe reminded Geir that his role as a defence lawyer was the same – to look after Breivik's interests and ensure that he received a fair trial after which Geir took the case (Lippestad, 2013, p. 33).

Many of the lawyers I interviewed and indeed others, present themselves as being motivated by a sense of justice – an "emotional purpose" (Schweingruber & Berns, 2005) driving them to fulfil their role obligations. This purpose is associated with feelings of pride at performing a vital role: providing defendants with a fair defence and achieving the best possible outcome. This contrasts with feelings of outrage that may arise when an injustice is perceived to have occurred. We see too then that, at times, as with Geir Lippestad, emotional purpose reminders might be needed.

Defence lawyers thus account for their legal role but they also account more specifically for the associated emotional performances and experiences. I have termed this latter form of accounting as "emotional accounts" (cf. M. B. Scott & Lyman, 1968; Jacobsson, 2008; Westaby, 2010). Whilst an accused rapist might awaken feelings of disgust or dislike outside of one's role of defence lawyer, when one is in that role, such feelings are irrelevant. Emotional accounts are thus used to justify the absence of otherwise expected emotions. This, in turn, facilitates loyalty to the client, which as Siri says is "easier than you think." She is therefore following the emotion rule that defence lawyers should not be influenced by personal feelings, in line with the professional code of conduct and emotional regime of law (Association, 2008). Defence lawyers present themselves as having a purpose that is in line with their role, in the same way the honour of the civil servant is linked to his or her ability to execute the order of superiors, "exactly as if the order agreed with his own conviction (...) Without this moral discipline and self-denial, in the highest sense, the whole apparatus would fall to pieces" (Weber, 1946, p. 97).

Emotional accounts are therefore a form of "character work" (Strong, 2001) assuring others of the defence lawyer's personal moral core. Consequently, defence lawyers must not only do "character work" (Strong, 2001) on behalf of their client in court, presenting him or her as morally upstanding, they may also need to do it for their own presentation of self. Emotional accounts are also a way of maintaining face and managing eventual face attacks in order to ensure the interaction continues smoothly, for instance, at dinner parties or other social occasions (Goffman, 1956b).

Emotional accounts may thus be used as a strategy to reduce "emotional dissonance" (Hochschild, 1983) by reframing a dilemma in order to ensure that one's emotional experience is in line with expectations and enabling loyalty (cf. Wettergren, 2010, p. 413). Defence lawyers talk about their professional role as shaping and even excluding emotional experience and moral judgement, enabling their role to be performed freed from such factors. This can also be a strategy for managing the emotions of others: attempting to allay fears or suspicions regarding their ethical or moral core.

Loyalty layers

The tendency for the defence lawyers I interviewed to elevate loyalty to the client is somewhat unexpected as defence lawyers have dual loyalties – serving "two masters, their client and the courts" (Newman, 2012, p. 4) – with both of these loyalties essentially based on achieving access to justice (see also McChrystal, 1992). Another quick look at the Swedish Bar Association's (2008, p 4) guidelines shows that there are indeed two parts to the defence lawyer's role: to show loyalty towards the client "within the established framework of the law and good professional conduct." This duality of loyalties is inherent to the adversarial system and is also relevant for prosecutors who are both ministers of justice and advocates for their clients – the victims (Bandes, 2006a).

However, loyalty to the law is only mentioned by a few of the lawyers I interviewed. I do not mean to suggest that lawyers in Sweden do not have loyalty to the law; however, the inclination to lift loyalty to the client in our interviews could be explained as a way for lawyers to professionally position themselves from other legal professionals – all legal professionals have a loyalty to the law, what distinguishes defence lawyers is their client loyalty. There will be more about this in the final chapter.

Defence lawyers may thus have competing loyalties simultaneously, which can be seen as different layers to be negotiated in order to determine which is the strongest or most prevalent layer in each situation and which shapes their actions (Bauman, 1989; Connor, 2007; Lundquist, 1988; Shapiro, 2003). Consequently, these loyalty layers are not static, rather they are mobilised relevant to the social situation at hand. Choosing which layer to act on can be seen as a form of resistance towards one layer, rather than an act of disloyalty, or as simply choosing one loyalty over another (Arvidson & Axelsson, 2017; Kirchhoff & Karlsson, 2009; Royce, 1995/1908). An example of this can be refusing to represent clients who have confessed their guilt but who wish to be defended as innocent – loyalty to justice is thus prioritised over loyalty to the client. However, beginning to cry when a plaintiff talks about an attack that one's client (the defendant) denies occurred may be viewed as a display of disloyalty by the client – that the defence lawyer has sided with the prosecution (see also Grodzins, 1956; Kirchhoff & Karlsson, 2009; Lipsky, 1980).

Furthermore, professional loyalties work on different axes, both vertically thus demanding loyalty to those higher up the hierarchy, but also horizontally – towards one's colleagues (Arvidson & Axelsson, 2014).

Professional loyalty therefore entails identifying various loyalties and gauging the strength of them, that is, identifying competing loyalties, placing them in a hierarchy and then acting based on the topmost loyalty layer. The foremost loyalty is loyalty to the principle of loyalty – the professional ideal – irrespective of whether that loyalty is focused towards the client or the law.

Vera is one of the lawyers who explicitly mentions the law and touches on her loyalty, telling me, "it's an enormous balancing act – the law at the same time as the relationship with client should work but if you have to choose, then the law has to go first of course." Lawyers may thus face ethical dilemmas where the client's interests are in conflict with the law. An example of this is in situations where one has a client who has confessed that he or she is guilty of the crime but who wishes to be defended as though innocent. For instance, when I ask George in our interview what he would do if a client told him that he or she was guilty, he replies:

> I would continue to defend the person although I do think that there are different opinions regarding this and my opinion does not agree with the Bar Association's. I am of the opinion that if a client tells me that he is guilty, then I am responsible for continuing to defend him, (...) If I step down from my role without giving a specific reason, then the implication is that I reveal my client's [guilty] position and I think that my client's interests go first. I think that the Bar Association has sometimes, I think in this regard at least, rules that are a bit too rigid. But what I am absolutely prohibited from doing is to call in evidence that supports something that I know is false. That's where the line is drawn – but showing weaknesses in the prosecutor's evidence – they are there – and I'm not doing anything wrong by showing them. (George)

Perry has a similar approach to George, telling me, in situations where a client confesses:

> There are two positions that lawyers can take: one that says that I have to step down because I can't defend you if I know that you are guilty. The other position is that I can defend you but that I won't call in evidence that is wrong, that I know is wrong. And that's the category I belong too. I will continue but if you try and call in a false witness or something that I knows is wrong because you have confessed, who says that you were somewhere else at the time [of the crime], if you try anything like that then I will step down. (Perry)

Martin tells me that his primary loyalty is to his client and recounts a classic question that lawyers discuss a lot:

> The client confesses in a case but says that I should defend him as denying the crime. It doesn't happen very often, but it is a classic question – are you allowed to continue in the assignment? The majority assert that you are not allowed to. But I would say that you can keep going, I mean, what the client tells me – they say a lot of things. But my working hypothesis is that I do my job based on the client's position or version of a certain sequence of events. I assume that what he or she says is right and then I work based on that. (Martin)

In such situations, George, Perry, and Martin choose loyalty to the client – continuing to represent him or her – over loyalty to the law – reporting that the client has confessed to the crime; however, not all lawyers are in agreement with this view. For instance, Lena and Siri both say that although they've never been in such a position, they would step down if a guilty client asked to be defended as innocent, as does Daniel. When I ask Daniel if it is a matter of interpretation he replies:

> My understanding is that it isn't [a question of interpretation], rather it's the position of the Swedish Bar Association that you cannot continue to represent a client [who has confessed], but of course, it can be difficult to do the right thing in that situation. (Daniel)

This indicates that the negotiation of loyalty layers is an individual accomplishment. Each lawyer places different loyalties at the top of the hierarchy and acts accordingly.

The way in which defence lawyers morally account for themselves is also relevant to explore here. In my interviews many of the defence lawyers present themselves as "hired guns" (Ebervall, 2002). That is, their clients do not hire a lawyer, rather they hire a morally neutral set of skills and knowledge. The hired gun, in turn, will fight for the client, irrespective of what is morally right, and irrespective of what is true or false. We see that the professional ideal of the loyal lawyer can help to determine which loyalty layer and thus moral priority, should be topmost and acted upon (Connor, 2007; McChrystal, 1992). For instance, lawyers who present themselves as hired guns place loyalty to the client as the most important layer with moral justifications and explanations stemming from this.

I will give an example of this to explain more clearly what I mean: imagine a murder case where the defendant is accused of killing a man at a party who had been having an affair with his mother. The defendant's father was also present at the party and was seen fighting the victim, together with the son, shortly before the victim was found. Despite the son being arrested with bloodied clothes and confessing to the crime, his defence lawyer begins to suspect that it is the father, and not his client – the son – who committed the murder. In such situations, the defence lawyer can choose between acting as a hired gun – following the client's instructions without questioning the client's reasons for claiming guilt. The defence lawyer therefore avoids posing moral questions regarding the ethics associated with representing as guilty a man who the defence lawyer suspects is innocent. In contrast, the defence lawyer can choose to be a "moral agent" (Ebervall, 2002), engaging his or her moral compass in order to decide whether he or she should continue to represent the client, or indeed, whether to convince the client to confess his innocence. This latter route arguably entails a greater array of ethical questions to be dealt with.

A similar example can be seen in the case where a client confesses to her lawyer that she committed a crime a number of years ago (see Ebervall, 2002, pp. 373–374). The client says to her lawyer that she thinks the crime will shortly be outside the period of limitations. The lawyer checks this and finds it to be correct. The client then asks "so if I stay out of trouble for the next six months, I can't be charged?" In such situations the lawyer may choose the hired gun route and repeat that the period of limitations will shortly be passed as answering "yes" to the client would be a violation of the Bar Association's code of conduct (both in Sweden and the U.S.). In such instances, the lawyer must balance loyalty to the law with loyalty to the client. Placing loyalty to one's self and one's own principles and morals could in contrast, entail encouraging the client to turn herself in to the authorities.

Loyalty, professional ethics, and professional practice are therefore tightly linked and enable a degree of personal engagement whilst still maintaining distance (Henriksen & Vetlesen, 2013; Weber, 1978). This also means that the responsibility for certain decisions and actions can be placed, not on the individual decision-maker, but on the regulations which have formed the decision or on one's position in the legal system, similar to migration board workers (Wettergren, 2010).

Another aspect to be considered here is the extent to which defence lawyers are able to avoid loyalty obligations. That is, to what extent can lawyers refuse clients? All of the lawyers I interviewed stated that they would accept all criminal cases, irrespective of the person or the crime, however, this is not the case with all lawyers. One of Sweden's most well-known and experienced criminal lawyers – Leif Silbersky does not represent clients accused of drug-related crimes. He states that there is no logic to his decision, only a feeling that he would not be able to represent such clients to the best of his ability due to personal feelings regarding drugs (Silbersky, 2018). Furthermore, as he believes that the biggest mistake a lawyer can make is to not be loyal to the client he has chosen to decline all such cases (Silbersky, 2014, 2018). Thus, as a defence lawyer, professional loyalty means one must be certain that one's personal feelings can be set aside in order to loyally represent the client.

However, this is not merely a balance of two loyalties: one's client and the law – this tightrope is further complicated by other commitments the lawyer may have, for instance to society, to their law firm and colleagues as well as loyalties to family and friends and even to their own personal values and identity (Arvidson & Axelsson, 2017; North, 1990; Rosa, 2013; Sennett, 1998).

Law firm cultures and loyalties

I will now highlight two of these loyalties for a moment: balancing loyalties to one's family with loyalties to one's law firm. In order to do this, it is necessary to present a brief overview of the culture of law firms with a particular focus on the gender culture of some law firms.

Research exploring law firm cultures, and indeed, the culture of law in general, has suggested that the legal profession has traditionally, and to some extent continues to be considered a masculine profession. This means that there may be a "work-hard, play-hard" culture which rewards loyalty to one's law firm. Explanations for this stem from the assumption that feminine tasks are "expressive and person-centred, helping, nurturing and empathizing," thus occupations requiring "coolness, detachment, analytic objectivity, or object-orientation such as law (…) are male occupations" (Epstein, 1970, p. 155; for an excellent overview of the literature see Kay & Gorman, 2008). This raises questions regarding the extent to which the legal profession has been feminised regarding two aspects: the representation of women in the legal profession and the extent to which it has been changed or influenced by women (Menkel-Meadow, 1987).

Regarding the first of these aspects, Rhode (2003, p. 4) suggests that although the overall number of women in the legal profession has risen in many jurisdictions, there are still concerns regarding "the structure of professional roles, and the inequality of professional opportunities." A closer look at the figures regarding women in law reveals that there are still inequalities regarding equal representation in different areas of law and in different professional roles. For instance, despite constituting the majority of law students in Sweden, England and the U.S., women are in the minority working as attorneys and are underrepresented at positions higher up the professional hierarchy (American Bar Association, 2018; Council, 2019; Persson, 2018). This stands in stark contrast with other legal professionals, for instance in Sweden in 2017, a total of 659 judges were female, compared to 602 men thus placing women in the majority (Domstolsverket, 2017). Similar figures are also found for Swedish prosecutors (Åklagarmyndigheten, 2017).

Part of the explanation for this has been presented as the "cowboy culture" (Dahlgren et al., 2014) at some law firms where long work hours and constant availability mean that lawyers are expected to place loyalty to the law firm at the top of their hierarchy of loyalties (see Sommerlad et al., 2010, p. 7 for a presentation of the masculine cultures prevailing in the legal profession in England and Wales).

The difficulties associated with this are reflected in research showing that in the U.S. and Sweden, female lawyers are less likely than their male colleagues to feel that it is possible to successfully combine a personal and professional life (Brodherson, McGee, & Pires dos Reis, 2017; Dahlgren et al., 2014). Thus far, it therefore appears that the second aspect of the feminisation of law has not led to a change in the cultural norms, rather a demand on women to adapt to them (Menkel-Meadow, 1987, p. 3; see also Spencer & Podmore, 1986).

All of this means that lawyers must manage their loyalties: either placing loyalty to one's firm at the top of the hierarchy thereby enabling a faster climb up the professional ladder, or placing a competing loyalty at the top, for instance one's family which may, at some law firms, slow one's professional advancement. I have had many informal conversations with lawyers who have talked about making the decision to not become partner as they have instead prioritised their family – a clear example of how loyalties may be drawn in different directions. Kate tells me that she has chosen loyalty to her family over loyalty to the law firm, saying that she explains to her client:

> I have to leave at a certain time most days because I need to pick up from nursery school and so I can't keep on taking a lot of work phone calls. I can't keep on answering a lot of calls during the evening – that's something that I try and teach my clients – that I work certain times. (Kate)

I therefore suggest that the loyalty of defence lawyers can be seen as a legal loyalty – a professional loyalty which shapes emotions, relationships and loyalty hierarchies.

Now that we know more about how defence lawyers talk about loyalty, my focus is going to switch to disloyalty – to those instances where the defence lawyer falls out of character – where he or she drops lawyer face, if only for a second. Such deviations can serve to reveal the underlying rules of how loyalty should be performed which will be the focus of the coming chapters.

Disloyalty

Defence lawyers endeavour to stay in character, keeping their place in the interaction. However, situations may arise when a discrepancy between the official projection and reality occurs that is, the defence lawyer falls out of face, deviating from their role and exposing unmanaged or inappropriate emotions – conveying the "wrong" impression (Goffman, 1956b, p. 33). The affective line of loyalty is dropped, the mask falls, if only for a moment. In short, the lawyer looks disloyal. By revealing these disruptions, we are able to see the rules that otherwise have remained hidden – the rules for performing loyalty (Goffman, 1959, p. 168; Goffman, 1961b).

Uncomfortable loyalty

We now know that loyalty as a necessary ingredient of a successful defence is discussed by all those interviewed. However, this is not always easy as Sandra tells me, "sometimes you have to put yourself in very uncomfortable situation [sic] in order to not be disloyal to your client." The following extract is a fairly typical example of such an uncomfortable situation. It is taken from an assault trial which the client denies. The defence lawyer begins her closing speech by saying:

> "This is a sad story." She goes on to state that her client was attempting to stop the plaintiff from committing suicide by swallowing tablets, and was therefore trying to force the tablets from the plaintiff's mouth – this is why her mouth was red and swollen. Another suicide attempt by the plaintiff is mentioned and the associated injuries are also described by the defence lawyer as resulting from her client intervening. As the defence lawyer goes through these charges, she argues that there is no evidence of abuse or assault. The plaintiff becomes upset and starts crying. The defence lawyer shows no reaction to this and continues with her closing speech. (Fieldnotes)

This excerpt shows several things. First, it illustrates how defence lawyers construct "sad tales" (Goffman, 1963b; M. B. Scott & Lyman, 1970) or account of events, by downplaying certain aspects and, secondly, it shows that defence lawyers' work may entail causing someone to cry. We see that the defence lawyer does not describe the case as "tragic" or "devastating" or the like, rather "a sad one." She says this in an expressionless manner – there is no emphasis on particular words, there is no softening of facial features or body language that one might assume to be appropriate in such situations. Instead, there is emotive recognition (stating that this is a sad case) aimed at controlling the emotive content and import: constructing a certain story, a certain version of events (cf. Flower, 2014). We see therefore that an aspect of defence lawyers' work is to use discursive means to make emotional plaintiffs and their emotional facts socially invisible whilst simultaneously drawing attention to their client's own sad story. This also involves openly threatening the face of plaintiffs by questioning their version of events, and in doing so, bringing the plaintiff to tears (Goffman, 1956b).

This is not a strategic production of emotions in the plaintiff aimed at achieving a specific goal rather it is an unintentional side-effect which can be quite uncomfortable for the defence lawyer (and of course, for others) and one which may lead to inappropriate emotions in need of management as Lena tells me, "it's never fun being the one asking the questions that make someone break down" (cf. Tracy & Tracy, 1998). Such feelings of discomfort should therefore be managed in order to display professionalism and loyalty to one's own client and to not risk showing disloyalty. A crying defence lawyer could indicate that he or she perceives the plaintiff's version of events as credible, a version of events which the defendant might insist is inaccurate (Neu, 2000, p. 14). Crying could therefore jeopardise the team performance and the performance of loyalty to the client thus communicating disloyalty – that the defence lawyer has sided with the plaintiff, as Sandra says:

> I would not have wanted my defence lawyer to well up with tears when [the plaintiff] described what they have been subjected to. I would really rather have wanted my lawyer to sit completely neutral and take it all in. (Sandra)

The social awkwardness of making someone cry can be emotionally accounted for by justifying one's actions based on one's professional role as I have previously discussed (M. B. Scott & Lyman, 1968; 1970).

Revealing the rules for performing loyalty

When the lawyers I spoke to talked about their ability to stay in role, all presented themselves as accomplished performers, able to stay in face throughout the performance, even when met with face threats, both to their own face or team face. I will present this in more detail in the next chapter; however, it can be seen in the following fieldnote extract from a cross-examination where the client actually confesses to one of the offences he has previously denied committing whilst being questioned by his lawyer:

> The defence lawyer does not show any reaction, no change in tone of voice, body language or facial expression, he just continues to the next question. At the end of the questioning the defence lawyer states that they are changing their plea from not guilty to guilty. The client looks at his lawyer and says something to which the defence lawyer replies "No, but now you confessed to it!" (Fieldnote)

Even when confronted with a confession in the middle of a trial, the lawyer's mask did not drop – he did not show surprise or irritation, he remained with a neutral facial expression, no gestures or other communicative movements were seen. The observant reader may have noted that the defence lawyer in the Danny Diamond trial at the start of this book had a similar non-response. The norm is thus to display the absence of overt emotional expression in such situations. However, on rare occasions, it is possible to see the mask slip. For instance, the following excerpt shows a rule break with the defence lawyer dropping her mask of professionalism for a brief moment during a trial where the defendant is accused of assault. The plaintiff has already been questioned by both the prosecutor and the defence lawyer. The judge then asks the plaintiff how drunk he was at the time of the assault (of which he is the alleged victim):

> The plaintiff replies, "I've been more drunk" to which the judge asks "you don't have any problems remembering the incident?" When the judge says this the defence lawyer blinks. She has not asked the plaintiff any such questions. (Fieldnote)

Rather than not reacting, we see a blink, arising from the defence lawyer's own (in)action – she failed to ask this important question herself. Instances such as this were unusual for me to see – there were only a handful of trials where I observed the defence lawyer's mask slipping indicating that the norm is to not react, with the rarity of such deviations indicating how important this strategy is in the defence lawyer's toolkit. This means that covert expressions become meaningful – they become unusual, revealing the unwritten rule which calls for a strategy I have named "stoneface" to be used in order to manage inappropriate emotions and to convey loyalty and professionalism. I will present a more detailed analysis of stoneface in the coming chapters; however, here it is important to note that stoneface constitutes one of the normative ways of conveying loyalty and professionalism, deviations from this strategy thus risk conveying disloyalty.

For instance, the following is an excerpt from a trial I observed where the defendant is accused of stealing a wallet and train ticket from someone's pocket which he denies doing. There is surveillance film footage from the train station where the theft occurred, which shows the event from several angles. We join proceedings just after the court has seen the film showing the suspect who bears a striking resemblance to the defendant and even has the same distinctive clothing. We see the suspect entering the train station and approaching the victim. The footage is shown on two large screens, one behind the prosecution and one behind the defence which affords me the opportunity to watch the footage and observe the reaction of the defence lawyer:

> The film shows the suspect talking to the victim. The victim has asked the suspect for help in finding his train. The suspect stands very close to the victim. He knocks the victim's leg with his leg, kicks the victim's bags and also claps him on the shoulder. It is during one of these exchanges that the suspect is said to have taken the man's wallet and train ticket. We even see on the video how at the end of the meeting, the suspect turns and walks away and is holding what looks to be a wallet in his hands. He is then shown on film footage from a different angle walking along, looking through the wallet and also holding something that looks to be a train ticket in his hands. When this film sequence is shown, where we see that

> the suspect turns and walks away from the victim with a wallet in his hand, that is, where we see the theft, the defence lawyer blinks. A big blink, more than a mere opening and closing of the eye as a normal blink would be. His face scrunches up slightly more than the other times he blinks. He has not blinked like this before and he does not blink like this again afterwards. (Fieldnote)

The defence lawyer has maintained a neutral facial expression throughout the majority of this viewing of video footage. However, when the theft is shown, he blinks an unusually large blink. As minor signs and symbols can convey social information, a blink may exemplify an inadvertent act giving off an inappropriate impression (Goffman, 1956b, p. 132, 1967). Here, it may convey the defence lawyer briefly falling out of his role.

Such "unmeant gestures" (Goffman, 1956b, p. 132) may serve to reveal the strong emotional undercurrents because, not only are clients talked about as being a source of face threat but, as we will see soon, they are also a source of irritation and frustration which should be managed. I therefore interpret the blink as a mask slip revealing the felt emotion during emotional concealment (cf. "micro-expression" Ekman, 1992, 2004). That is, the blink might reveal the concealment of an underlying hidden emotional experience such as irritation, disgust or surprise that is in need of management.

I observed the blink as a mask slip in various trials, for example, one concerning the handling of stolen goods where there were two defendants. The first defendant states that he did not know that the goods were stolen when he is being questioned in court, however, as I captured in my fieldnotes, "the second defendant says that he knew he was buying stolen goods. The defence lawyer of the other defendant blinks four times in rapid succession."

This failure to align expressions with the reality being presented by the defence team could also serve as an example of the defence lawyer taking the opportunity to drop the mask when the audience's attention is elsewhere – watching the surveillance footage or whoever is being questioned (Goffman, 1956b, p. 34). This creates a backstage area for the defence lawyer to break from his role, probably observed only by the ethnographer in the courtroom.

Another example of a mask slip is sighing. I observed and wrote down the following exchange in one trial:

> *Prosecutor:* Did you threaten her?
> *Defendant:* No.
> Defence lawyer keeps on writing notes.
> *Client:* Or, maybe what I said about the windows [he threatened to smash her windows]
> Defence lawyer gives a small sigh. (Fieldnote)

We see that when the client says that he didn't threaten the plaintiff, the defence lawyer uses stoneface – he does not react, he continues to write notes in order to hide inappropriate emotions (such as surprise or irritation) which could lead to a loss of team face if shown. When the client then changes his version of events and says that he might have threatened the plaintiff the defence lawyer falls out of role by giving a small sigh – his mask slips.

Another way in which disloyalty may be communicated is by physically distancing oneself from one's client. Sandra tells me about this, recounting an uncomfortable situation her colleague found herself in during a trial. Sandra says:

> Sometimes you have to sit with a client who has done completely disgusting things and so, one time, this lawyer realised she had moved her chair away from the client in the courtroom because in some way, it was so terrible, child pornography for example, but then she thought no, [move] back again, it's us, I represent you. It's those kinds of feelings you have to put to one side. (Sandra)

Later on in the interview, Sandra states that she thinks that the lawyer probably managed to save the situation and that it was hardly noticeable. This points to the importance that defence lawyers place on such gestures and the role of facework and emotion work in the courtroom as I will also show in the next two chapters. The comment also illustrates that at times, defence lawyers are aware that they have dropped the mask and must attempt to recover it. These small revealing signs such as moving away one's chair must be kept hidden so as not to damage the impression of loyalty.

Failing to use stoneface and showing doubt in a client's version of events could therefore threaten the team performance as Vera talks about here:

> If we show [doubt] in some way, then we show the client that we don't believe in their case (*sak*). And it might become obvious for the client as well, which in turn, makes the client worried and maybe answer incorrectly or think, "yes, oh, what did I do now?" and "maybe my lawyer isn't doing their best" or something. Rather it's our job to react like [shows nothing]. (Vera)

Vera presents stoneface as critical to the justice process. If her performance deviates from the team line (the version of events being presented by the defence team), by showing disbelief in her client's version of events, this could lead her client to question, not just Vera's professionalism, and, in turn, loyalty, but also the entire interaction, in this case, whether or not he or she (the client) has received a fair trial (cf. Schudson, 1984). Vera is therefore saying that her "emotional cues" (Clark, 1990; Waldron, 2000) may be interpreted by her client as communicating disloyalty, which may lead to the client feeling anger or disappointment. These cues can also be construed as Vera positioning herself outside the defence team, i.e. distancing herself from the client, which, in turn, signals a break in Vera's professional role obligations.

When I describe these instances of doing disloyalty, I am describing situations where the loyalty layer guiding the defence lawyer's performance is something other than loyalty to the client (Arvidson & Axelsson, 2017; Connor, 2007). Implicit to a shift in loyalty layers is therefore a shift in the emotional performance: different layers require different performances.

Disloyal eyework

Another subtle way in which loyalty and indeed disloyalty can be communicated is with eye contact. Eye contact is used to initiate and sustain social interaction and is thus an expected action (Goffman, 1963a; Kendon, 1990; Shilling, 2003). In the literature on courtroom practices, eye contact is described as being important when addressing the judges or indeed whomever one is talking to (Blomkvist, 1987; Mellqvist, 1994). In particular, during cross-examination, eye contact is seen as an important part of persuasive communication and should be made when questioning witnesses (Ball, 1994, p. 4; Blomkvist, 1987). I therefore expected to see eye contact in the courtroom interactions I observed. The analysis of my fieldnotes shows that eye contact is indeed made when defence lawyers question witnesses and plaintiffs and when they are talking to the judges or prosecutor. Furthermore, I noted that when defendants are questioned by the prosecutor, the defendant looks at the prosecutor. If the judge addresses the defendant, eye contact is made.

This routine use of eye contact in these interactions thus revealed the systematic absence of eye contact between defence lawyer and defendant. My fieldnotes show that frequently there is no eye contact made between these teammates during long stretches of proceedings. For instance, near the start of one trial I observed, I wrote "the defence lawyer first looks at his client at 9.43am (proceedings started at 9am)."

This absence is particularly notable during the defence lawyer's questioning of his or her own client. Even then there is often no eye contact made between teammates. When I asked defence lawyers about this in the interviews, all of them claimed that they do make eye contact and many reacted strongly when I told them what I had observed, deeming this act of avoidance as unprofessional. This reluctance to acknowledge the lack of eye contact may stem from the shared understanding of the importance of mutual glances for uniting individuals in an interaction (Simmel, 1921, p. 358). Defence lawyers are therefore reluctant to acknowledge the absence of this otherwise expected action, an absence which could indicate the absence of a union or interaction.

The defence lawyers I interviewed gave various accounts for this situated behaviour. For instance, Peter tells me that perhaps I cannot see it because of where the spectator seating is positioned. However, in nearly all of the observations I conducted I was able to have a direct, uninhibited view of the defence team's interactions.

The placement of the microphone on the desk in front of the client was also used as an explanation by several lawyers: the client and lawyer both face the microphone when speaking, not each other. Others explained that clients receive information before the trial informing them that they will be recorded by a film camera in the middle of the courtroom when they are questioned; therefore, defendants tend to look into the camera when speaking.

Other accounts provided include defendants looking at the judge who presides over the trial and who therefore becomes the natural focus when speaking. For instance, when I told Lydia how unusual it was to see eye contact between defence lawyer and client she replied, "I think that [clients] think they are [answering questions] for the court's sake." This is supported by studies showing that gaze orientation indicates who one is addressing (Sacks, Schegloff, & Jefferson, 1974). However, the gaze of both defence lawyer and client is usually fixed in the middle of the courtroom, the no-man's land of neutral territory that does not belong to the prosecution or the defence. It is akin to that used by patients during physical examinations – however, in contrast, in this courtroom interaction both parts are gazing into the distance, rather than just the patient (or client) (Heath, 1988).

Yet another account given by defence lawyers uses the fact that the client and lawyer sit side-by-side making eye contact difficult. This close physical proximity may encroach on the interactants personal space, or "use space" (Goffman, 1972, p. 34) leading to the interaction being experienced as too familiar and intimate. Such deviations from the normal rules of interaction may make it easier to fall out of role which both parts want to avoid. Accordingly, eyework in the form of gaze avoidance, can uphold the interaction (cf. Goffman, 1957).

A sociological explanation is that gaze orientation or eye contact can lead to individuals revealing information about themselves that they would prefer to keep hidden (Kendon, 1967, 1990; Robinson, 2006). Gaze avoidance may thus be a form of civil inattention, in order to avoid seeing the client's vulnerability or shame if such is the case (Goffman, 1956b; Rossing & S. Scott, 2014; Simmel, 1921).

The defence lawyer's avoidance of eye contact with the client could also be a way of communicating the form of their relationship. Eye contact can provide emotional support, thus the avoidance of eye contact can convey the professional nature of the relationship being based on legal support (cf. Katz, 1999, p. 295). Indeed, many of the lawyers I interviewed state that emotional support falls outside the remit of the defence lawyer's role.

The most readily available explanation is that the client avoids eye contact because he or she is lying, based on the common perception that gaze aversion is linked with deception (Team, 2006; Vrij, 1995). However, a comprehensive overview of the literature shows that there is little association between gaze avoidance and lying (DePaulo et al., 2003). This was an explanation that was not given by any of the defence lawyers.

The avoidance of eye contact can therefore be seen as a way of upholding the role performances and the formal relationship between teammates whilst showing consideration for the situational discomfort of being a defendant in a criminal trial. As the avoidance of eye contact is therefore the norm when questioning one's client according to my observations, eye contact becomes unusual – a relatively deviant case – thus highlighting the underlying norm (Strong, 1988, p. 236). I argue further that when eye contact is used between teammates, it is used instrumentally as a form of dramatic production drawing attention to facts and reinforcing the team impression as we see in the following excerpt when the defence lawyer is asking questions to his own client:

Defence lawyer:	"Was this something that you had planned?" He makes direct eye contact when asking this.
Client:	No.
Defence lawyer:	It was a complete whim?
Client:	Yes. (Fieldnote)

On another trial I observed the defence lawyer only made eye contact once when posing questions to his client – asking him if he would have committed the crime had he known it was illegal at the time. The defendant replies "absolutely not!" Eye contact is made here as a form of factwork – intentionally drawing attention towards something and building it up as a fact. This will be explored in more detail in the next chapter.

Lydia tells me that she might not look at her client during questioning as she has prepared the client and therefore already knows what he or she is going to say, "it's more like, ticking off the answers based on what you expect." The lack of eye contact is therefore seen as conveying the team impression – I know what my client is going to say. This means that making eye contact with a client might be an unmanaged response to an unexpected answer, inadvertently drawing attention to certain information, as we see in the following excerpt:

> There are two defendants – Dave and Kevin – in this trial for theft. The plaintiff is being questioned by the prosecutor about the break-in. Dave's defence lawyer sits with his arms crossed over his stomach, looking at the plaintiff over the top of his glasses. He glances down at his papers briefly and occasionally makes small, quick notes, but otherwise he looks directly at the plaintiff throughout the whole time she is questioned by the prosecutor.

> When the plaintiff says that she only recognises one of the defendants – Dave – his defence lawyer looks directly at him and gives four rapid blinks. Proceedings began over half an hour ago and this is the first time that he has looked at his client (although eye contact is not made). Another half hour passes without eye contact. It is then time for him to question his client, Dave. He does not make eye contact with Dave when asking questions, instead he looks at the space in the courtroom in front of them both. (Fieldnote)

In the above, we see Dave's lawyer looking at the plaintiff but avoiding looking at his client throughout proceedings, even when questioning him. The only time he does look at him is when destructive information is presented. The strategy of stoneface is not used, rather rapid blinking and looking at his client. Eyework can thus undo teamwork and convey disloyalty.

Doing disloyalty or stoneface?

All of this leads to the question – is stoneface a performance of professionalism, loyalty, and indeed, teamwork, or is it a way of communicating distance from one's client? It could, for instance, be argued that defence lawyers perform stoneface in order to save their own professional lawyer face by creating distance from their clients' incriminating testimony. Defence lawyers may thus be doing distance rather than doing professionalism, loyalty, or teamwork. However, the defence lawyers interviewed state that when they accept a case, they should represent the client's version of events; therefore, even if the client's story seems farfetched, the defence lawyer will follow the team line. Indeed, removing oneself from a case is talked about in the interviews as being unethical and could lead to questions pertaining to the client's innocence as legally, the defence lawyer cannot represent as innocent a client who has confessed his or her guilt. Consequently, by removing oneself from a case, the defence lawyer is threatening the face of the client, giving the impression of guilt.

When an exception to this rule arises and a client wants to drive a case despite the defence lawyer advising that their version of events will be deemed implausible, the defence lawyer can create distance discursively by avoiding alignment to the client, stating in court "my client claims that he was not at the scene of the crime" (cf. Potter, 1996, p. 148). This can be seen as an instance of the defence lawyer placing "self-loyalty" (Arvidson & Axelsson, 2017) which is loyalty towards oneself or integrity, highest in the hierarchy of loyalties to be performed. This is a strategy seen in research from other countries, for instance, barristers in England may state: "I have been instructed to say…" (Harris, 2002, pp. 569-570). In this way, the emotional display of professionalism is merely symbolic with lawyers using "coded oral messages to signify their detachment to other legal professionals present" (Harris, 2002, p. 575; see also Adelswärd, Aronsson & Linell, 1988). This can be seen as a professional break-sign similar to the way that newsreaders achieve the appearance of neutrality, by attributing a controversial description or statement to a third party, or by the use of quotation marks, seen as a shift in alignment (Clayman, 1992; Goffman, 1979, cf. Goffman, 1972). This approach is, however, frowned upon, both in the legal literature but also by the lawyers I interviewed (Borgström, 2011, p. 101). I observed doing distance in only a handful of trials, for example in the following excerpt:

> *Prosecutor:* I've read somewhere in the preliminary investigation that you have boasted to others that you hit a security guard.
> *Defendant:* That's bullshit!
> The defence lawyer blinks rapidly three times then puts his left elbow on the desk again, with his chin resting on his hand, writing in his papers with his other hand. His arm and elbow look like a barrier between him and his client. (Fieldnote)

The elbow on the desk forms a symbolic boundary between the client and defence lawyer, constituting a break-sign, in contrast to the "tie-signs" (Goffman, 1972) which have thus far been presented. The defence lawyer may be distancing himself from the reality that his client is presenting but he may also be distancing himself symbolically from the client's break of the ceremonial order seen in the use of the word "bullshit" conveying a lack of respect and manners.

In another trial, the defence lawyer distanced himself from his client who claims that he has no other choice but to steal to fund his drug habit as he can't get accepted on a rehabilitation program, to which the defence lawyer replies, "just because you can't get onto rehab program doesn't mean you have to steal." However, Sandra discusses how there is nothing to be gained from distancing oneself from the client, she tells me:

> There is no reason to somehow send some kind of double message, to have a double agenda, to try and show the court that, "you understand that I think that this seems crazy" or "now he's lying again" or whatever. (Sandra)

For these reasons, I do not consider stoneface to be a case of "derisive collusion" (Goffman, 1956b, p. 119) where the performer does not really agree with the version of events being presented, and communicates this in subtle ways to the audience. Neither is this how defence lawyers present themselves in the interviews. The guiding premise is that the shared identity and shared reality of teammates means that it is unacceptable to "sell your client out" in the courtroom as one defence lawyer interviewed states. The risk is therefore that one is perceived as "doing disloyalty" when doing distance.

Concluding comments

In this chapter, I have presented an overview of loyalty before exploring defence lawyers' loyalty talk and the various ways in which loyalty is central to their role. I conclude by showing that although loyalty is a key role obligation and one that is a source of pride for defence lawyers, at times this performance ruptures and disloyalty is shown, even if only for a fleeting second. These deviant performances constitute the exception thus revealing the underlying performative rule which will be the focus of the coming chapters. Defence lawyers' loyalty talk and the rarity of breaks in performance reveals the strength of the emotional regime of the criminal court and the importance placed on performing one's legal principle and thus duty.

Note

1 Hirschman (1970) has focused on this in terms of consumer loyalty. For instance, customers and members will remain with a certain product or organisation for longer than they otherwise would have as they expect that the product or organisation will be remain the same if they are satisfied, or improved if they are dissatisfied – they use their "voice" as Hirschman (1970) writes. They do not need to look elsewhere to satisfy their interests or needs – or "exit" (Hirschman, 1970; see also Törnqvist, 2017 for how prosecutors use exit and voice). Loyalty thus provides an informal barrier to consumers leaving, without the need for formalised barriers preventing it.

Chapter 5

The facework of defence lawyers

The inherent coordinated conflict of a criminal trial in Sweden stems from the competing realities at play within the overarching agreement as to the situation at hand. That is, whilst all are in agreement as to the nature of the interaction – a criminal trial – it may be fundamentally based on two competing versions of reality: the prosecution's assertion that the defendant is guilty of the crime, contrasting with the defence team's claim that events did not take place as the prosecution asserts. Consequently, there is an overhanging risk for face threats and interactional disruptions, particularly if certain performers are uninitiated into the ritual. In this chapter, I show that the role of defence lawyer entails the expectation to perform, uphold, support, and at times, threaten, different faces. I present the various forms of facework the defence lawyer should perform: presenting one's own, or lawyer face, along with upholding the face of others such as one's client, as well presenting a united defence team which I present in terms of team face. These performances, which centre on the conveyance of loyalty, should follow the interaction order, ceremonial order, and emotional order of the criminal trial, which, in turn, are formed by the emotional regime of law.

Defence lawyers' courtroom interactions and performances are shaped by official guidelines and, in particular, the legal principle of loyalty (cf. Flam, 1990a, 1990b). It is therefore the principle of loyalty that guides their performances and it is loyalty that is the underlying meaning to be communicated to others (cf. Jacobsson, 2008). Furthermore, as the role of the defence lawyer is to represent defendants, integral to the defence lawyer's role performance is the construction of the defence team. Teamwork and loyalty are thus inextricably linked. This leads to the question: how do defence lawyers accomplish this? Defence lawyers do not receive training regarding the professional performance of loyalty and as we saw earlier, how these rules should be performed is not set out (Flower, 2014, 2016a). My analysis in this chapter thus centres on how defence lawyers accomplish their role – how they communicate loyalty, professionalism and teamwork. The themes in this current chapter centres upon are: how do defence lawyers present self, other and team? And, how are loyalty and teamwork accomplished by defence lawyers in the courtroom? Although it is impossible to disentangle emotions from interactions, for analytical ease I nevertheless endeavour to focus on the strategies used by defence lawyers to construct and communicate their role in this chapter, before moving on in the next chapter to explore the emotions involved.

Lawyer face

We now understand that dramaturgical performances should entail performing the task, not the performer's characteristics, and this is particularly true of the defence lawyer, who should not be influenced by personal factors (Association, 2008, p. 4; Goffman, 1956b, p. 47). This performance is particularly challenging for defence lawyers in Sweden as the Swedish courtroom lacks many of the easily recognisable symbols representing justice and the execution of law, such as robes, wigs, a dock, or even a jury. I argue that the lawyer must depend on the "presentation of self" (Goffman, 1956b) to uphold their lawyer face – to perform professionalism and loyalty, bereft as they are of these typical ceremonial props (cf. Roach Anleu & Mack, 2017, p. 165). I will now begin to describe the ways in which defence lawyers present and construct this role and, in the next chapter on the emotion work of defence lawyers, I build on this.

Identity work

My analysis shows that one way in which the role of defence lawyer is accomplished – constructing lawyer face – is by positioning their performances away from others, for instance, from Stockholm lawyers,[1] celebrity lawyers, and prosecutors (the latter of which will be discussed in chapter seven). Stockholm lawyers and celebrity lawyers (who have a high media-presence) are presented by Daniel as being "a bit more confrontational" and "a bit more aggressive" as Andrew says. Martin uses a highly publicised drug smuggling trial in Sweden (Södertäljemålet[2]) to explain that situations – which he likens to a "state of war" between prosecutors and defence lawyers – may arise in Stockholm. Martin claims that such performances do not benefit clients and occur due to defence lawyers wanting to appear "tough."

All of the lawyers I interviewed positioned themselves away from the kind of cocky and aggressive courtroom demeanour Martin talks about, and many others also echo Martin's position that it is used as a strategy for garnering clients. Indeed, George tells me that a well-known criminologist in Sweden, Professor Leif G. W. Persson, commented a few years ago that these so-called "star lawyers" don't win any more cases than anyone else, it's just that they're good for their clients' self-confidence (Persson, 2009).

Aggressive, Stockholm lawyering is therefore not talked about as a good lawyering practice in order to achieve the best possible outcome for the client, rather it is presented as a marketing strategy to gain clients. It is also depicted as the defence lawyer adjusting his or her performance to make the client happy – good for their self-confidence. George also describes how clients consider the defence lawyer's performance to reflect upon them (the clients). In dramaturgical terms, George is saying that the defence lawyer's face is the client's face, pointing to their shared identity, a concept which, as I have already mentioned, I have termed "team face" (and which will also be discussed in more detail later on in this chapter). Here, we begin to see that the teamwork of a defence team is an interactional accomplishment – that the performance of one's teammate is, by extension, a reflection on the other teammates.

Stockholm lawyers are talked about as being too involved with their clients – perceived by the lawyers I spoke to as having broken interactional and emotional boundaries (Goffman, 1957, p. 52). These performances are thus considered to disrupt the ceremonial order, breaking rules of propriety, the consequence may be that the focus moves from what is being said to who is saying it.[3] For the defence lawyer, this means that he or she risks being viewed as unprofessional and overly-loyal. It also means there is a risk that an important argument that he or she has made is overshadowed by the performance given leading to the argument losing weight. All of the lawyers in this study talk about the importance of the manner in which their role is performed – their demeanour as presented on the "personal front" (Goffman, 1959). This will be explored in more detail further on.

I argue that Martin, George, and the other defence lawyers I interviewed are constructing, presenting, and sustaining a professional identity in order to produce sense, significance and meaning, that is, they are using "identity talk" (Snow & Anderson, 1987). This is achieved by distancing themselves away from Stockholm lawyers – who may be seen as the Swedish equivalent of Pierce's (1995) "Rambo litigators" – and who are perceived as breaking the ceremonial order of the criminal trial which calls for good manners – their aggressiveness is talked about as being bad conduct. They consequently also risk breaking their role in the interaction – not being personally involved, along with breaking the emotion rules – showing aggression in the wrong way. Interestingly, very few of the lawyers I interviewed had actually seen "Stockholm lawyers" in action and when I visited the courts in Stockholm, I didn't observe any instances of aggressive lawyering. It seems that there is a cultural understanding of Stockholm lawyers as being aggressive based on only a few first-hand experiences or, perhaps based on the same mediated view of the court as the general public receives where sensational and explosive trials and its actors are reported in the newspapers. There is therefore a shared understanding of Stockholm lawyers that may not necessarily be based in courtroom interactions, rather it may be an attempt to construct a coherent identity in line with professional expectations.

This shows that defence lawyers' social identities are relational, characterised as much by what they are not as what they are, through a process of "dis-identification" (S. Scott, 2017, p. 5; Williams, 2000). Lawyers are thus able to interactionally accomplish their identity category, that is, lawyer face is negotiated in interaction with others enabling them to position themselves into a certain identity category, in contrast to another identity category, that of aggressive, Stockholm lawyers (cf. McKinlay & Dunnett, 1998). This counter identity affirms their own identity. I will return to this in the final chapter of the book to explore how defence lawyers and prosecutors construct their professional identities and counter identities.

Clothing and props

Giving a professional and loyal impression can be accomplished by conveying information on the "personal front" (Goffman, 1959): via clothing, voice, and props. It involves looking like a (loyal) lawyer. This can be seen by contrasting the performances on the personal front of two defence teams from a trial regarding drug dealing that I observed. There are two defendants: one of them is represented by one lawyer, the other defendant has two lawyers representing him. We join the trial just after the prosecutor has presented the facts of the case and the judge has asked the defence lawyers if they would like to add anything. The contrast in defensive facework strategies to convey a professional impression used by the two defence teams is striking:

> This defendant has two lawyers, one of whom is wearing a bright yellow tie and a smart, expensive looking suit. His hair is coiffured. His associate is younger and is also wearing a smart suit and has slicked back hair and black framed glasses. Mr Yellow Tie presents his client's version of events whilst his associate hands out a document that is about an inch thick. The document is colour-coded with post-it notes sticking up. The prosecutor, judges and the other defendant's lawyer all get a copy. Mr Yellow Tie then gives a short presentation stating that their client denies the accusations and can't be linked to the email account which is central to the prosecution's case, and thus cannot be connected to the crime.
>
> The second defendant's defence lawyer is not as snappily dressed as the others, not as polished-looking. His hair needs cutting and he has a slightly ill-fitting suit. He compliments the prosecutor for a "detailed presentation of facts" and states that he doesn't really have anything to add. The tone of his voice is monotonous with only slight emphasis when stating that his client "has not" used the email account that the prosecutor also accuses his client of using, linking him to the crime. Halfway through there is a loud noise of a walkie talkie which is the defence lawyer's and which he has evidently forgotten to turn off. He apologises and turns it off and there are slight murmurs of amusement amongst everyone in the courtroom. (Fieldnote)

Which of these two lawyers would you rather have? Which of these two performances conveys professionalism? It is apparent here that facework fulfils an important function in communicating professionalism.

We see several impression management strategies in the first team: firstly, the use of the compendium filled with post-it notes and colour coding which can be seen as a way of drawing attention to the professionalism of these two lawyers (Mr Yellow Tie and Mr Slicked Back Hair): it conveys a sense of thoroughness, well-preparedness, and confidence. I interpret this document as a prop used to convey the impression of professionalism; therefore, I consider it to be an impression management strategy rather than an emotion management strategy. It should be briefly noted however that props such as documents can also be used as a tactical emotion management strategy aimed at creating hesitation or anxiety in others. Another of the lawyers I interviewed, Richard, tells me that sometimes during questioning:

> As a control question you can just, "but what you just said, is that really the same as what was documented [in evidence]?" And it could very well be that it is the same, I mean, with what we know is written down, but just the knowledge (…) that I am perhaps a second away from pulling out a document that can reveal a lie – then people show their true colours. (Richard)

The second way in which impressions are managed in the fieldnotes with Mr Yellow Tie is through clothing. The first defendant's lawyers are smartly dressed in expensive looking suits and ties with trendy yet age-appropriate eyewear. This contrasts to the slightly scruffy-looking lawyer for the other defendant. The importance of clothing in making a certain impression is discussed by Charles who tells me that, in the 1980s, celebrity lawyers got clients because they sat in "ridiculously fancy offices, wore tailor-made suits, and so people thought that they looked successful even though they had no professional experience."

So what about this scruffy lawyer? Has he used facework strategies? Perhaps his ungroomed appearance is meant to imply that the client does not need an expensive, well-dressed lawyer as he has not committed any crime? Or, is the impression conveyed that he simply did nothing – he didn't hand out any compendiums! Is this an "act of commission" – rejecting the expected action, or is it an "act of omission" – a passive failure to act? (S. Scott, 2017, p. 3). It is difficult to know if his appearance and performance are giving the intentional social information conveying his client's innocence or whether he is unintentionally giving off a display of indifference (Goffman, 1959, 1969; see also Blumberg, 1967). The point is that clothing and props convey meaning. They thus constitute an important strategy for communicating meaning in a ceremonial setting devoid of many of the usual sacred props.

In my interview with Lena, we discuss how clothing has become more relaxed in Swedish courts for the legal actors; however, most are still smartly dressed. I jokingly asked her if she thought it would become even more relaxed, with lawyers wearing shorts, she replied:

> I hope not! [Laughs] (…) Personally I think that I wear, I dress quite formally. I don't always have a suit but I normally have a blazer when I'm in court. And I think that, somehow, I signal that I take this seriously. (Lena)

Clothing is therefore talked about by Lena, and many of the other lawyers I interviewed, as a way of ceremonially conveying professionalism. It is a way of symbolically communicating loyalty to the legal system and its ceremonial order and the gravity of it, as well as loyalty to one's client: that one takes one's role seriously as reflected in one's clothing.

Presentation of self regarding one's appearance using costuming and props communicates not only the individual's social status but also whether he or she is in a formal or informal situation (Goffman, 1959). Lena discusses this when I asked her if she is aware of how she looks in the courtroom:

> I'm very aware that, partly that you dress in a way so that you get into your role. Today I haven't been in court so I look like this [casually dressed] but I wouldn't dress like this in court, I would dress a bit more, to get into my role. (Lena)

We see here that Lena wants to make me aware that her informal appearance reflects her current position of interview respondent and the informal situation we are in, as opposed to her appearance when she is in her role of defence lawyer in the courtroom.

Other studies have shown that lawyers in jury systems dress in a certain manner in order to please the jury; however, the lawyers I have spoken to talk about clothing in terms of appearing professional and not about influencing the judges (see Levenson, 2007 for a discussion). Clothing can nonetheless be used by lawyers to go into character and create a certain impression. In this way, defence lawyers are similar to service workers who put on a uniform and go into a role that is habituated and routinised (Bergman Blix, 1996; Leidner, 1993). For instance, George tells me that he puts on his lawyer role when he puts on his suit. For George and Lena, as we also saw here, clothes help one enter one's role – both dramaturgically speaking but also, in extension, regarding emotional performances.

Voice

It is not just clothes, props and sitting down that maketh the lawyer, but also sounding like a lawyer as Lena explains:

> The worst thing, I think, is when you feel that you didn't quite nail it, that you get a bit uncertain, then you're always a bit afraid that it can be heard

> that you're not quite, you want it to sound like you are as sure as possible and then I think that people listen and believe you more than if you sound uncertain. That's what you think yourself if someone is talking and you think, "this person sounds really uncertain, not credible." (Lena)

Other lawyers I spoke to also talk about the importance of sounding confident in the courtroom. A confident voice is therefore a facework strategy aimed at both giving oneself face, but also in undermining and building up facts – sounding certain of something gives it more weight. Defence lawyers talk about being aware when the prosecutor sounds uncertain as Richard tells me:

> You notice on a counsel who is inexperienced and has a tendency to be nervous and stressed, stammer. You notice in different ways that this wasn't quite what they thought. It's a question of habit being able to stay cool in such situations. (Richard)

Both sides of the adversarial courtroom watch each other for signs of nervousness or stress which are then utilised to one's advantage thereby showing the interactional and emotional nature of an adversarial trial: a prosecutor sounding unsure may be inadvertently revealing a weakness in his or her own case, a weakness which can then be focused upon by the defence. This also means listening not only to how a witness sounds in court – an uncertain-sounding testimony from a witness can be questioned for its credibility – but also reading the performance of one's own client as I will explore later on in this chapter and the next.

Maintaining a confident façade and interpreting the performance of others is therefore an important part of the defence lawyer's performance. Edward, one of the lawyers I interviewed, even describes a confident façade as a "weapon" in business law.

Whilst lawyers do not have rules regarding the standardisation of intonation and body language as in some of the service industries, there are nevertheless expectations or informal rules regarding tone of voice (see Leidner, 1993, p. 111). Not only should one sound confident, but also, not once did I hear a defence lawyer shout when questioning someone. A louder voice was occasionally used in the closing speech in order to emphasise certain emotional elements of a case, but this too was unusual. One reason for this could be that a louder voice is associated with an authoritarian position which, in the case of a trial, is held by the judge (cf. Roach Anleu & Mack, 2017, p. 131). This can be seen as an aspect of the ceremonial and emotional order of the criminal trial: voices should remain at a normal volume and calm, expressing emotions in an appropriate way in order to remain courteous and polite.

We thus see again that the emotional regime of law which stifles emotions calls for subdued emotional displays. This may come into conflict with the client's expectations and lead to disappointment and disruptions as I show in the next chapter.

Other strategies

During the entire time I conducted fieldwork, I only saw a defence lawyer stand up during a trial once. This was when a defence lawyer walked over to the witness to ask her to specify more clearly on a diagram where she was standing when she witnessed the crime. This was met with slightly raised eyebrows and a look which I interpreted as mild amusement from the judge indicating that it was perceived as a role break, a performance outside the remit of the defence lawyer's usual repertoire. The reaction of the judge served as an implicit rule reminder, revealing that the defence lawyer had broken the interaction order of the criminal trial – this is not something one expects a defence lawyer to do (cf. Hochschild, 1983; Rock, 1993).

I began to think that standing up was not permitted and asked about it in my interviews. Perry sums up the general consensus amongst the respondents when he says that standing up "seems a bit over the top" whilst Daniel tells me that it should "only be used if you have back problems" and goes on to say that he has thought about doing it and has other colleagues who have done it but says, "personally I think it would have looked silly." Daniel even mentions colleagues who have stood up in court, in particular one colleague who was so unusual as to be memorable. There is therefore a consensus amongst defence lawyers that standing up in the courtroom is inappropriate.

The accepted courtroom conduct is thus to remain seated throughout proceedings, an expectation which can be seen through its absence in the performance of defence lawyers. Sitting down is thus an implicit, informal rule. Standing up means standing out which is against social expectations and may thus also break the etiquette of the criminal trial. This is also true of prosecutors in Sweden who should not attempt to stand out, indeed, George mentions a prosecutor who used to stand up but the prosecutor was seen as being odd by everyone else because of this (see Törnqvist, 2017). Such behaviour would not comply with English Crown Court rules either; however, in jury systems such as the U.S., lawyers may walk around the courtroom, moving towards the jury to make a point or for dramatic effect (Pizzi, 1999, p. 126; Scheffer, 2010). This implies that it is not simply a case of whether or not a jury is present as juries are a part of the English Crown Court and the American criminal trial.

Staying seated is consequently an example of an invisible interaction rule that is a shared understanding despite its unwritten and implicit origin. Deviations from the performance of this rule lead to one being viewed as unusual, even stigmatised (Goffman, 1963b).

Another way in which lawyers can uphold their presentation of lawyer face on the personal front is by asking for a break if they feel they are losing concentration or falling asleep, and consequently in danger of losing face. When I read through my fieldnotes, I found that on certain trials I too was struggling to stay awake, noting things like "this is the longest hour, ever." On several occasions, I also observed how the lay judges looked like they were falling asleep, but rarely the judge, a contrast that I explore in more detail in the final chapter.

This problem of staying in role and always looking vigilant is described by Martin who says, "you have to sit there and look like you are interested the whole time. It can be damn difficult at times I can tell you." Taking a short break enables the defence lawyer to gather himself or herself backstage and return to the courtroom with lawyer face in-tact.

Stoneface as lawyer face

Now I want to return to a form of facework – stoneface – that I mentioned in chapter four and which will be a recurrent theme throughout the rest of the analysis as it is used to manage threats to different types of face. This strategy is explored in more detail here as a tool for performing professionalism and thus defending lawyer face. Later on in this chapter I go on to show how it can also be used to project the impression that the client and defence lawyer are a united team and thus constitutes a strategy for sustaining team face.

All of the lawyers I interviewed associated professionalism with the ability to deal with unexpected problems and with being well prepared. Situations where they risk losing lawyer face by showing that they have not prepared appropriately, for example, that they have not properly thought through the line of questioning, must be managed in order to sustain the performance of professionalism. In such interactional emergencies, defence lawyers talk about using stoneface – looking "neutral in the moment" as Daniel says – as a pre-prepared strategy for covering up mistakes.

Stoneface is an "act of commission" (S. Scott, 2017), a demonstrative doing nothing that is actively chosen, rather than an omission or passive failure to act. By not showing any visible reaction, the lack of response is, in itself, a response and a symbolic act. Actively doing nothing, in interaction with others, is therefore, simultaneously, the production of something, in this case, of professionalism.

Stoneface involves actively hiding certain emotions and producing a face of stony professionalism. It entails hiding social and emotional information that may be inappropriate in order to convey the appropriate impression. It is therefore an emotion management strategy, aimed at managing emotions inappropriate to the situation such as shame or embarrassment at being unprepared, and ensuring that one's performance is in line with the emotional regime of the criminal trial and one's professional role.

We therefore see the underlying emotion rule – surprise or disappointment should remain hidden if it is associated with a lack of professionalism. The hierarchy of acceptable emotions thus positions these displays as inappropriate for defence lawyers. Siri tells me that if something happens during a trial and "it's something that I am really surprised about then I don't want anyone else to know. You try and like, just, yes, that was part of the plan, let's carry on." It is consequently a strategy arising both as a result of the social situation, but also formed by the social situation. In this respect, it is a professional emotion rule aimed at performing the lawyer's situational disinterestedness (cf. Parsons, 1954).

In this section, I have shown the strategies used by defence lawyers to construct and perform their professional face: lawyer face. I have also begun to distinguish the invisible rules guiding performances and associated emotion management strategies. I now turn to the ways in which the defence lawyer manages the face of others, in particular defendant face and defence team face with the focus on courtroom interactions.

Defendant face

The defence lawyer also has to ensure that clients stay in face by initiating them into the interaction order, ceremonial order and emotional order of the criminal trial (cf. Adelswärd et al., 1988; McBarnet, 1981). This is aimed at conveying the impression that they are a credible interactant. My analysis here will focus on preparing the defendant's personal front and the ways in which the ceremonial order – good courtroom manners – are introduced to the defendant – the defence lawyer's client. These preparations can be seen as face-saving strategies.

Clothing and props

Preparing the client for trial includes advising him or her how to convey an image in line with normative societal expectations. This includes the client's presentation of self: what to wear and how to act (Goffman, 1956b). Such preparations can take place backstage, prior to the frontstage trial. For instance, on the frontstage, the client should convey the appropriate body language, posture and tone of voice also in order to show respect. Lena tells me that it is important for the client to make a good impression, saying:

> You usually say to your client to behave themselves, give a good impression and I think that, if you confess, that you, "yes, I stand for what I did and I apologise" then I think that you can absolutely get the court on your side. (Lena)

Good behaviour is presented as positively influencing the court. Lena is talking here about the client showing contrition thereby ensuring that he or she fulfils the expectation of showing regret for one's deviant actions. She is thus talking about encouraging the client to follow the emotional order with its associated emotional expectations. I will explore this in more detail later on in this chapter and the next.

A few of the lawyers I spoke to said that preparing the client's personal front regarding clothing is irrelevant – it doesn't matter what the client wears in court. However, the client's appearance and manner in court are discussed by many of the other lawyers I spoke to as being important in conveying a certain impression that can influence the judges. Siri discusses one client's appearance in a trial, telling me:[4]

> He wore a very political t-shirt in court with a slogan from a racist party (…) and I tried to like, because we were going to go up to the Supreme Court, then I thought, maybe you shouldn't wear that again, like, because it doesn't give that good an impression, you don't win the court's sympathy if you wear that (…) The court doesn't know [you]. It's about giving a good impression. (Siri)

Several of the lawyers I spoke to said that they advise clients to dress and act naturally although perhaps dress a little bit smarter than normal, or as Lena says, to dress "credibly." The importance of giving a credible impression is also discussed by Perry who recounts the case of a client who turned up to court in a suit (a form of clothing that is associated with formal occasions and certain professions in Sweden), an occasion so novel it made him chuckle to recall it.

Siri, Lena, and Perry therefore tell me that the client's personal front should be in line with defendant face, that is, the image that the client and indeed, defence lawyer, are hoping to portray of the client. In this way, the defence lawyer is attempting to portray the client's social identity in a particular light, using information on the personal front to communicate this identity (Goffman, 1956b). By extension, portraying a virtual social identity by the use of impression management strategies using clothing and manners may lead to assumptions being made that the client's actual social identity is also in line with this socially communicated identity (Goffman, 1963b).

The defence lawyers I interviewed present inappropriate or non-credible clothing as possibly leading to conclusions being made about the client's character and which could have implications for how credible his or her testimony is considered to be (Simmel, 1957; cf. Dahl et al., 2007; Kaufmann et al., 2003; Wessel et al., 2006). Clothing communicates meaning, for instance, holes in a suit may reflect more than poor tailoring, they reflect social standing, character, and morals (Simmel, 1957). Accordingly, by managing the client's personal front, encouraging him or her to dress naturally and credibly, the lawyer is attempting to construct the client's face.

One aspect of personal front that many of the lawyers I spoke to agreed is inappropriate, is wearing a cap in the courtroom. During my fieldwork, I saw only a handful of people wearing a cap during a trial. Most commonly it was someone in the public gallery and, on rare occasions, the defendant. Wearing a cap is often a cause for sanctioning by the judge with the defendant being asked to remove it in the courtroom (but not spectators sitting in the public gallery). There are no official rules regarding caps and hats; however, it is talked about in terms of breaking the ceremonial order of the criminal trial: showing bad manners towards the official office of the court as reflected in sanctions by judges. As a cap can be associated with deviancy in Sweden, this shows that the meaning it communicates crosses over from the outside world to the inside world of the courtroom and reveals that there are similarities in the ceremonial orders inside and outside the courtroom (cf. Hillyard, 2010; Rypi, 2017; Schuster & Propen, 2011).

Lawyers advising their clients not to wear a cap is therefore not just about showing good manners, it is also a way of managing the appearance of the client in order to create the impression that the client is non-deviant – constructing and conveying social information regarding him or her.

Other aspects of the client's personal front that should be prepared include the use props, which, as we have already seen, may be used by defence lawyers to convey a certain impression (cf. Goffman, 1956b, p. 143; Waldron, 2000). Scheffer's (2010, p. 174) study of English Crown Court criminal trials includes an observation of a defendant accused of indecent assault being encouraged to bring his well-dressed and well-behaved girlfriend to court in order to give the appearance that he was capable of a normal relationship (which had been questioned by the probation service). The use of such props, or "disidentifiers" (Goffman, 1963b, p. 59) as a way of distancing the client from a stigmatised or deviant identity, in this case as violent and impulsive, in order to create a competing impression of normal, is not mentioned by the lawyers I spoke to.

The defence lawyer is thus expected to prepare clients and present them on the frontstage of the courtroom, an aspect of their legal role that is not expected in judges or prosecutors to the same extent, if at all. This is therefore a unique aspect of their role performance.

There are occasions, however, when the client intentionally deviates from their expected performance, as can be seen in the following excerpt from a cross-examination in a trial for assault and robbery. The perpetrators of the crime arrived in a car and, contrary to his police statement given at the time of his arrest, the defendant is now claiming that he was not in the vehicle. The prosecutor continues the questioning:

Prosecutor:	How long did it take for you to walk [to the scene of the crime]?
Defendant:	Don't remember.
Prosecutor:	Where were you before that?
Defendant:	Don't remember.
Prosecutor:	Have you seen the car?
Defendant:	No.
Prosecutor:	Did you know that [your accomplice] had a weapon?
Defendant:	No.

> The questioning continues in this vein for a while longer with the defendant giving monosyllabic responses. Within the space of a few minutes, the defendant replies "no" 16 times, "yes" 8 times, "don't remember" 3 times, and "don't know" once. The defence lawyer shows no reaction to any of this. (Fieldnote)

The strictly ordered interaction of a criminal trial does not provide many opportunities for the client to use defensive facework to defend his or her own face; however, one strategy I observed on many occasions was "hedging" (Goffman, 1972) – acting as though they were not totally committed to the interaction, for instance by maintaining a joking relationship with the trial in order to show how unseriously they take it (Goffman, 1952, p. 462). This can be seen in the excerpt above. This performance by the defendant can be construed as displaying disinterestedness or rudeness – bad manners. I interpret this deviation from the ceremonial order not as resulting from a lack of initiation into the interaction order but rather as the performance of a seasoned performer. It shows a repeat offender familiar with the system who intentionally deviates from the rules of interaction in order to display disrespect for the ritual he is forced to interact in (cf. Collins, 2004). The defendant is performing his lack of commitment or reluctance to play his assigned role, distancing himself from it in an interactionally constraining situation (Goffman, 1961b). Such instances may constitute an interactional challenge for the defence lawyer requiring him or her to direct the client back into face as I will describe later on in this chapter.

Defence team face

So far, I have discussed the facework strategies of defence lawyers regarding the presentation of lawyer face. This was seen in terms of giving a professional impression and accomplishing one's role with particular focus on how this is achieved through clothing, voice and gestures. I then went on to show the ways in which defence lawyers protect defendant face by preparing the client's personal front and by explaining the rules of interaction, again in order to ensure the client's presentation of self as an adequate interactant of the social situation at hand. I also introduced how the client's presentation of self can bring interactional challenges for the defence lawyer.

I will now go on to show how the defence lawyer and client can be seen as a team and how this team performance can be analysed as such.

Constructing the defence team

Goffman (1956, pp. 48–49) writes that performances can be analysed as team performances when there is co-operative activity within the team and when the performance is aimed at staging a "single routine." My analysis also shows that many of the lawyers I interviewed talk about the client and themselves as a "we" or a team. In Goffman's (1956b, pp. 48–49) vocabulary, a dramaturgical "performance team" sustaining a "team impression." Both client and lawyer therefore unite behind a shared reality – which is based on the client's version of events – and social identity: the defence team. I therefore suggest that it is appropriate to talk about the presentation and management of "team face" which I will analyse as such (cf. S. Scott, 2016, p. 11). Defence lawyers must therefore not only present lawyer face, but also work towards sustaining team face. This became clear in my interview with Vera when she said that "*we* managed to change the decision" of the court when it was appealed at the Supreme Court. I asked her to whom she was referring when she says "we":

Vera: I meant, like, me and the client.
Lisa: But that's how you think, in terms of "we" and not "I?"
Vera: Yes, at least I do! [Small laugh]

Collective facework is required within the defence team in order to uphold their shared identity and the shared reality they are united behind (S. Scott, 2016, p. 11). This involves presenting defence teammates as capable performers, thus requiring them to help each other back in line when their performances falter or when team face is threatened.

This team impression can be accomplished explicitly but also more implicitly. For instance, as I have already mentioned, the team impression is immediately visible in the Swedish courtroom with the tie-sign of them sitting next to each other communicating they are a team. The courtroom layout also enables specific social interactions which assist in maintaining team face (cf. Goffman, 1972; S. Scott, 2015; Åkerström, 1997). I have observed defence lawyers placing a calming hand on the client's leg as well as exchanging notes and comments (on one occasion I even observed the lawyer winking to his client). We can also see the performance as a team in the following interactions between a defence lawyer and his client during a trial regarding possession of weapons (amongst other charges):

> During the prosecution's presentation of facts, the defence lawyer points to things in the file on the desk in front of him and his client. He is explaining things and asking questions every now and then. A little later on, the defence lawyer leans over and asks the client something about the photos being presented and asks "are you sure?" to the client's response. Everything is spoken in a whisper. The defence lawyer pours himself a glass of water then offers to pour one for the client but the client declines. (Fieldnote)

This teamwork is particularly striking when contrasted with a fieldnote from my observation of a trial at an English Crown Court:

> The defendant sits at the back of the courtroom, in the dock. There is thus no interaction between the defendant and his barrister. Once or twice the defendant's barrister turns and gestures or points towards him when arguing the case but the defendant appears more as a prop than an actual actor involved in proceedings. (Fieldnote)

The team impression is also communicated in more subtle ways that depicted in the previous extract in the Swedish courtroom, and must be upheld even when threatened. I suggest that there are two sources of a face threat to the presentation of team face: it can either stem from a source outside the team – such as the plaintiff, witnesses, prosecutor, and others – this comprises an external face threat, or it may stem from one's teammates thus constituting an internal face threat. I will now describe what I mean by this before going on to show the ways in which these face threats are managed in order to convey and uphold team face.

Face threats

Upon initial analysis, many of the face threats I have discussed in this book thus far appear to originate from the prosecutor, plaintiff, or witness, constituting face threats coming from outside the defence team. Indeed, as I have already mentioned, the adversarial nature of the criminal trial constitutes a face threat to the defendant, which may be based on the prosecutor questioning the defendant's version of reality and presentation of self as innocent.[5] However, I would like to problematise the face threat of the trial in order to show how an external face threat can lead to an internal face threat arising from within the team, and furthermore how, due to team membership, a face threat aimed at the defendant is rather a face threat to the team and in extension, lawyer face.

Source of face threat

Here are two examples of what may at first glance seem to be an external face threat, can also be seen as an internal face threat. The first extract from my fieldnotes regards a defendant who is claiming that the police coerced him into a confession. We join the trial as the prosecutor asks the defendant more about this:

> *Prosecutor:* You are going to have to explain what happened.
> *Defendant:* It felt a bit leading. The [police] wanted me to confess.
> *Prosecutor:* I've never heard of this happening before! [Said in a tone of voice conveying scepticism].
>
> Defence lawyer does not alter his facial expression or what he is doing. (Fieldnote)

In the second excerpt the defendant, who is accused of committing a crime whilst wearing a balaclava, is mocked by the prosecutor when the prosecutor asks him why the police happened to find a similar balaclava to that worn during the crime in his wardrobe at home:

> *Defendant:* I usually go on skiing holidays.
> *Prosecutor:* You go on skiing holidays?!
> *Defendant:* Yes.
> The prosecutor asks if he has any other skiing equipment.
> *Defendant:* It's in the wardrobe.
> *Prosecutor:* Yes, I'm sure it is!
> The prosecutor says this with heavy intonation on "sure" which I immediately interpret as expressing sarcasm or disbelief. The defence lawyer keeps on writing notes showing no change in facial expression. (Fieldnote)

In these extracts, the prosecutors are intentionally threatening the face of the defendants by questioning their version of events and presentation of self by implying that they are lying ("I've never heard of this happening before" and "Yes, I'm sure it is!"). We see that the prosecutor thus constitutes an external face threat to team face, whilst simultaneously building up the evidential facts of the case (cf. Archer, 2011a; Harris, 2011a; Penman, 1990).

However, I argue that these and many of the other exchanges I present can also be seen as internal face threats. Using this approach, I interpret the performance of the defendant in both the forced-confession and the balaclava excerpt as undermining or weakening the version of events the defence team is attempting to portray. For instance, in the balaclava trial, the defendant presents a version of events that are responded to by the prosecutor as unlikely or unbelievable. They are therefore examples of "incompetent role performance[s]" (S. Scott, 2015, p. 10) thus calling for collective facework strategies being employed by the defence lawyer in order to bring the team performance back in line.

Face threats from within the defence team

Although the defence lawyer and client constitute a performance team they are not mutually dependent and there is an imbalance when it comes to obligations and expectations. On the one hand, the responsibility of the team performance is shared as both the client and the lawyer have to be present and in agreement as to team membership. With these requirements in place, they are able to work together to unite behind a joint version of reality: that the client has not committed the crime or that there are mitigating circumstances.

However, on the other hand, the defence lawyer has obligations to the client as a function of his or her role as defence lawyer. This brings with it expectations from the client as to what the lawyer will do, expectations that can be disappointed if one is not aware of what to expect (as is discussed in the next chapter on emotion work), yet the lawyer cannot expect or depend on the client's dramaturgical co-operation and loyalty (Goffman, 1956b). The defence lawyer cannot assume that the client will stay in role, follow the rules of conduct and uphold the version of events the team is attempting to convey. Furthermore, the defence lawyer has little possibility for choosing his or her teammates to ensure a successful performance (as is the case in many other team performances) – as the majority of lawyers I spoke to said that they take all cases they are offered and none of them said that they would turn down a case because of who the client was (excluding, of course, conflicts of interest).

Linked to this is the fact that the client does not take an oath to tell the truth and is free to change his or her version of events presented in court. As the defence lawyer's performance is, at least in part, based on his or her client's version of events, this places even greater demands on an already dramaturgically demanding situation. All of this makes the client one of the sources of face threat to his or her own team face. The risk of the client as a face threat becomes even clearer if we compare criminal law, where the client is present in the trial, to business law, where clients aren't always present during the pre-trial hearing because, as Edward tells me, they leak so much information to the other side before the settlement has even begun. The client therefore risks inadvertently conveying information which the lawyers would prefer to remain hidden.

All of the lawyers I spoke to talk about the client being a major source of potential internal face threat which the defence lawyer must manage throughout the trial. This kind of internal face threat is not discussed in previous interactionist work (cf. Rossing & S. Scott, 2014).

The risk for internal face threats arises, not just when the defendant is being questioned by the prosecutor, but also when being questioned by his or her own lawyer. Vera talks about how the situation of a criminal trial can lead to the defendant becoming nervous and changing their version of events:

> You can have gone through it a hundred times: what happened? Did you know that there were things [such as weapons] there or whatever, or, what were you thinking when you fought and then they tell you and based on what they say I can tell [the court], sure this and this has happened but there was no intent. And then when they are in court, they say something completely different! Because either they feel pressured or uncertain in the situation and they think that perhaps it sounds better if I say this. And suddenly you have created intent which the whole time [the defence] has

> said wasn't there (…) It's also dangerous because, often when the lawyer is going to ask a question, the client relaxes because they know that we are on their side and then maybe they answer even worse because [their lawyer] asked the question. (Vera)

The bond of the defence team can inadvertently lead the client to relax and reveal facts that the team either had hoped would remain hidden such as facts that are damaging to the case, or facts that are new to the defence lawyer posing a potential face threat, not just to team face but to lawyer face. This can, in part, be due to the other partner in that specific interaction, namely the defence lawyer who is doing the questioning which may lead to the client relaxing more perhaps associating the interaction with a backstage situation. However, it may also be due to the client interacting in a situation where the rules of interaction are unclear. This internal face threat coming from within the team described by Vera is an unintentional internal face threat, based on the client's lack of initiation in the interaction order of the courtroom (cf. Tracy & Tracy, 1998). This differs from the interaction I described earlier on in this chapter where the client gave monosyllabic answers which can also be seen as an internal face threat. However, in contrast to the one described here, the monosyllabic performance does not arise from a lack of initiation, rather, I argue, from familiarity with the interaction order which one does not take seriously (Goffman, 1961b).

The client's presentation of self as damaging team face is talked about by all of the lawyers I spoke to. Clients who present themselves in court as aggressive may convey an image that deviates from the impression the team is attempting to present, for instance, that the client is not a violent person and has not committed the offence. Defence lawyers therefore try to prepare their clients beforehand as to how they should portray themselves in the courtroom. I explore this in more detail in the next chapter and, later on in this chapter, I show the strategy of directing the client by using "staging talk" (Goffman, 1959, p. 173).

It is not only the defendant who can internally threaten the defence team, but also the defence lawyer if he or she inadvertently poses a "fatal question" as lawyers describe it, the answer to which is unknown or unforeseen and the consequence of which may be damning for the case. The unpredictability of a trial means that it is not always possible to know what this "fatal question" might be as can be seen in the following excerpt from my fieldnotes of a robbery trial. We join proceedings as the defence lawyer is asking the plaintiff about how he perceived the defendant during the attack:

> "How was [the defendant]: [his] state of mind?" The plaintiff replies, "he was as cold as ice, I got goosebumps. He was either a professional criminal or he was drugged." The defence lawyer replies, "that wasn't what I asked, was he threatening in any way?" (Fieldnote)

Here, the response of the plaintiff is damaging to team face as the defence team is attempting to portray the defendant as non-violent. The plaintiff thus comprises an external threat to team face. However, the lawyer has also posed a "fatal question," the answer to which damages team face therefore he has inadvertently threatened both his lawyer face as well as the reality the defence team is presenting. Inadvertently posing such a question may require corrective facework in order to give the impression that the answer was expected and/or to attempt to reduce the impact which may have unintentionally built up the prosecution's facts rather than undermining or weakening them.

The fatal question is the subject of folklore amongst defence lawyers. For instance, Siri tells me about a murder trial she has heard tales about:

> The witness points out a man for murder and, as I say, this isn't my case, and the defence lawyer asks, "how can you be so sure that it was the man you are now pointing out?" And the woman replies, "because it was the most beautiful man I had ever seen." (Siri)

Now think about your own reaction when reading this and place yourself in the shoes of that defence lawyer who must keep up normal appearances when dealing with this (beautiful) face threat. The ability to manage face threats is a key lawyering tool.

Keep calm and carry on

So, face threats can either come from within the defence team or from outside the team. Whatever the source of the threat, it places dramaturgical demands on the defence lawyer, as Richard says, "it becomes a kind of crisis management in the moment." My analysis shows that it is the source of such destructive information that shapes the strategy used to manage it. There are three ways in which face threats may be managed depending on the source and the type of information presented: (1) External face threats may be managed by highlighting or over-communicating information. Here, the defence lawyer uses strategies to draw attention to information that threatens team face. These are called "dramatic productions" (Goffman, 1972); (2) External face threats may also be managed by the defence lawyer downplaying or under-communicating destructive information thus drawing attention away from damaging information that is threatening team face. I have named these strategies "dramatic reductions"; (3) Internal face threats tend to be under-communicated with dramatic reductions as they constitute a misalignment to the team performance.[6]

What is important to note here is that all of these facework strategies can involve subtlety and understatement in line with the ceremonial order and emotional order of the courtroom which demands emotional restraint, civility and politeness.

I begin by introducing the strategies that defence lawyers use to draw attention towards face threats before moving on to show dramatic reductions which actively construct disattention (Goffman, 1959).

Dramatic productions

A defence lawyer may manage face threats and do teamwork by aligning to the client via a dramatic realisation of loyalty. This can be achieved by rhetorically[7] and gesturally supporting the client's version of events and questioning the claims of the prosecution. This is done by drawing attention towards damaging information or evidence that is presented in the court which threatens the impression of reality the defence team is portraying and which therefore constitutes a face threat. The defence lawyer is thus dramatically highlighting certain facts in order to sustain team face (Goffman, 1956b, p. 19). Such symbolic gestures communicate support for the client's version of reality and consequently loyalty to the client. We can therefore see that loyalty and teamwork are interactionally intertwined.

This is perhaps what we would expect to see defence lawyers do in a courtroom: represent their client by reacting to the prosecution's evidence which the defence claims to be inaccurate. What is interesting to highlight here, however, is how this can be analysed as a performance of facework. Such performances can then be used to contrast the other end of the extreme where defence lawyers use strategies to draw attention away from information presented by not appearing to react, which will be discussed further on. Typically, the employment of props and emotional displays are included in the facework of teamwork.

The strategy of dramatic productions will now be introduced by presenting an excerpt taken from my fieldnotes from the closing speech of a murder trial where the defendant denies the crime. We see how the defence lawyer acts as though an external face threat has been committed and that the worst possible interpretation of events might occur: that the judges deem the prosecution's version of events to be strong enough to find the client guilty:

> The defence lawyer begins his closing speech. He takes off his glasses and states that "the prosecutor is *wrong* in making these claims!" He leans forwards, forearms on desk, hands clasped, and asks the judges to experiment themselves at holding the weapon in the way the prosecution claims the defendant was holding the weapon at the time of the murder. He shakes his head and raising his voice and speed of delivery states that it is impossible that the incident transpired as claimed by the prosecutor. He points a finger on the desk, waves it in the air, points at the prosecutor and, raising his voice even more states that there is *no* evidence for the accusations. His voice becomes slightly higher in pitch emphasising his client was in *shock* after the incident. He states that "I don't claim that this *is* what happened,

> rather than it *could* be what happened" whilst pointing a finger at the judges. The defence lawyer continues that the claims of the prosecution "are pure speculation" said in a tone of voice implying incredulity. His voice then softens stating, "my client is not the same person now as he was when taken into custody" which makes the defendant's mother start to cry. The defence lawyer then states that the charges will never be accepted by the defence and looks to the mother when he says this, before saying in the softest tone of voice yet that his client should be released immediately. (Fieldnote)

The defence lawyer uses facework in the form of bodywork by using his body as an impression management tool to draw attention to the face threat: leaning forwards, shaking his head, pointing his fingers, in order to draw attention to certain facts and thus sustain team face. This bodywork supports what is being said when he presents an alternate version of events (this could be what happened). It is also used to draw attention to the destructive information presented by the prosecutor that goes against the team's version of events (the prosecutor is wrong). In this way, the defence lawyer uses symbolic gestures to loyally sustain the impression of reality the team is projecting, thus supporting team face.

Bodywork is consequently used to align to the team performance and is also a way of building or undermining facts, hence it is appropriate to talk of it being a form of "factwork." By this I mean that the defence lawyer is using gestures and emotions to build facts and/or undermine facts. He is presenting and shaping facts in the courtroom using interactional techniques, similar to the way that deviancy or normalcy can be collaboratively constructed in the courtroom (cf. Holstein, 1988; Holstein, 1993). Factwork involves "working up" (Potter, 1996, p. 123; cf. Staske, 1996) an account (based on the client's version of events) to make it appear as a fact, whilst simultaneously "working down" (S. Scott, 2015, p. 68) another account – undermining the facts presented by the prosecution.

The dramatic production in the closing argument presented earlier also involves emotions, stretching from outrage to indignation to incredulity to sympathy, all in the space of ten minutes. Garnering such emotional engagement from the court, in part by evoking sympathy for the defendant, is an important part of defending one's client (Althin, 1994). The defence lawyer's voice builds momentum, becoming louder and louder, faster and faster, with emphasis on certain emotive words: "wrong" and "shock" to build up a sense of emotional outrage at the accusations against the client. It is a way of aligning to the client and producing a team performance by performing emotional expressions.

Towards the end, the tone changes notably, becoming much softer and quieter. The emotions of the defendant's mother are now also included and reinforced. This can be seen as another way of using emotions as an instrumental tool; however, in this case, it entails the utilisation of another actor's emotions – namely the mother's – it is a rhetorical tool using pathos (McCormack, 2014; Sobota, 1994).[8]

We thus see a contextual aspect to the performances: in the closing speech it is acceptable to show a wider range of emotions and use impression management tools such as props, the body and rhetoric, in a more explicit or obvious manner, compared to other parts of proceedings. I suggest this is because the closing speech signifies "the culmination of the representational project" (Scheffer, 2010, p. 156) and therefore more dramatic strategies are used.

So, facework can involve defence lawyers interactionally constructing or deconstructing facts in order to perform team face. Whilst this can be accomplished more conspicuously as in the example I have just presented, often, the performance of teamwork and loyalty is subtler. Team face is more usually sustained by using a combination of understated non-linguistic gestures together with a muted verbal performance (Blomkvist, 1987, p. 83; Flower, 2016a, 2016b; Hägg, 2004).

This can be seen in the following interaction where the prosecutor is presenting the facts of the case at the start of a trial and is reading aloud a report written by an expert witness for the prosecution regarding the extreme temperatures that can be reached inside a car on a warm day and the consequences this may have for leaving an animal inside. The defendant denies all the charges and claims the car had been left in the shade. The findings of this report are thus of importance for the defence's case and when the exact temperatures are read out:

> The defence lawyer looks up sharply and says, very quietly but also very forcibly "what?!?" (*nämen*) The defence lawyer looks at the prosecutor, then the judge and then his client and shakes his head. Later on, when it is the defence lawyer's turn to talk, he sits up straighter in his chair, speaking rapidly and in a loud tone of voice states that he became "quite annoyed" when hearing the report which he claims includes incorrect details. (Fieldnote)

The claims of the prosecution's expert witness are an external face threat as it implies that the client has been criminally negligent, thereby opposing the social position and impression of reality that the defence team is attempting to portray. However, the defence lawyer must ensure that his team performance communicates his support of the team line by challenging or undermining the facts presented by the prosecution – the face threat – whilst simultaneously following the flow of interaction and ensuring that his performance of adversarialism remains appropriate. His emotional performance of annoyance is therefore accomplished verbally by saying "what?!?" and changing his tone of voice and nonverbally by looking up and sitting upright. This form of dramatic production remains appropriate to the interaction order, ceremonial order and the emotional order of the criminal trial: non-confrontational, muted and polite whilst also being appropriate to the context. He uses bodywork to convey alignment and meaning to the situation in an interactionally confined context (cf. Goffman, 1972, pp. 11, 125).

We see then that the scope for responding to such face threats is consequently limited to subtle verbal responses and gestures ensuring the continuation of the interaction flow. Responses of "what?!?" or similar are recurrent in numerous observations and demonstrate the normative nature of the emotional regime. Quietly mumbling "what?!?" is therefore the Swedish equivalent of shouting "objection!" in an American courtroom, a difference in performance stemming from the difference in display rules between the two legal cultures thus pointing to differences in the "societal emotional regimes" (Bergman Blix & Wettergren, 2015, p. 3).

In such situations, the defence lawyer is performing what I have named "vicarious facework" as in this situation and context, the client is unable to save his own face as such protestations would disrupt the flow of the criminal trial. As I mentioned at the start of this chapter, the dramaturgical scope for the defendant's defensive facework is fairly limited (although displays of nonchalance may be used). The defence lawyer must therefore save the client's face on his behalf.

This is a form of collective facework that differs to the current literature on collective facework strategies as it is not aimed at aiding interactants within the team to regain face when they have let their own face slip (cf. Lee, 2009). In the excerpt above, vicarious face-saving is done by the defence lawyer, for the client, when the face threat arises externally (from the prosecutor). This also functions to maintain the defence lawyer's professional face as it is part of his role to question evidence that goes against his client's version.

At the end of the following excerpt, we see the defence lawyer dramatically producing attention towards certain facts by exclaiming "very strange!" thereby giving face to the client. It is taken from my fieldnotes of a trial where the defendant is accused of various crimes related to the possession of narcotics with intent to supply:

> When the defendant is being questioned by the prosecutor, he claims that he doesn't know how the cocaine ended up under his mattress which the police found when they searched his flat. He thinks that he might possibly have tidied it away there the night before (after a party that he had at his house) but he doesn't remember doing this. He does remember seeing a white powder but didn't know that this was cocaine. He goes on to say that he only uses a small amount of marijuana every day but that he had no intention of selling the large amount that was found in his residence – it was all for his personal use. The prosecutor points out that this is a large

amount of marijuana to buy if he only uses a small amount but the defendant stands firm that he was not going to sell it. The lawyer does not visibly react throughout.

When the defendant is being questioned by his defence lawyer, she asks him about his bank accounts. The defendant says he has no idea how one million Swedish crowns [€96,000] ended up in one of the accounts: he never uses that bank and can't imagine where the money has come from. He explains that he doesn't use the card that is connected to the bank account and therefore that it wasn't him who made all of the purchases visible on the bank statement. When he is talking about this the lawyer makes the comment "very strange!" saying this in a serious tone of voice. (Fieldnote)

Not only does the defence lawyer draw attention to the facts the defence team are presenting – that the defendant is unknowing as to why such a large amount of money is in his bank account, but also, in the middle of this excerpt, we see the defence lawyer using another strategy, namely the dramatic reduction of stoneface which I introduced in chapter four and which I will now develop further.

Dramatic reductions using stoneface

In the excerpt I have just presented, the defence lawyer draws attention to certain facts by commenting "very strange!" and draws attention away from others – for instance, that the defendant does not know how the narcotics came to be under his bed – by not reacting. These are the two extremes of how destructive information to the team impression should be dealt with: either highlighted or downplayed.

There are numerous examples in my data of defence lawyers using dramas of reduction wherein normal appearances are upheld by not responding to destructive information given by the client in order uphold team face (Goffman, 1969). Dramatic reductions include various strategies, one of which I have already introduced as a way of upholding lawyer face (for instance by covering up mistakes) namely stoneface. However, stoneface can also be used as a strategy for upholding team face by downplaying face threats or destructive information coming from either within the team or from outside the team. It is also used to build and undermine facts and is therefore a tool to convey loyalty to the team and the team's version of events.

I return now to the excerpt from the opening of this book and where we are now able to see stoneface being used. This excerpt is taken from a criminal trial where the defendant is accused of breaking and entering into a flat and stealing various goods. There is a witness who has given a description of the suspect and seen him entering the property in question empty handed, and, after a short while, leaving with a large bag which is full. The police were called to the scene and caught the defendant leaving the area, wearing plastic gloves and carrying the stolen property in the bag described by the witness. He is therefore arrested. We join proceedings as the prosecutor is asking the defendant for his version of events:

> The prosecutor asks the defendant how he came to be in possession of the stolen items and the defendant claims that he bumped into an acquaintance who gave them to him. When asked to describe the acquaintance, the defendant claims he does not remember what his acquaintance looked like or what he was wearing. When asked what the acquaintance is called, the defendant thinks a while and says, "Hmmmm, Erving." Coincidentally, this also happens to be the (very unusual) name of the defence lawyer. The prosecutor points out to the accused that in his police statement he stated that the acquaintance he bumped into was called Danny Diamond, which the arresting police officer has also testified to. When asked why he was wearing plastic gloves at the time of his arrest, he replies that it was because he thought that the items could possibly be stolen and he didn't want to get his fingerprints on them; therefore "Erving" gave him his plastic gloves along with the items.
>
> Throughout all of this, the defence lawyer stares, almost without blinking, at the prosecutor. His facial features do not move: no raised eyebrows, no shake of the head. He is still: glasses in hand, body turned fully towards the prosecutor, not looking at his client. (Fieldnote)

Take a moment here to reflect upon your own reaction upon reading the above excerpt again. Does it sound credible to you? Did you raise your eyebrows when reading it? Perhaps smile or shake your head? I have presented this extract at various conferences and seminars and it is always met with amusement and incredulity; therefore, this may be seen as the expected reaction in such a situation when one is presented with a version of events that seems very unlikely. However, the defence lawyer does not react as you or I would react, or indeed perhaps as he would react upon hearing such an unlikely tale if heard outside his professional role as a defence lawyer.

As we have seen in the guidelines for the Swedish Bar Association (2008), the defence lawyer above should not allow any personal opinion regarding the version of events being presented by the client, and therefore, the team, to affect his performance (providing, of course, the version is not overly far-fetched). This means that even in instances such as that described here, where the version of events is unlikely, the defence lawyer should nevertheless uphold it. Additionally, he must convey the qualities integral to his role which includes ensuring that his expressions are coherent with the reality being presented – he should keep up normal appearances (Goffman, 1972). This means that he should use emotion work to ensure that his emotional display is in line with the reality the team is presenting. He should also follow the appropriate emotion rules in such situations, for instance, disbelief should not be displayed. There may also be other emotions in need of management such as embarrassment, as the client appears to commit a faux pas by fabricating the name of his acquaintance – a name that only 0.1 per cent of the population of Sweden have as their given name (SCB, 2017).

In such situations, defence lawyers use stoneface as a form of factwork in order to build up alternative facts[9] which otherwise would not have existed (S. Scott, 2017). By acting as though nothing unusual is happening, the defence lawyer is supporting the version of reality that the client has constructed, giving it credibility (cf. Emerson, 1970; Porter & ten Brink, 2009).

Stoneface is therefore used here as a form of emotional factwork involving the modulation of responses. For instance, had the defence lawyer in the Danny Diamond excerpt shown disbelief, he would have granted that the facts presented were not quite believable and thereby inadvertently supported the opposition's facts. By not showing any surprise or disbelief in the client's version of events, the defence lawyer is supporting it, thus sustaining team face. This can be demanding, particularly when the defence team are joined in a "polite fiction" (Burns, 1992) whereby the team members agree to unite behind a reality that both are perhaps not completely convinced is accurate – as may be the case in the Danny Diamond excerpt, and as Sandra also tells me:

> I can do a closing speech where I know that some of the things I say are going to be very difficult for the court to believe in because it's, it's not especially likely that it was like that, but I hope that, that it's not noticeable that I also think it seems a bit unlikely. (Sandra)

Stoneface can also be used as a counter-move against the prosecutor's attempts at discounting the defence team's reality. For instance, in one of the previous excerpts I presented, the prosecution openly questions the reality of the defendant as being unusual (when the defendant claims he was coerced into a confession the prosecutor exclaims "I've never heard of this happening before!") – yet the defence lawyer continues to stay in line. He uses stoneface to construct, define, and sustain a reality that contrasts to that claimed by the prosecution.

The presentation of facts thus requires the appropriate performance, drawing on the appropriate emotions in order to achieve the strategic goal of proving the client's innocence by questioning the validity of evidence, by showing weaknesses in the prosecution's case, or by hiding weaknesses in the defence. Stoneface highlights how this fact production and reduction is accomplished using nonverbal communication, not just verbal.

I consider stoneface to be a "dramatic reduction," building on Goffman's (1972) concept of dramatic productions. It is based on the premise that even the absence of an action is still an action. Dramatic reductions are thus active commissions, rather than passive omissions, aimed at keeping facts hidden (remember – stoneface can also be used to hide professional mistakes as I presented at the start of this chapter) (cf. Goffman, 1956b; S. Scott, 2017).

This is another performance on the "personal front" (Goffman, 1956b, p. 14) using bodywork as a tool for impression management, in order to align oneself to the team by not showing any reaction, even small facial expressions such as a slight frown as Charles says, "you really try and control yourself, you really do."

All of the lawyers I spoke to talk about using this strategy which they called doing "stoneface," "poker-face," or "blank-face" in order to convey the appropriate impression (Goffman, 1969). The observant reader will have noticed that several of the fieldnotes presented in this chapter have already shown the defence lawyer doing stoneface: for example, in the balaclava trial, the defence lawyer remains still-faced, writing notes. Here is another example of stoneface taken from my fieldnotes of a trial where the defendant denies being at the scene of a crime:

> *Prosecutor:* Why were you at (the scene of the crime)?
> *Defendant:* I wasn't there!
> *Prosecutor:* But you were arrested there.
> The defence shows no reaction, just keeps on making notes. (Fieldnote)

The defendant is caught out in a potentially face threatening situation: a lie. Similar to the client's presentation of self in the Danny Diamond extract, the client's performance may be deemed embarrassing to the team thereby comprising an internal face threat to team face.

We see then that the client may contribute to undermining the version of events the team is presenting – an internal face threat – and it is up to the remaining team members – the lawyer – to manage this gaffe. Dramatic reductions are therefore another instance of vicarious face-saving and maintaining lawyer face. This contrasts to the vicarious face-saving in dramatic productions as now the source of the face threat is the client himself (in earlier examples, the source of the face threat was external).

Stoneface is thus used here, not as a defensive strategy employed by defence lawyers to sustain their own lawyer face as I presented at the start of this chapter, rather it is used as a collective strategy to protect the team's dramaturgical fate, that is, saving team face and protecting the team's image. Stoneface can thus be performed for the team – a form of "emotional teamwork" (Waldron, 2000, p. 80).

Stoneface is discussed by the defence lawyers as coming with experience and the successful use of it during trials is talked about admiringly with defence lawyers recounting tales of being complimented for their stonefacing. Stoneface reveals an invisible emotion rule outlining the expected emotional display, learned through a process of implicit socialisation (cf. Flower, 2014).

Stoneface is therefore a form of facework used to accomplish teamwork and loyalty. Teamwork demands dramaturgical co-operation on the side of the defence lawyer in order to sustain the team performance. If, as is sometimes the case, there are several defendants, the defence lawyer has no bond to the other defendants and may react with disbelief at another's claim to reality; however, commitment should be shown to one's own client thus highlighting the "team" aspect of dramaturgical loyalty. Taking the team "line" means simultaneously taking the loyalty "line" (Goffman, 1967). We see again that teamwork and loyalty are interlinked.

Dramatic reductions using props

In the extract from my fieldnotes from the closing argument of a murder trial that I presented earlier in the section on dramatic productions, we see dramatic production using the body as a facework tool in the form of nonverbal gestures such as finger pointing and other gestures in order to dramatically realise the client's version of events. Props are also seen in this excerpt when the defence lawyer takes off his glasses in a performative gesture. The use of props as an impression management tool during jury trials has been discussed, although in general, they have gained little sociological attention (Ball, 1994; Hägg, 2004, p. 182). I will now discuss the use of props to symbolically communicate meaning in more detail where most illustrations will focus on their use in dramatic reductions to do factwork and facework (cf. Waldron, 2000).

In situations where destructive information is presented constituting a face threat, the defence lawyer sometimes uses props to tone down or under-communicate the potentially damaging impact. Props can therefore be used to dramatically reduce or undermine facts. In the following trial, the defendant denies the crimes he is accused of and we join proceedings as the arresting police officer recounts what the defendant said when he was taken into custody:

> The police officer says that the defendant stated he wanted "to kill the man" that he stabbed in the neck. When the police officer says this the defence lawyer takes his mobile phone out of his trouser pocket and checks it, holding it on the desk in front. The policeman goes on to say that the defendant told him "they screamed when he assaulted them." The defence keeps looking at his mobile phone. The policeman then states that the defendant said "they screamed and screamed." The defence lawyer checks his fingernails: he holds up his left hand in front of his face, palm facing him, fingers curled over and bites the edge of one of his nails. The gesture of moving his hand to check the nails is very sudden. He then goes back to leaning forwards with hand on chin and cheek. (Fieldnote)

In all instances in the above extract, the defence lawyer either looks at his mobile phone or fingernails when destructive information is presented.

Looking at mobile phones is a recurrent occurrence I have observed in many trials and does not garner any reaction from the judges, which may point towards it being viewed as acceptable. Indeed, in interviews, defence lawyers state that they may need to check email during proceedings. (However, as we will see in chapter seven, the ringing of a mobile phone in the courtroom is a breach of norms.) On the rare occasion the mobile phone of either the judge or lay judge rang, they responded with visible embarrassment: blushing, shaking of head, rapid movements to turn it off, and statements of apology indicating that this comprises a deviation from the ceremonial order.

The inspection of fingernails is a strategy used by many defence lawyers at times when testimony is being given which could be perceived to be damaging to the defence. It is thus used to manage face threats. Once again, there is a reaction here, but the response is not outwards, performing outrage or frustration, rather it would appear to be a performance designed to reduce the impact of statements undermining the facts. It may therefore be seen as a dramatic reduction with the use of props. In the majority of trials I observed, there is at least one instance of this kind of strategy ranging from the inspection of fingernails, to the use of toothpicks, to polishing glasses.

Other examples of props being used to draw attention away from evidence are plentiful in my fieldnotes. The following excerpt is taken from a trial where the client is accused of assault and we join proceedings where the plaintiff is being questioned by the prosecutor and is giving her version of events:

> The plaintiff is describing in detail when the defendant chased her and pushed her into a window. The defence lawyer glances at the clock, the prosecutor, the judge, his client, and then his notes. The plaintiff goes on to describe how she was pinned to the floor and was choked by the defendant, with his hands around her neck, lifting her head up and hitting it on the floor. The defence lawyer takes out his mobile phone from his blazer pocket and checks it before putting it away again. When the plaintiff says "it really hurt!" the defence lawyer checks his fingernails. The plaintiff goes on to say that "it felt as though my arm broke" the defence lawyer's hand goes to the pocket with the mobile phone again. The plaintiff then goes on to talk about the children's involvement. The defence lawyer stops reaching for the phone again. He reads the papers in front of him instead and makes notes. Later on, he takes out chewing gum and starts chewing when the plaintiff is talking about another incident where she was attacked and strangled by the defendant. (Fieldnote)

The next excerpt also comes from another trial where the plaintiff has claimed that the defendant assaulted her in front of their small children:

> At the most delicate point of the proceedings, when the plaintiff is describing how scared and upset her small children became when witnessing

> the defendant's attack on her, the defence lawyer brushes some (invisible) crumbs from the front of his jumper. This occurs mid-morning so the gesture is unlikely to be the result of a recently eaten meal. (Fieldnote)

A prop or a gesture can also be used as a sign of something else than the ostensible usage, in this case, showing that the plaintiff's testimony is, at the least inaccurate, at the worst, untrue as the client claims he has not committed the assault in both of the cases above. A mobile phone, fingernails, or brushing away crumbs may be used as a subtle way of manipulating reality (cf. Goffman, 1956b, p. 162).

Another example is seen below where we meet a witness giving evidence regarding the abuse and assault committed against the plaintiff. The witness is describing one such incident recounted by the plaintiff to the witness after the event:

> The witness details one instance where the defendant attempted to smother the plaintiff by placing a pillow over her head. Halfway through the witness' testimony the defence lawyer takes out some throat sweets, offers one to her client who declines by a very small shake of the head, and then takes one for herself and replaces the packet back in her pocket. The defence lawyer has not shown any signs that her throat might have been causing her discomfort and this is the first and only time she takes out a throat sweet. (Fieldnote)

The defence lawyer takes out throat sweets when the witness is describing an attempted murder. The timing of this action, at the most delicate moment in proceedings, would appear to indicate that it is designed to achieve a goal, namely to reduce the impact of the witness's statement. Rather than showing sympathy or openly objecting to a witness's testimony which should only be done delicately, the defence lawyer performs in a way aimed at neutralising the emotional impact of the statements given: she is doing something very mundane, as if trying to counterbalance or deconstruct the facts in the witness' dramatic statements. The defence lawyer is "figuratively erasing" (Katz, 1999, pp. 320–321) herself from the scene by not showing the emotion that would be expected in such a situation. In producing such invisibility by using the body to simultaneously guide attention away and towards it, defence lawyers in such instances deviate from the emotional norm of showing sympathy when hearing a tragic story as would be expected in a different situation. An alternative explanation could be that defence lawyers use props to manage their own inappropriate emotions that might arise from hearing sad accounts. However, I posit that as props are used in an array of situations ranging from descriptions of attempted murder (which could, in other situations, provoke feelings of sadness in the defence lawyer) to descriptions of minor incidents (which would not be considered to be emotive), they can be understood as strategies for drawing attention away from facts, rather than strategies for managing one's own inappropriate emotions.

The defence lawyers' performances here are thus of teamwork and loyalty – the client has claimed that the plaintiff or witness is lying; therefore, reacting in a more sympathetic manner might jeopardise this.

It should also be noted that this deviation from the emotion norm of showing sympathy or compassion in such a situation and instead retaining a cool countenance, could lead to the defence lawyer appearing heartless to the non-legal actors in the courtroom as they may be unaware of emotional order of the criminal trial (cf. Goffman, 1967, pp. 10–11). Again, we see an explanation for the preconception I presented in the introduction that questions whether or not defence lawyers have feelings (cf. Goffman, 1967, pp. 10–11).

All of the excerpts in this section show that props tend to be used when the source of the face threat is external to the team. However, once again, the observant reader may notice that writing notes is often used when doing stone-face, both when managing external face threats and when the source comes from the client, internal to the team. Writing notes is therefore another face-work tool used to distract attention from a potential face threat which I have observed on numerous occasions in the courtroom. Whilst the defence lawyers interviewed state that writing notes is necessary to remember what has been said, it is also talked about as a form of staying focused and awake and strategy for covering up face threats.

Directing the defence team

In the theatre of the courtroom, it is the defence lawyer who directs the defence team performance, constructing a convincing story for the court and ensuring that the team performance stays on track (Dershowitz, 1986; Ebervall, 2002; Levenson, 2007). The strategies used to direct the team impression will now be discussed.

Tell it like it is

A successful team performance should conceal any prior consultation regarding the party line between team members which is done backstage (Goffman, 1959). If this has not been possible then there is a risk that the frontstage performance falters, revealing cracks in the team performance. As we have already seen, documents and clothing can be used to create a certain impression. These performances on the personal front can be prepared in advance. Another important factor is for team members to "get their story straight" (Goffman, 1956b, p. 54) beforehand, in order to identify and then follow the "party line" (Goffman, 1956b, p. 53).

Whilst studies from the U.S. show that defence lawyers prepare their clients for cross-examination in the courtroom (Pizzi, 1999), the lawyers I spoke to say that their "staging talk" (Goffman, 1959, p. 173) is aimed at counselling their client to "tell it like it is." However, they do request that the client tells them the version that they are going to present in court, and to stick to that version. This backstage talk enables lines and positions to be established so that past and possible future disruptions or performances can be discussed and agreed upon.

Preparing the case is not always possible for a defence lawyer, for example the client might not reply to contact from the defence lawyer before the trial. This makes it difficult for the defence lawyer to know the client's version of events, which, in turn, makes it difficult to know how to question a client in the courtroom. In other words, the "party line" becomes a "thin party line" (Goffman, 1956b, p. 52) and can negatively affect the impression given by the lawyer in the trial, leading to them appearing to be unprepared, nervous or less confident in court which, as already noted in the beginning of this chapter, is damaging for one's lawyer face. The lack of such preparatory discussions can also threaten team face as it makes it harder for teammates to unite behind an impression of reality if the defence lawyer is uncertain as to what that reality is. Lydia talks about the frustration that can arise on such occasions, yet this frustration between teammates must remain hidden as it could threaten the defence team's bond and integrity and lead to a disruption in the interaction order (S. Scott, 2015). Just to remind the reader, the interaction order is based on the definition of the situation: a criminal trial which is a social situation that expects the defence team to be united. The defence lawyer is the legal voice of the defendant. If the defence lawyer is not seen to be representing the defendant, then one facet of this social situation has broken down, and the interaction order is no longer upheld.

Frontstage direction

Sometimes the backstage work of teamwork fails and is revealed frontstage in the courtroom. This shows a breakdown in team face and the defence team appears weakened. The following is an example of where such dramaturgical co-operation breaks down. It is revealed to us in the courtroom that the defence lawyer has used backstage "staging talk" (Goffman, 1959, p. 73) in order to give face to the client in the courtroom by presenting him as willing to take part in mediation.[10] However, the client fails to uphold the line the defence lawyer is attempting to project:

Defence lawyer: Are you still willing to take part in mediation?
Defendant: What's mediation?
Defence lawyer: Are you still positively inclined to meeting and talking to the plaintiff?

The defendant does not look at all open to the idea of meeting and talking to the plaintiff. He looks blank.

Defence lawyer:	Is it the case that you are open to mediation?
Defendant:	Uuuuuuuh.
Judge:	Perhaps you would like to discuss this with your client?
Defence lawyer:	Yes, it might be that I have misunderstood. (Fieldnote)

The defence lawyer's attempt at giving face to the client backfires in court as the defendant does not appear to know what mediation is. It deteriorates into a breakdown in team performance making them appear disunited. We see once again, that the defence lawyer is not able to rely on his team members' dramaturgical co-operation and the (lack of) backstage preparation is accidentally revealed frontstage.

Thus, even if one has prepared with one's client backstage there may still arise occasions where maintaining a team performance involves one team member directing the other in order to bring him or her back into line (Goffman, 1963a, pp. 34–35). The lawyer, as the director of the team performance, must ensure that the performance remains dedicated to this shared team identity. This involves a process of idealisation of the other team member's roles. In the extract above, we see a failed attempt by the defence lawyer to present the client in the best possible light, as positive to mediation – a form of idealisation (Strong, 2001).[11]

Frontstage directions take place in full view of the courtroom with the defence lawyer playing the role of "cooler" (Goffman, 1952) as Andrew talks about here:

> If I feel that it's getting like, that [the client is] starting to get worked up then I always angle the microphone away and then I lean in and I talk calmly with them, calm them down. And then if it's the case that they are sitting there bouncing then I ask for a break if I know they're about to explode so to speak, because I want a client who "behaves themselves" [shows citation marks]. I mean, if your client is suspected for a violent crime for example, then I don't want the person in question to sit there and show violent tendencies because then it's like, "yes, yes, it was like the prosecutor said." Bit like that. Instead, behave yourself, pull yourself together. (Andrew)

Andrew has the strategy of asking for a break if the client is about to deviate from the rules of interaction which prescribe turn-taking in speech and acting in a calm and controlled manner. Just as lawyers talk about taking a break in proceedings if there is a risk to their own face, taking a break is also presented as a way of cooling the client down if he or she has "flooded out" (Goffman, 1961a, 1967) or is on the brink. This is necessary as such emotional outpourings may reveal something regarding the client's character that the defence team is attempting to keep hidden. As Andrew describes, if the client is accused of a violent crime, then his or her possible violent tendencies should remain hidden. Taking a break can therefore ensure that the client stays in face. In the next chapter, I explore in more detail how defence lawyers prepare their clients in order to avoid such situations arising.

The following excerpt from my fieldnotes is another example of frontstage direction, taken from the part of a trial where the defence lawyer is questioning his client regarding a charge of drink-driving (I will return to this excerpt in the next chapter to further explore the production of regret):

> The defence lawyer angles his chair slightly towards his client and says "of course, you regret that you drove?" to which the client replies that he does. The defence lawyer then states "you were in a spiral of drinking too much." His head is tipped slightly to one side and his voice is softer when he says this.
>
> Later on in proceedings the defence lawyer is questioning his client about the assault he is accused of and asks "do you mean that the plaintiff is making it up?" As he says this, he looks at the defendant and nods. It is a large, single nod of the head. The client replies "yeees, yes." (Fieldnote)

This is an unusual performance as it shows the defence lawyer quite clearly leading the responses of the client. Although this is the point in proceedings where the defence lawyer is supposed to be questioning his client, the questions are more statements aimed at constructing the defendant's identity as regretful by forming the client's answers in order to produce a performance of regret with a tinge of sympathy ("you were in a spiral of drinking too much") (cf. Althin, 1994; Gathings & Parrotta, 2013; Snow & Anderson, 1987). We also see frontstage direction aimed at producing regret in the following excerpt:

> When the prosecutor is questioning the defendant, the defendant admits that he "did stupid stuff" and looks at his defence lawyer when he says this. His lawyer nods and says "say what you did" in quite a soft but fairly stern voice. His client continues that he stole some items, looks again at his lawyer who nods again. It is the first time there has been any interaction between them and the first eye contact that has been made. (Fieldnote)

Rather than facework (aimed at maintaining appearances in the present) this can be seen as "character work" aimed at showing the client's "moral core" and therefore, "future behaviour and the effects of the individual on society at large" (Strong, 2001, p. 42). The use of eye contact also serves to strengthen the united front between client and lawyer.

By this rationale, a great deal of defence lawyers' work, if not all, is indeed character work, ensuring the court that the client is not a danger to society. In the earlier example, we clearly see the defence lawyer attempting to portray the client as having sound moral character demonstrated by showing regret: the normatively expected emotion both inside and outside the courtroom when one has done wrong.

When the defence lawyer asks his client in the drink-driving excerpt if he meant that the plaintiff has fabricated the assault, the client has previously not mentioned anything that would indicate that he thinks the plaintiff is lying, only that the plaintiff's version is not the same as his own. It is the defence lawyer who constructs the fact that the plaintiff is lying, thereby threatening the face of the plaintiff. The client is clearly directed as to how to answer this question as the defence lawyer gives a large affirmative nod. Again, the defence lawyer is steering the impression given by simultaneously using bodywork, giving an individual performance whilst also producing a performance in the client, by pulling forth details that otherwise would have remained hidden, in this case, the client's regret, and by nodding in order to indicate the "proper" response. In this way the defence lawyer is managing and partly performing the client's emotions (cf. Thoits, 1996). In much the same way that competency can be interactionally achieved in collaboration between a patient and defence lawyer, the above episodes are ways of "teaming up" to construct facts (Holstein, 1993).

We also see in these two excerpts that facework in the courtroom can also have multiple goals (Penman, 1990). I have previously shown how the prosecutor often threatens the defendant's face and also presented an excerpt where the defence lawyer threatens the face of an expert witness by reacting with indignation in order to protect team face. The two current extracts shown here present defence lawyers intentionally damaging their own client's face by encouraging them to admit the crime – "say what you did" – in an attempt to reduce the severity of the sentence.

While outside of the courtroom such strategies might lead to the receiver of the face damage feeling aggrieved, in the courtroom they are permitted by the courtroom norms (Archer 2011b, 6; Goffman 1967, 14; see also Harris 2011b). Although the defence lawyer's actions in the drink driving example can be seen as an intentional face threat to the client's face – painting him as having an alcohol problem – the goal is nevertheless to strengthen the team's version of events: that the client was unable to stop himself. I therefore argue that the face threat is intended to accomplish an instrumental goal and should instead be seen as an "instrumental face threat."

More specifically this instance shows an internal instrumental face threat, coming from within the team. However, an instrumental face threat can also have an external source, for instance the prosecutor, who is attempting to give the defendant another face than the one he or she has claimed. This is, I believe, implicit in Goffman's (1967) theory but it is in need of greater clarification.

Internal instrumental face threats can also be seen as a form of facework where the defence lawyer gives the client an opportunity to repair the situation by intentionally damaging the face of the client (as an alcoholic) and the plaintiff (as a liar) whilst simultaneously maintaining lawyer face and team face (Penman, 1990). It balances this open-face threat by attempting to accomplish normality by weakening or "working down" (S. Scott, 2015, p. 68) the deviant identity of drinking too much, and "working up" (Potter, 1996, p. 123) another identity. In this way, the defence lawyer is attempting to construct a social identity that is socially approved: a person showing regret for their actions. In contrast to previous interactionist work on identity construction, in this case, it is the defence lawyer who is actively constructing an identity for his client, rather than the client constructing his own (cf. Potter, 1996, p. 114).

This, in turn, can also be seen as another form of dramatic production and reduction: dramatically producing one identity and dramatically reducing another. Both facts and identities can be built up or undermined.

The performance of instrumentally damaging the client's face should be handled with care as disclosing to the court the client's improprieties may lead to the client questioning his or her lawyer's loyalty. This is a balance of engaging in an open-face threat to one's own client whilst at the same time ensuring that the client understands that this face threat is coming from a place of loyalty.

This extract displays the emotion work of teamwork demanding the active production and reduction of emotions in self and others. The defence lawyer as the director of the team performance demands that he or she encourages the appropriate personal front, including emotional expression in team members (Goffman, 1956b).

Backstage direction

As already shown, directing clients to remain in face during the trial occurs mainly backstage, prior to the trial, as the lawyers I spoke to talk about reminding clients to remain "poker-faced," with one defence lawyer even saying that she writes this on a note to be shown to the client at pertinent points in proceedings. The surreptitiousness of the note placed on the desk in front of defence lawyer and client, means that this direction remains backstage, despite being performed frontstage. It thereby avoids any threat to the flow of interaction (Goffman, 1959).

The reader may remember from my methods chapter that my positioning in the courtroom afforded me a view of more intimate interactions between the defence teammates. I have thus observed hidden directions in court as we see in an extract from my fieldnotes from a trial regarding the possession of various firearms, explosives, and drugs:

> The client is now going to give his version of events and states that he has only a very weak memory of things and would rather be asked questions than speak freely. He starts to shake his legs again – he has done this throughout proceedings. He sits with his feet crossed at the ankles, knees

> out to the sides and bounces his legs back and forth. When he does this, his lawyer touches him on the leg to make him stop. His lawyer does this at least ten times throughout the questioning which lasts around 30 minutes. He stops shaking his legs for a few seconds then starts again. The lawyer keeps touching his leg to make him stop. His lawyer is sitting with his hands resting on the side of his leg so that he can make the movement without it being visible to the rest of the courtroom. On one occasion, the lawyer shifts in his chair slightly and at the same time taps the client on the leg to make him stop again. (Fieldnote)

As fidgeting can signify hostility or anxiousness, this constitutes another example of the defence lawyer attempting to direct the client into giving a more credible performance in line with team face: a tapping leg might convey guilt (Levenson, 2007).

Another example of directing the client that is discussed by several of the lawyers is kicking the client in the leg under the desk during the trial. When I asked Andrew what he would do if he needed to calm down a client in the courtroom, he points to his desk and, whilst assuring me that he is joking says, "you know, this is why they have these in a courtroom [points to the front side of his desk that obscures his legs] so that you can kick your clients in the leg! [Laughs]."

Although Andrew tells me he is joking about kicking clients, other defence lawyers I interviewed talk about using this strategy. Whilst kicking the client in the leg can therefore be an effective way of directing a client backstage to calm him or her down or be quiet, out of sight behind the cover of a desk, such strategies risk accidentally becoming frontstage. Martin explains that such strategies should be agreed on beforehand as "once, the client asked me why I kicked him in the leg" thereby moving the discrete backstage direction to frontstage. Perry says that he has never kicked anyone but tells me about a colleague who failed at hiding direction during a trial by accidentally stabbing a client in the leg with the sharp end of his pen when attempting to quieten him.

The danger in hidden, situationally backstage direction becoming frontstage is that it can reveal information that the lawyer would otherwise prefer to have remain hidden, for instance, weaknesses in the team performance or information regarding the defendant's character. As many of the defence lawyers discuss this strategy, it appears to be a shared understanding and expectation that directing one's client is part of one's professional role.

Concluding comments

To summarise, in this chapter I have analysed how defence lawyers talk about presenting themselves, others and the defence team and shown how this is accomplished in the Swedish criminal trial with its inherent adversarial competing realities, in order to show the invisible rules of interaction guiding dramaturgical performances.

Central to the role of defence lawyers is the performance of loyalty and the accomplishment of the defence team. My analysis has therefore centred on how the abstract principle of loyalty is performed in a criminal trial and how teamwork is done. I have shown how the subtle and nuanced facework of defence lawyers remains aligned with the emotional regime of the criminal trial which may be seen in and is upheld by the interaction order, ceremonial order and emotional order. In the next chapter, I continue to explore the emotions involved in these performances.

Notes

1 Stockholm is the capital of Sweden. All of the interviewees come from another part of the country.

2 "Södertäljemålet" is a case regarding gang murder and organised crime. The prosecution accused the defence of raising too many procedural questions and interrupting the prosecution whilst the defence lawyers in turn accused the prosecution of being poorly prepared and introducing new evidence.

3 The same can be true of clients – if they break the interaction and emotion rules they risk being seen as incapacitated, which is a disruption that should be repaired (Goffman, 1961a, 1967).

4 In the U.S., lawyers are more likely to attempt to change the client's look in preparation for a trial in order to influence the jury (Levenson, 2007, p. 4). Again, the absence of the audience of a jury in Sweden and the presence of judges making decisions implies for many lawyers that there is no-one possible to influence in the Swedish courtroom.

5 Although it should be noted that in some trials, guilt to some degree may have been acknowledged.

6 It was unusual to observe the defence lawyer drawing attention to missteps. Indeed, I only saw this on a handful of occasions, for instance, when the defendant reacted strongly to a mistake made by the translator thus justifying the outburst.

7 I follow Potter's (1996, p. 108) use of "rhetoric" seen as "a feature of the antagonistic relationships between versions: how a description counters an alternative description, and how it is organized, in turn, to resist being countered."

8 Although my study may have overlaps with research on rhetoric (which is considered one of the central lawyering tools) as I show how defence lawyers discuss and perform emotional and interactional means of persuasion, my focus is nevertheless on the ways in which the emotional regime of law shapes and guides courtroom emotions and performances, not on how arguments can be used to persuade others (Bakken & Graver, 2013; Graver, 2010). I am interested in the accomplishment of a role and a principle, not how a case is argued.

9 I am not using "alternative facts" in the Trumpian sense of the term, rather Potter's (1996, p. 107) approach to constructing "descriptions and alternative descriptions."

10 Mediation involves the perpetrator and the victim of the crime meeting together with an impartial mediator to talk about the crime and its consequences.

11 Pizzi (1999, pp. 196–197) writes that in the U.S.A., lawyers attempt to humanize the client by placing an arm around him or her.

Chapter 6

The emotion work of defence lawyers

As is now clear, my central premise is that the structurally embedded emotional regime of law forms the emotional performances of legal professionals (and indeed, lay participants). These performances are guided by unwritten rules pertaining to the specific role and thus principle one is performing. This is because, as we have also seen, there are no explicit guidelines beyond phrases such as having "good professional conduct," and not being influenced by "personal gain or inconvenience or any other irrelevant circumstances" (Association, 2008, p. 4; Heuman, 2013; cf. Jacobsson, 2008). I suggest that encompassed in these terms is emotional experience; therefore, professional responsibility is associated with the separation of emotion. We can consequently see the emotional regime of law conveyed in these guidelines, and in this chapter, I will show how it can be seen in defence lawyers' presentations and performances of their institutionalised social position.

In the previous chapter, my focus was on showing the invisible rules for how defence lawyers dramaturgically accomplish their role, now I turn to the emotional accomplishment by analysing how defence lawyers talk about emotions and emotion work and by analysing their emotional performances in the courtroom. I thus move from focusing on the underlying meaning to be communicated to the emotions involved.

I first discuss how defence lawyers talk about emotions before exploring different emotion management strategies. Defence lawyers' emotion talk and emotional performances reveal the social and professional expectations they perceive they are faced with pertaining to their legal role which demands that emotions are professionalised and rationalised. These expectations constitute a set of invisible guidelines for their role performance and a resource for emotion management (Jacobsson, 2008; Törnqvist, 2017; Wettergren & Bergman Blix, 2016).

Themes to be addressed here are as follows: how are emotions talked about and performed by defence lawyers? How do defence lawyers manage their own emotions and the emotions of others?

Managing own emotions

As I have presented in the chapter on previous research, the professionalization of everyday emotions is an integral part of many professions and involves rendering or managing inappropriate emotions into suitable ones (Hochschild, 1979, p. 551). My analysis shows that defence lawyers talk about "everyday emotions" (Ashforth & Humphrey, 1995) as inappropriate to their professional role thus requiring management into what I have termed "professional emotions." These professional emotions are aligned with defence lawyers' professional code of conduct, which, in turn, upholds the false separation of rationality and emotionality. This is exemplified by Charles who tells me that, "people act in affect. A lawyer must not do that" (cf. Association, 2008; Hochschild, 1979, p. 551; Wettergren & Bergman Blix, 2016).

I begin by showing how defence lawyers talk about and manage their own emotions and, in particular, the emotion rules for the performance of loyalty. I am thus interested in how they construct and uphold lawyer face with emotion talk.

Switching off emotions

In my interview with Andrew, he talks about some of the difficulties of working closely with clients and the emotion work demands it places on him. He begins by talking about the hopelessness in defending clients who are obviously guilty saying:

> Sometimes, the clients, you can feel like this: come on, seriously? What the hell am I doing? (…) You begin to doubt your professional role – that everyone has the right to a defence. It's there that it starts to crack when I feel, come on! An example: you're sitting with a client who is accused of a number of violent crimes for which there is solid evidence, it's not just testimonies from the plaintiff but also there are maybe medical records, there are witnesses, I mean, like, [the client] is fried. Full stop. But the client is in their own little world: "this hasn't happened. It wasn't me." And, sometimes, it can feel a bit like this: seriously, I mean, can't you just open your eyes and see how it looks? (Andrew)

Andrew then goes on to discuss how he responds to a similar version of the how-can-you-defend-a-rapist question, namely "how can you defend a paedophile?" He dwells not on how he responds to others' questions regarding this, but instead on how he reasons with this question on a more personal level:

> It can feel a bit like this: why am I sitting here, trying to give you as good a defence as possible when you clearly aren't listening to anything I say (…) People ask, "can you take any case?" "How can you defend a

> paedophile?" for example, that kind of thing. Sure, at times you can ask yourself, if you're sitting in that kind of trial where there have been so many atrocities and perhaps there is overwhelming evidence against the client, then I think that you can reason internally, on the personal side, now let's grit our teeth and go forwards and try desperately to keep that wall in place between the professional role and what it demands of you and perhaps your personal feelings. (Andrew)

Andrew gives us a glimpse of the smörgåsbord of emotions that he should manage in his professional role towards the client such as irritation, doubt, and disgust as well as frustration and anger towards the legal system as a whole (see also Törnqvist, 2017). I will focus on these specific emotions shortly, but now I would like to focus on the way in which these emotions are talked about.

I have already touched upon how defence lawyers present personal feelings as irrelevant to the professional role and my analysis shows further that emotions are talked about as possible to "switch off" or "suffocate" (Hochschild, 1983; Maroney, 2011a; Sutton, 1991 cf. Harris, 2011a,b). For instance, George tells me that when he had to look at photographs of child pornography that had been introduced as evidence, he "just sat there and categorised the photos" according to severity. He goes on to say "I didn't have any of those feelings [of disgust], I just [did it]."

This ability to "switch off" emotions is presented by defence lawyers as a strategy for professional survival (cf. Kemper, 1978; Westaby, 2010). Andrew tells me that at his law firm:

> We usually say that, when you come, when you are new, then you are filled with idealism – belief in the future – you are going to stand there and weigh the scales of justice and everything. And you take a lot of things personally. You get personally engaged. If you are going to make it, if you are going to work with criminal cases, then you have to develop a circuit breaker inside yourself [points to the base of his skull], which says, "now I am at work," "now I am not at work." Because, frequently, you are in investigations and it can be anything from criminal investigations, if you sit with clients who are suspected of atrocious deeds and if you take it all personally I mean, let it in, and take it home with you, then you don't feel well. You don't do that. You have to be able to switch off, that's how it is. (Andrew)

This finds support in other interviews, for instance, Daniel tells me, "you have to be able to cut yourself off because otherwise, ultimately, I don't think you can cope with working [as a defence lawyer]." Similarly, Perry compares his role to that of medical doctors, saying, "you have to be professional. I mean, if it's a doctor taking care of someone who is going to die, then they also have to suffocate their feelings and I would say that we have to do that too."

This expectation is talked about as something that defence lawyers are socialised into as Andrew says earlier: when you are new, you take the work personally and as Martin also says, new defence lawyers should learn they "have to switch off and look at everything with professional eyes." However, Martin goes on to tell me that this can lead to you having an "occupational injury – you become a bit like a machine" akin to the flight attendants in Hochschild's (1983, p. 135) study who "go into robot" as a form of distancing themselves from the job.

Defence lawyers' emotion talk thus presents a "wall" between personal and professional emotions. Everyday emotional experiences and professional emotional experiences are presented as controllable things lying within them – psychological states that can be suppressed or turned off and on (cf. Maroney, 2011a; Burkitt, 2002). We see that when discussing professionalism, defence lawyers often neglect the interactional nature of emotional experiences and their "sociality" (Ahmed, 2004; see also Collins, 2004; Durkheim, 1912/1995).[1]

The illusionary division of rationality and emotionality is thus upheld and reproduced by defence lawyers by presenting emotions as possible to "switch off" or "suffocate." However, as my analysis will go on to show, this presentation can be more appropriately depicted as a process of strategically managing emotions (Wettergren & Bergman Blix, 2016).

Transforming emotions

My analysis of defence lawyers' emotion talk regarding disgust shows that rather than using a strategy of suppression as presented by the lawyers above for these inappropriate feelings, it is more accurate to describe an engagement and transformation process wherein everyday emotions become professional emotions (cf. Lehrberg, 2014). This is a cognitive process which involves engaging with the object of emotion – for example, child pornographic images as George described earlier – and first appraising it as something that is morally offensive before then reappraising it either by changing how it is perceived, how it is evaluated, or according to the goal (Maroney, 2011a, p. 1508; Maroney & Gross, 2014). This situated professionalisation of everyday emotions thus entails engagement and transformation – not suffocation or suppression – transforming an everyday emotion into a professional appropriate tool (cf. Harris, 2002; see also Bandes & Salerno, 2014). This is described by Siri who says:

> If you look at physical examinations and you see, like, a close up of someone's anus basically, yeah, you look at it very clinically. It's a photo that I don't really want to see but I have to look at it. (Siri)

Siri is describing how she engages in the image and appraises it as a photo that she doesn't really want to look at, then reappraises it in order to perceive it as evidence. Peter also describes this, telling me:

> When I read [the investigation report], I focus on the evidence, what is there? Are the bruises different colours? Then they weren't caused at the same time. Are there a lot of bruises? This could indicate abuse of alcohol, especially if the colour is different. (Peter)

Siri, Peter, and others present this transformation as cognitively re-defining the image to legalese: to finding evidence that supports or opposes one's case. Defence lawyers thus learn to define the viewing of gruesome evidence through a legal lens (Maroney, 2011a; Smith & Kleinman, 1989; see also Wettergren, 2009). This involves a process of engagement and cognitive reappraisal in order to normalise emotional experiences (Maroney & Gross, 2014; cf. Harris, 2002). Looking at explicit or unpleasant images thus becomes normalised – just another part of one's job. This has already mentioned by George when he described looking at child pornographic images, and is also described by Lena here who says, "you look at it very technically somehow [laughs]. You talk about and read about things that, yeah I mean, it becomes a job, law, nothing else, that's how you have to tackle it." Andrew likens this to the normalisation process that pathologists go through, telling me that when he is looking at gruesome images:

> You look at it a bit clinically, I mean, I think that it's kind of like, when I talked with a doctor who was a pathologist, then the first time they were going to do an autopsy on a body, like, "eeeeeeew" [draws back in disgust] like this, but, after a while then it becomes scientific work, it's not, I don't know what to call it but you distance yourself, you see it in another way. (Andrew)

This normalisation enables the achievement of specific goals whilst simultaneously ensuring that emotional experiences, expressions and performances are in line with the emotional regime of law (cf. Ashforth & Humphrey, 1995; Cahill, 1999; Maroney, 2011a; Smith & Kleinman, 1989).

We also see again that defence lawyers employ emotional accounts – they use their position in the legal system to explain, justify, create meaning and make sense of their role and the absence of expected emotions (Baker, 2002; Ogletree, 1993; Rennstam & Wästerfors, 2015; M. B. Scott & Lyman, 1968; 1970). They thus use the law as an emotion management strategy. This is akin to the way that medical students use science as an emotion management strategy by defining contact with dead bodies and intimate examinations of patients as part of scientific medicine (Cahill, 1999). In this way the lawyers I interviewed, like medical students, present themselves as able to separate their feelings from the object invoking them and instead focus on the "impersonal facts of the subject matter" (Smith & Kleinman, 1989, p. 61). Their emotion talk presents a division between emotionality and professionality that is also in line with the emotional regime of law (Barbalet, 2001).

This process of learning to manage one's emotions – the professionalisation of emotions – in particular, disgust, can be seen in the way that Andrew talks about gruesome images as becoming scientific after one has worked as a defence lawyer for a while. Vera also describes how a young intern working at her law firm first reacted to seeing photographic evidence in a murder case:

> She was completely horrified, she just "aaaaaaaaaah! [screams] No, I don't want to see, it's a lot of blood, I'm sensitive when it comes to blood" and all that whilst the rest of us, we were just, "yeah, ok" [laughs]. She was like, completely new, but of course, it's like doctors, I mean, you get used to it, you don't see it in the same way as you did the first time you saw it. (Vera)

Here, we find support that defence lawyers are expected to learn to look at evidence, such as photographs or autopsy reports that would be considered gruesome in other situations without reacting in the same way as those who are not accustomed to viewing such material.

I posit that defence lawyers learn this transformation and normalisation process via professional emotional socialisation as there is little mention of emotions or emotion management strategies on law programmes in Sweden (Flower, 2014; cf. Boon, 2005; Cahill, 1999; Harris, 2002; Westaby, 2010). The focus on law programs is instead on learning analytical skills, rather than interpersonal skills leaving law students and lawyers to learn strategies implicitly (cf. Hess, 2002; Lehrberg, 2014).[2] The goal is for this emotion management to become habituated (Bergman Blix, 2010). As we have already seen, this socialisation process also entails learning to "switch off" inappropriate emotions and acting professionally.

Unlike medical students who may act "as if" a body was no longer a body but rather a cat or a toaster in order to transform it into a non-specific thing, the defence lawyers I interviewed did not talk in such terms (Hochschild, 1983; Smith & Kleinman, 1989). The body remains a body but it is transformed into evidence through a process of making discomfort with anatomical issues personally insignificant yet legally important (cf. Lief & Fox, 1963).

The underlying emotion rule is therefore that disgust is an inappropriate everyday emotion that should be managed (cf. Smith & Kleinman, 1989).

Although my focus at this point is on the management of the defence lawyer's own emotions, in particular disgust, it is relevant to show here that there is also a tactical dimension to this. By succeeding in managing one's own emotions and looking at gruesome pictures, one is also, in extension, managing the emotions of others as Andrew describes here:

> I look at it from two perspectives: evaluating the evidence, how can this be tied to my client in one way or another and then it's less about pictures and more about the technical investigation that has gathered evidence. And then of course, at the same time, I keep in mind that ok, how is this

> going to influence the court if it's shown and what can I do to dampen the possible impact that it might have on the trial? It's those two [perspectives]. (Andrew)

George also talks about this when he tells me more about looking at child pornographic images which had been introduced as evidence:

> It's a bit tactical because I think that, in this case, by avoiding looking at these pictures at the trial, then I got the judge on my side. Uh, so I created a more positive climate for my client because, uh, they were not nice pictures. I think that the court would have been negatively influenced in relation to my client by showing these pictures so it was also a tactical reasoning on my side. (George)

George and Andrew thus reappraise images in order to achieve a certain goal (Maroney, 2011a). Learning to look clinically at gruesome details is a vital "trick of the trade" aimed at enabling oneself to look at the images professionally but also in order to prevent shocking images being shown in the courtroom which may negatively influence the judges.[3]

We also see here that Andrew and George have the shared expectation that the judge and lay judges may not be able to view the photos through the same "rational" lens as they themselves view it – that the judge and lay judges would not be able to transform personal emotions into professional focus on the evidence. This, in turn, might influence their judgement. So, whilst defence lawyers often talk about their performance as not influencing the judges, the presentation of gruesome photos is seen as swaying them. I suggest that this is because photos are considered as evidence which should be judged according to their legal value, performances are not.

Appropriate and inappropriate emotions

The role of defence lawyer involves client contact and, due to the interactional nature of emotions, this may lead to the emergence of emotions in need of management in order to perform one's professional role. I will shortly focus on how specific emotions are talked about, but before this I will touch upon how defence lawyers talk about winning and losing as a way of managing inappropriate emotions.

If you want to win, be a prosecutor

As already noted, around 93 per cent (Nordén, 2015) of trials lead to a conviction due to the nature of the legal system as prosecutors do not bring a case to trial unless they determine that the evidence they have gathered will lead to a guilty judgement. So, how do defence lawyers continue to work in a role which almost always leads to the client being found guilty of a crime they claim they did not commit?

My analysis shows that defence lawyers also use emotional accounts to align winning or losing with their role-based emotional purpose which, as we have just seen, is presented as fighting for justice. Winning is therefore seen in terms of achieving justice – providing the client with legal representation and achieving the best possible outcome for him or her. As Daniel says, "winning a criminal case doesn't have to be about getting some freed, it can be about them getting the appropriate sentence." Winning is thus not talked about in terms of conviction or acquittal as it might be viewed in the eyes of the media or general public, but rather in terms of role fulfilments: if one has fulfilled one's role as a competent defence lawyer then this counts as a win. This is a form of emotion management making it possible to sustain one's self-image as an accomplished lawyer – lawyer face – even in the face of repeated "losses" (cf. Törnqvist, 2017). The otherwise expected emotions of disappointment associated with losing are thereby managed.

Another strategy for accounting for losses is for defence lawyers to present themselves as the underdogs, indeed Lena tells me, "if you want to win then you should probably be a prosecutor instead" (cf. Pizzi, 1999). Losses are accounted for as a result of the justice system, for instance, Lena describes the workload of preparing a case for trial as being unequal between prosecutors and defence lawyers, saying, "prosecutors have far more resources behind them, I mean, prosecutors work with a load of police (…) Having a client to defend, you are very alone."

Losing is thus presented as arising from external factors, such as the client not having a strong enough defence case to begin with. I have seen a similar tendency to place the blame on situational factors amongst law students accounting for academic failures by blaming the teachers (for example, for not preparing the students correctly or for setting an exam that was too difficult) (Flower, 2013).[4] Some lawyers even remove themselves one step further stating, "I don't lose a case, my client does."[5] This can be seen as a protective face saving strategy and a way of the defence lawyer cooling themselves out in a situation where they are at risk of humiliation (Goffman, 1952, 1956b).

Whilst some of the lawyers talk about winning in terms of professional competencies, viewing one's own role as the decisive factor in winning or losing a case can be problematic according to Andrew as then a loss can be seen as arising from one's poor performance. This may, in turn, lead to feelings of shame.

Dislike and fondness

Personal feelings towards a client should not influence one's performance according to the Swedish Bar Association (2008), irrespective of what these feelings might be. Siri describes this succinctly when she tells me, "you want to do your best even if you think the person is a real asshole, you still want to do your best. You don't want to go to court and make a fool of yourself." Siri is describing the importance of maintaining face in the courtroom (Goffman, 1956b). Her fear of being negatively evaluated in the eyes of others, that is, the fear of embarrassment arising from deviations in her professional role performance, leads to an increased awareness, and increased management, of inappropriate emotions (Cooley, 1922; Flower, 2014; Scheff, 2000).

Siri is also presenting professionalism as entailing the separation of her everyday emotions of dislike from her role-based professional emotions. This successful separation leads to feelings of pride in her performance. Once again, this emotion talk upholds a division between emotionality and professionalism. However, whilst disliking a client is presented as an inappropriate emotion in need of management, liking a client can be an acceptable source of motivation as Andrew tells me:

> If you take your professional role seriously then you treat [all clients] exactly the same. Full stop. But, I'll put it like this [gets a pen and places it on the desk in front of him], here are all the measures I can take and here is the line for all the measures that are required in this specific case. If I have fulfilled these measures then I have fulfilled my obligations as a defender in relation to the ethical rules and legal requirements and everything. Full stop. You never mess with that but then, of course, I'll put it like this, if I have a client who I like, then perhaps I go [shows moving over the line where the pen is lying on the table]. It's not that I do a better or worse job in relation to procedural responsibility but that maybe I do that little bit extra. (Andrew)

Disliking a client is presented as something that does not hinder or inhibit their role; however, liking a client is a legitimate motivator of performance (cf. Lipsky, 1980). This shows a new aspect of emotion management theory. Hochschild (1979, p. 564) discusses the rules regarding the extent, direction, and duration of feelings. However, here the defence lawyers are talking about how much a feeling is permitted to *influence* them. Defence lawyers therefore present a distinction between positively valenced feelings[6] (liking a client) which are permitted to influence one's performance, and negative valenced feelings (disliking a client) which should not influence one's performance at all (cf. Hochschild, 1983; Maroney, 2011a; Sutton, 1991). Negative emotions are thus seen as inappropriate and in need of control whilst positive emotions are more acceptable (cf. Wettergren, 2009).

Irritation

In any social interaction, personal feelings towards the other interactant will arise. This is also the case for the interactions between defence lawyers and their clients. For instance, when I asked Perry what the biggest cause of irritation is in his professional role he replies:

Perry: The thing you often get most irritated at is, and I hardly dare to say it, but it's your own client.
Lisa: Because? Or what is it that makes you irritated?
Perry: They're stupid. Yes, it's often so. You're not in court because you're an honourable and honest and wise person, many [clients] can be pretty stupid.

Although Perry's remark is unusually outspoken, Lydia also tells me that she can feel irritated at clients who don't make use of her services, saying "I can think that it's a bit rubbish if they haven't been in touch before [the trial] because often, it's enough with a phone call, it's nothing!" As both Perry and Lydia talk openly about feeling irritated by their client, it signifies that it is acceptable according to the feeling rules. Furthermore, irritation may even be displayed more explicitly in the backstage situation of our interview. For instance, during my interview with Perry a client rang him repeatedly and sent text messages leading him to say in response to a question I had posed, "can you repeat the question? I get so distracted by all this with the client, he drives me insane!" This irritation should, however, not be displayed towards the client in client meetings (perhaps only in extreme cases) or in the courtroom as Martin says "you can get irritated with the client, but of course, you don't show that." In order to perform loyalty and teamwork, inappropriate emotions, such as irritation, must be managed (cf. Roach Anleu and Mack, 2017, p.168).

Here, we can see the differing contexts of the emotional regime of the criminal trial at play: irritation with a client may be felt and displayed in the backstage of an interview situation with a researcher, however, such emotions are prohibited to be displayed in the frontstage context of the courtroom and may be shown to varying degrees in the client meeting. Irritation is thus permitted according to the feeling rule, but its display is dependent on context.

Happiness and sadness

We have seen that there are a number of inappropriate emotions in need of management in order for defence lawyers to accomplish their role. As I mentioned in chapter three, the emotional regime of law provides the framework for emotions in legal interactions taking place in different settings, for instance, the courtroom (which is the focus of my study), other areas of the courthouse, and law offices. These spaces can be discussed in terms of being frontstage, where the team performance takes place, and backstage, where the performance is prepared and problems or frustrations may be ventilated (Goffman, 1959). The law offices can consequently be seen as backstage: a place where the frontstage performance of the trial is prepared – both lawyer face and team face are worked on. Although it should be noted that the law offices can also be seen as both frontstage as lawyers may still be performing in their role of defence lawyer when meeting clients there, I would still argue that, even in the lawyer-client meeting there is a relaxation of the rules of emotional interaction, particularly in contrast to the stricter rules to be followed in the courtroom.

The backstage nature of the law offices with its relaxed emotion rules is described here by Vera who tells me that an intern at her law firm once remarked that it was sometimes like a "playground" at the law offices as there was so much laughing and joking. Vera says:

> We work with tough things every day and therefore it's incredibly important to have fun at the office. That you can admit if you have made a mistake. That you can go and ask for help. I mean, all of that, you have to have something easy-going and we always have fun here and laugh and joke, and like, laugh every day. We have had interns who have said, "sometimes it's like a playground here." You see, they come with a completely different seriousness and don't understand that you need this contrast, so that when you do the important stuff, you can go out in the corridor and joke a bit, kid each other and tease each other and then go and work again. (Vera)

Vera presents the law offices as a place where she can relax and have fun which she sees as a vital aspect of being able to fulfil her professional role and obligations.

This backstage emotional space is also a place where professionally inappropriate emotions can be vented which arise from working with "other people's shit or society's or whatever you want to call it" as Andrew says (cf. Clark, 1987; Fineman, 2006; Goffman, 1956b; Korczynski, 2003). Returning briefly to the "crying taboo" (Lively, 2000, p. 39) in the courtroom, whilst this is unacceptable for litigators in the U.S. in both backstage and frontstage areas – both the law offices and the courtroom – in Sweden the crying taboo only pertains to display rules in the courtroom.[7] Crying is therefore acceptable in the backstage setting of the law offices which can constitute an emotional refuge from the stricter emotion rules of the courtroom (cf. Reddy, 2001, pp. 128–129).

The law offices can thus provide a safe haven where the rules governing frontstage interactions are relaxed, permitting different emotions. Losses of face can be dissected: embarrassments and mistakes revealed and processed and face given to colleagues – even pride from successfully questioning a witness can be shown, a display that is strictly prohibited in the courtroom (Goffman, 1956b).

The backstage office is therefore a place where potentially disruptive emotions are encapsulated and segregated from one's ongoing role of defence lawyer thus showing the hierarchy of emotions (Ahmed, 2004; Ashforth & Humphrey, 1995, p. 104; cf. Roach Anleu & Mack, 2005). This is a place where colleagues can reciprocally support each other in order to ensure that they can continue to perform their role requirements appropriately (Hochschild, 1983; Lively, 2000; Wharton & Erickson, 1993).

The "emotional buffering" (Scarduzio & Tracy, 2015) as presented by the lawyers I spoke to, differs to that found in studies in the U.S. which showed that the need for such emotional support results from one's position in the occupational hierarchy (Lively, 2002). In contrast, the lawyers I interviewed talk about the stressors that arise from their occupational role in the legal system, that is, it is predominantly their client contact which leads to the need for buffering (cf. Lively, 2000).

It should be noted that such buffering systems are not taken for granted as an important part of professional life for defence lawyers, as both Daniel and Sandra had experience of working at law firms where "communities of coping" (Korczynski, 2003) were absent. It appears as though the emotional climates are different at different law firms, with some firms encouraging the display of emotions that may be deemed inappropriate such as sadness. Others appear to follow the pattern found in the U.S. where "acknowledging the role of emotion may brand one as not merely weak, but downright unlawyerlike" (Bandes, 2006b, p. 5). I see this in terms of differences in the legal settings that constitute backstage and frontstage settings, which, in turn, shows how strict and how encompassing the societal emotional regime of law is (cf. Bergman Blix & Wettergren, 2015, p. 3). In Sweden, the emotional regime may be deviated from in the refuge of the law offices where display rules permit the expression of otherwise inappropriate emotion, whereas in the U.S. the display rule prohibits such expressions, both in the frontstage of the courtroom and the backstage of the law offices.

Empathy

Empathy is presented by the defence lawyers I interviewed as a vital tool of lawyering. My analysis of the way in which they talk about this – their empathy talk – shows that it upholds a traditional approach to empathy as constituting two separate processes: cognitive empathy which is presented by them as understanding the other's feelings and which is associated with rationality, whilst affective empathy is talked about as emotionally engaging in the other (feeling their feelings). Accordingly, their empathy talk upholds the emotional regime of law by reproducing the false dichotomy between rationality and emotionality. This stands in contrast to the emotion sociological approach which sees empathy as inherently and simultaneously cognitive and emotional (see also Clark, 1997).[8]

Defence lawyers also talk about using empathy to achieve specific goals. I will now present a typology of this "strategic empathy" (cf. Davis, 1997; Wettergren & Bergman Blix, 2016) and explore their empathy talk.

Relational empathy

Empathy is presented by the lawyers I interviewed as being used to create a relationship with the client. This type of empathy, which I have termed "relational empathy," entails understanding the situation and emotions of the client by taking his or her role in order to build the lawyer-client relationship (see also Bandes, 2006b). Empathy is thus used to build the defence team.

Defence lawyers present the empathy work of teamwork as requiring the management of inappropriate emotions and the display of emotions appropriate to an empathic demeanour when talking to clients as Lena explains:

> I try to show clearly that I don't think it's tough listening, I mean, I'm listening, you can tell me anything, I won't be emotionally affected by it. Because then I have, or at least, I've understood and tried to learn through the years, that if you think it's tough then they eventually notice that, and they try and gloss over the truth and that's why I try and say that you can tell me anything, I don't think it's tough, and that I, yes, that I'm here, I don't judge anyone. (Lena)

Lena is saying that displaying empathy when meeting the client, may involve managing away personal emotions of discomfort, dislike, disgust or surprise in order to encourage them to tell their story. Lena also says, "I try and show that I really understand their feelings because otherwise I don't think they're going to open up if I just sit there." By managing these emotions, she believes that she is able to produce the appropriate countenance and produce feelings of trust in the client.

Lena is also saying that an important aspect of this relational empathy is communicating to clients that she does not morally judge them which she accomplishes by "showing clearly" which I interpret to mean that she uses emotion work. This means that teamwork may also entail the performance of the suspension of moral judgement in order to convey the joint identity and in order to be able to unite behind a shared reality (Goffman, 1956b). In this way, the relationship of these teammates differs from other relationships where moral suspension is not required (cf. Jacobsson, 2008; Goffman, 1972).

Relational empathy is also presented by the lawyers I interviewed as an important tool not just to one's client but to others during a trial. Lo, another criminal defence lawyer I interviewed, describes how this is important as she "needs to create a relationship to [others] in court, even if it's just for the short time you're in there."

Defence lawyers talk about other legal professionals sometimes lacking relational empathy. In particular, this failure in judges is talked about disparagingly. For instance, all the defence lawyers I interviewed present themselves as understanding that a trial is not just about the law, rather it may be a life-changing event or the culmination of months of worry and may constitute a social situation filled with uncertainty and emotional strain for defendants.

Lo also tells me that she can get irritated at judges whom she perceives as not understanding that participating in a trial can be very difficult, for elderly people in particular. Judges are also criticised by Lo as well as Lena for not being able to understand the emotional despair and life experiences that can lead to a crime being committed. Lo says that:

> In criminal cases there are so many situations to understand. I mean, many of the people we represent are young people who see things in a completely different way than the older judges see them perhaps, so I think that's probably quite important, and I think that they, they have perhaps a bit of a sheltered life in court. As I say, we meet the clients more. (Lo)

The empathy of judges is thus questioned at times, in particular, their inability to be able to place themselves in the shoes of those from a different socioeconomic background.[9] Judicial emotional understanding is therefore expected by Lo and Lena. Defence lawyers, on the other hand, present themselves as being able to understand their clients' situations more easily due to the nature of their role which demands client contact, unlike judges (and prosecutors). This supports my claim that the emotion work demands on defence lawyers may be higher than for other legal professionals in some contexts.

Relational empathy is presented as pertaining to a rational understanding of the client's situation and emotions, but without emotionally engaging in the client: without feeling their feelings. Here, it should be noted that defence lawyers do present themselves as engaged in client's cases in terms of wanting to attain the best possible outcome; however, they present themselves as emotionally unengaged in the client's feelings (cf. Kemper, 1978a). The beneficial aspects of emotional engagement are not talked about in the interviews, with perhaps the exception of discussing how liking a client can lead to increased motivation (cf. Bandes, 2006b, p. 24). There is thus a resistance to talking about the beneficial aspects of emotional engagement, such as helping to build trust between lawyer and client (Genty, 2000; Gerarda Brown, 2012; Westaby & Jones, 2017). Defence lawyers' relational empathic talk thus reproduces the traditional emotional regime of law by presenting it as possible to separate rationality and emotionality.

Preparatory empathy

Empathy is also presented by lawyers as being used to understand how others, such as the judge and the prosecutor, will view the case. I have called this "preparatory empathy" as it is used in preparing for trial. Andrew tells me, "I think that you have to have empathy (…) to put yourself in someone else's shoes in order to be able to see the case from all sides." Andrew talks about empathy as a necessary lawyering emotional tool, similar to the way in which prosecutors use empathy (cf. Wettergren & Bergman Blix, 2016). Both prosecutor and defender need to be able to determine the strength of the case which, for the prosecutor, leads to the decision to press charges or not and for the defender, leads to them determining which parts of the client's version should be over-emphasised or under-emphasised (cf. Lehrberg, 2014, pp. 28–29).

Consequently, preparatory empathy highlights a time dimension to the concept of empathy as defence lawyers should use their empathic imagination to understand how the prosecutor and judge will view the case at a future point (see Cooley, 1922). Similar to relational empathy, preparatory empathy is talked about in rational, cognitive terms in order to anticipate how others will understand the case at trial.

Strategically directing empathy

Empathy is also talked about as being strategically directed by defence lawyers during the trial in order to manage the emotions of others in the moment (cf. Bandes, 2006b). An example of this can be seen in the following excerpt from my fieldnotes where the defendant is accused of assaulting a civil servant. We join proceedings during the closing speech, after the defendant has left the courtroom having reacted strongly to evidence given by the plaintiff:

> The defence lawyer says his client is diagnosed as having problems with social interaction and communication, and therefore easily feels threatened. The plaintiff's evidence led to his client feeling threatened, which is why his client reacted so strongly. The defence lawyer states that this is obviously not the best thing that could have happened, but that it can also be used to explain the assault that his client is accused of, as his client also felt threatened at that time. He asks the court to use his client's behaviour in the courtroom to try and understand how his client must have felt when being confronted by the civil servant – his client felt threatened and had to defend himself. His actions should therefore be seen in terms of self-defence. (Fieldnote)

We see here that the defence lawyer is directing the court to put themselves in the shoes of his client, implicitly saying: "you saw how he reacted here when he experienced being under pressure, imagine what he must have felt during the incident itself." The defence lawyer is encouraging the judges to emotionally engage in his client's feelings at the time of the assault. This, in turn, may lead to the charges against the client being viewed as a less serious crime. This strategic direction of empathy is therefore also a form of factwork – a dramatic production aimed at directing the judge's attention to certain facts (cf. Dershowitz, 1986; Ebervall, 2002; Goffman, 1972; Potter, 1996).

My findings thus partly support previous research indicating that "empathic communication is a critical dimension of lawyering." (Fletcher & Weinstein, 2003, p. 135; see also Westaby, 2010; Westaby & Jones, 2017). I say it only partly supports this, as emotional engagement with the client is not openly acknowledged by the lawyers I spoke to indeed, the successful use of empathy is talked about as entailing the separation of emotion from cognition and is also discussed as necessary to control as I will now show.

Controlling empathy

My analysis up until now shows that defence lawyers depict their work in a way that uncouples emotional understanding from emotional engagement. Rationality and emotionality are thus separated. Emotional understanding is presented as a beneficial lawyering tool, however, even this should remain under control as Andrew says, "I have to be able to have empathy (...) but at the same time I have to control it so that it doesn't take over." Andrew says that too much emotional understanding can lead to him becoming emotionally engaged which then risks "taking over" – becoming overly involved with the client (Clark, 1987; Cooley, 1922; Fletcher & Weinstein, 2003; Goffman, 1957; Ruiz-Junco, 2017; Wettergren & Bergman Blix, 2016). This, as we have already seen in the previous chapter, can lead to one being viewed as a deviant interactant. Such a break in the empathy rules is consequently considered unprofessional.

Sandra also talks about controlling herself from taking the client's role *too* much, saying:

> I need to stay cool, I can't give way, and somehow burst into floods of tears and think about my own children and all the other terrible things, because it's a lot – another person showing you their feelings – that you enter into something and it's like, there's no room for that. It's not why I am there, to share all of these feelings. I am there to take care of my client's interests and the best way of doing that is not by me bursting into floods of tears. (Sandra)

What is interesting is that Sandra tells me in this excerpt that she has to do emotion work in order to not cry – she describes how she has emotionally engaged in the client's feelings and appraised that she should not react on them (Maroney, 2011a). Sandra is describing the constant simultaneous presence of emotionality and rationality whilst, at the same time, denying it. I argue that this emotional control and resistance to the acknowledgement of emotions stem from the emotional regime of the law which encourages and reproduces the divide which supports strict emotion management and focuses on rationality. Linked to this is the finding that defence lawyers talk about the need to "control" empathy. This, in itself, implies emotion work.

Defence lawyers thus present themselves as having "empathic walls" (Hochschild, 2016) in place which protect against what they consider to be the wrong type of empathy: affective rather than cognitive, which, as we have now seen, present as being separate capacities.

Mapping empathy

Empathy should therefore be "selectively" (Bandes, 2006b) directed towards certain people, in accordance with institutionally determined "empathy maps" (Hochschild, 2013, 2016). These maps lay out the distribution of empathy in relation to the specific situation, interaction, and interactants. In this case, whom defence lawyers should use empathy towards, which type of empathy should be used (remember, they distinguish between cognitive and affective empathy), and the amount of empathy (in order to avoid becoming overly involved) (cf. Hochschild, 2016; Ruiz-Junco, 2017, p. 426).

My focus however is not on whether the recipients of empathy are morally deserving, as both Hochschild (2013, 2016) and Ruiz-Junco (2017) use the term, rather I argue that in this context, the determining factor for whom should receive empathy is based on one's particular professional role (cf. Ruiz-Junco, 2017). For example, defence lawyers talk about how they should not feel empathy for the plaintiff as this may risk conveying disloyalty to the client. Martin explains this when I ask him about which emotions can inhibit him in his work as a defence lawyer:

> You have to perhaps not be too emotionally affected by the person sitting on the other side, the person who has been subjected to the crime. That's probably something you have to be careful with. It goes back to the fact that it's the client sitting on my left that I'm backing 100 per cent now. Then it can also be the case in rape trials, when you come in, and [the judges] have had their deliberation and they release your client, that is, that he is going to be freed, then, in that same moment, you look over and see the girl sitting over there who, of course, in some cases, has been raped, but, in that moment that the guy is freed, she is, not a liar, but many think that maybe, then, in that moment, emotions, or at least in my case, are connected to her. (Martin)

Martin begins by talking about how he, as a defence lawyer, should not emotionally engage with the plaintiff's feelings during a trial but he finishes by saying that after the trial, when the plaintiff is no longer a plaintiff, rather someone who has made a false accusation of rape, then it is acceptable for him to emotionally engage in the "person sitting on the other side" (see also Bandes, 2006b; Bitsch, 2018a, b). That is, when no longer performing in the role of defence lawyer, he may follow a different empathy map. The end of the trial signals a shift in roles from professional to personal and thus a shift in professional emotions to everyday emotions, navigated by the appropriate empathy map. After the trial it is possible to act as a fellow human, as Peter tells us in chapter four.

I suggest that there is not only a contextuality to empathy, but also a temporality as Lena says, "you have to also be able to leave it of course, when you're not working any more." Empathy rules thus encompass how long one should empathise with a client (or plaintiff), not just how much (cf. Hochschild, 2016). Once the case is closed, the empathy should cease. Similarly, when the defence lawyer leaves work at the end of the day, empathy for the client should not follow them home.

I therefore extend "empathy maps" (Hochschild, 2013, 2016) to include not only the amount of empathy to be given to the appropriate recipient but also a temporal aspect – when empathy may be elicited. Furthermore, my analysis suggests that what is permitted to elicit empathy is also charted – legitimate "empathy triggers" as I would like to call them. Research on prosecutors indicates that they also have empathy triggers (Törnqvist, 2017; Wettergren & Bergman Blix, 2016).

This further complicates defence lawyers' presentation of empathy towards the plaintiff as inappropriate as I have just depicted. It is more accurate to say that there are certain facets of the plaintiff's role in a trial that permit the defence lawyer's empathy. For example, defence lawyers say it is acceptable to show understanding for the plaintiff's emotional experience of the interactional situation at hand – taking part in a trial – as recounting one's personal life in public can be a traumatic experience. However, as Martin talks about above, empathy towards the plaintiff's version of events may be inappropriate as this may be a version of events that the defence lawyer is refuting. This aspect is not deemed to be "empathy worthy" (Ruiz-Junco, 2017); therefore, empathy should not be triggered.

My data therefore suggests that competing versions of reality do not trigger empathy. The observant reader may have noted that I have already presented other instances of this, such as in the previous chapter where we saw a defence lawyer using throat sweets when faced with a version of reality in contrast to the defence team's thus conveying a lack of empathy. This means that empathy triggers can be used to explain the cultural preconception of lawyers being "cold" or without feelings.

Professional empathy

We therefore see that defence lawyers talk about professional empathy in terms of emotional understanding. Professional empathy differs from everyday empathy as the latter also permits emotional engagement. In this way, defence lawyers talk about empathy as a cognitive process, denying the inherent and inseparable emotional component (cf. Cuff et al., 2016). Professionalism is once again associated with rationality whilst unprofessionalism is linked with emotionality. Navigating these empathic waters is an important aspect of lawyering and a source of professional pride (Bandes, 1996, 2009, 2015a; Westaby, 2010; Westaby & Jones, 2017; Wettergren & Bergman Blix, 2016).

I thus support previous research finding that empathy performances are institutionalised and situated responses to empathy rules which are aimed at ensuring that one's role in the justice system is performed, communicated, and upheld (Ruiz-Junco, 2017, p. 424). It is based on the defence lawyer's position in the justice system: as a loyal lawyer, one should build the defence team which demands the strategic use of empathy. This social situatedness is apparent in the way in which defence lawyers talk about empathy and the ways in which it should follow the "emotive-cognitive" (Wettergren & Bergman Blix, 2016, p. 1) framework of the criminal trial. Empathy should therefore be felt in the right amount, at the right time and towards the right person (cf. Hochschild, 1983; Maroney, 2011a).

We see also that it is not merely the case that, as Andrew says earlier, "you have to have empathy" as a defence lawyer. The rules regarding empathy are more nuanced than this. This can explain why George found it difficult to answer my question regarding the role of empathy. He responds that he was about to say that he didn't understand the question before going on to explain:

> I mean, the question is damned difficult to answer because, first, I can never know what my client actually experienced and uh, and, uh [sigh] I mean, it [sigh], it links together a bit with what we talked about earlier, about getting carried away with your feelings whilst at the same time, you should do your job. (George)

For George, the concept of empathy was slippery: should he try and understand the client's version of events if the client doesn't even understand it? Or should he empathise with the client's current situation?

In this section, I have shown that defence lawyers present themselves as separating personal emotions from professional emotions which includes transforming inappropriate emotions into appropriate tools. I then presented a typology of empathy. Empathy is seen as a vital lawyering tool, however defence lawyers' empathy talk and emotion talk upholds the false dichotomic relationship between emotionality and rationality. The focus has been on showing how defence lawyers talk about and perform emotions revealing some of the emotion rules guiding their performances and the emotion management strategies used to accomplish this.

Managing others' emotions

In the previous chapter, I showed how the defence lawyer is expected to prepare his or her client, with the focus on preparations on the personal front – clothing and appearance. This section will now show how the defence lawyer also has to manage the client's emotional expectations by initiating them into the emotional order of the criminal trial. The goal of this aspect of loyalty work is encapsulated by Sandra who tells me "the client should feel that I am on their side" – this is the feeling to be produced in the client.

Expectation management

I will begin this section by showing that defence lawyers do a type of emotion management which I have called expectation management. By explaining the procedure of a trial and the role of the defence lawyer and others along with how these roles should be performed, in particular how emotions will be performed, the defence lawyer is attempting to align the client's expectations with what they may experience in the courtroom (Barbalet, 1996; Roach Anleu & Mack, 2005; Georg Simmel, 1950; Westlund & Eriksson, 2013). Expectation management thus involves explaining to the client what will happen during the trial, not just juridically, but also with regard to the performances given.[10] This is needed for several reasons, many of which stem from the client's uncertainty surrounding the social expectations and obligations attached to participating in, what may be, the alien social interaction of a trial (Goffman, 1956b; Hochschild, 1983).[11] Expectation management is therefore a form of pre-emptive or preventive cooling out in order to produce the appropriate emotion in the client and avoid him or her "flooding out" (Goffman, 1961a, 1967) during and after the trial. This calibration of expectations has three goals.

Firstly, the alignment of expectations and experience is a form of building trust – trust work – both trust in the defence lawyer and also trust in the justice system (Thelin, 2001; Tyler, 1988, 2003, 2006). This is central in building the client-lawyer relationship and is consequently a form of teamwork (cf. O'Keefe, 1990).

Secondly, if the client's experience is in line with his or her expectations, it can also lead to feelings of satisfaction with the defence lawyer and the trial. If expectations are misaligned, this could lead to the client questioning the quality of his or her defence and, in extension, the legitimacy of the justice system (Ojasalo, 2001; Thelin, 2001; Tyler, 1988, 2003, 2006). Expectation management thus also reduces the likelihood of anger or disappointment, which may need to be managed by the defence lawyer at a later stage (Wettergren, 2009).

Finally, expectation management is also aimed at aligning the client's emotional performance with the emotional regime of the criminal trial, thus avoiding the client displaying inappropriate emotions in the courtroom (Goffman, 1961b). It should be noted that, whilst defendants may have more emotionally expressive leeway than the legal actors in the courtroom, their emotional performances should still be appropriate.

My focus will be on the last of these, on the strategies used by the defence lawyer to align the client's social and emotional expectations with the emotional regime of the criminal trial. This entails preparing the client's expectations regarding the procedure, the defence lawyer's performance, the client's own performance, and the verdict.

The procedure

A study by the Swedish National Council for Crime Prevention (Westlund & Eriksson, 2013) found that there is uncertainty regarding various aspects of participating in a trial for those who have never done so before (for example, how to find the court, how a trial works, and who will be there). Many of the defence lawyers I spoke to confirmed this finding, saying that clients are often unsure as to what happens during a trial; therefore, they have to explain trial procedure, for instance, that there are only certain opportunities for the defendant to speak (Aronsson et al., 1987).

The defence lawyer's performance

However, the defence lawyers I interviewed add that defendants' lack of knowledge regarding trial procedure also pertains to the role and performance of the defence lawyer. Vera tells me that some of her clients:

> Think that it's really tough: why am I not saying anything? "We've sat here half a day and the prosecutor is still talking and you're not saying anything!" They have trouble understanding at times that, "yes, but we're still on the presentation of facts" [laugh]. (Vera)

This could lead to the client questioning the performance of the lawyer during the trial, which may lead to a disruption in the presentation of team face they are attempting to uphold. It also risks leading to a disruption of the trial if the defence lawyer misses evidence or testimony which may then have to be repeated, a time-consuming and costly interruption. It may also lead to the defence lawyer becoming distracted and losing concentration if the client's comment is not relevant to the specific context (Gould, 2014).

Defence lawyers thus perceive themselves as having to explain to the client the invisible rules that pertain to their – the defence lawyer's – role performance. Like Vera, Lena tells me that she explains what will happen in the courtroom, for instance, that she may not say much (including that she avoids posing the fatal question as discussed in the previous chapter),

> *Lena:* Because otherwise they think that you haven't done enough. Because then it can be, "why didn't you ask that question?" and "why didn't you say, why didn't you say it" and all that. You usually have to say that to them, because otherwise I think that they can get the impression that you have been far too passive and you aren't doing anything for their [case].
>
> *Lisa:* Do they ask these questions during the trial?
>
> *Lena:* Yes
>
> *Lisa:* What do you do then?

Lena: Then I usually say to them that I ask the questions that I think need to be asked. It's preferable to never pose a question that you don't know the answer to, but they don't understand that because they say, "but [the plaintiff] is lying," "yes, maybe you know that, but it's not something that [the plaintiff] is going to say here." I think some clients want a lawyer who is more vociferous.

Daniel also tells me that he has to explain what he will do during the trial, a performance which may include doing nothing, or stoneface. He says:

> You have to be clear towards the client about what they can expect and explain to them that, "it might well be the case that I don't say anything and that's not because, I mean, it's because I think that it's in your best interests." I think that as long as you prepare them and are clear towards the client what they, I mean, what my role is, what they can expect, how the trial will go, then I find that most of them buy this. (Daniel)

We see that defendants have expectations according to the lawyers I interviewed, not only of trial procedure, but also regarding the defence lawyer's performance. Accordingly, they also have expectations regarding how the defence lawyer's teamwork will be performed, which uses the client's version of events as the basis for the performance ("she's lying!"). As the invisible emotional order and its subtlety, the interaction order and its strictness, and the ceremonial order and its civility may be unknown to the client, doing nothing is perceived to be exactly that: doing nothing, rather than the strategic doing of something (S. Scott, 2017).

Many of the lawyers I interviewed thus present their clients as often being uninitiated into the ritual of a criminal trial. Clients therefore experience doing nothing as doing nothing, and, as I will soon come back to, they perceive unintentional face threats as malicious – in need of retribution as would be expected in many other interactions. The socially situated interaction order of the criminal trial should thus be explained to them.

It became apparent in my interviews that defence lawyers say that many clients have unrealistic expectations regarding the defence lawyers' role performance (and indeed, their own performance), often drawing assumptions about Swedish trials from interactions they have seen in depictions of American courts (see also Adelswärd, 1989). I asked Andrew about the difficulties this can lead to and he picks up on this shared cultural knowledge regarding both the trial and his trial performance:

Lisa: Do you prepare your client before you go in [to a trial], that it won't be like "objection!"?[12]

Andrew: Yes, yes, and I can tell you that it's become more and more common that clients, that they damn well believe that it's like

> on TV, and not just that, but they think it's like on crime shows, they think it's like CSI,[13] they took my DNA yesterday, why isn't it ready now? (…) And then we have the trial performance, that you should be aggressive, that you should really, you know, give 'em hell! Exactly like you said, "*objection!*" like this! Then I try and explain that, first of all, TV is TV and reality is reality (…) You also have to say that, "we have the prosecutor there and the judge and the lay judges there and they think you should be found guilty and blah, blah, blah and they don't give a shit which way it goes. They go in like small baby birds and we're going to feed them. The prosecutor knows exactly and we know exactly and if we go in and appear aggressive and threatening and really difficult then they are going to think a little bit less about you aren't they?" "Yes, yes, that's true." "So we maybe want to have a nice trial with a good atmosphere instead of making a fuss." "Yes, that sounds wise." A bit like that you see. Then you get a better climate for the hearing too.

Andrew talks about how clients may expect him to be a "Rambo litigator" (Pierce, 1995): aggressive, fierce, and intimidating. We have also just read Lena's comment that some clients want a more vociferous lawyer, something that is also mentioned by many of the other lawyers I interviewed. I suggest this expectation stems from medialized representations of criminal trials that clients have seen on American (and other) TV shows shown in Sweden, which depict defence lawyers as aggressive (cf. Fielding, 2006).[14] Such sensational, aggressive lawyering may also be what is reported in the media regarding Swedish trials (Barthe, Leone, & Lateano, 2013).[15]

In short, the client may expect a performance of aggression which is prohibited by the emotional regime of the criminal trial. There may thus be a clash of emotional expectations, specifically regarding how aggression may be displayed and its role in the criminal trial. Defence lawyers therefore have to negotiate the different agendas, expectations, and senses of justice that the lawyer and the client may have in order to calibrate the client's expectations with their experience of the defence lawyer's performance (Sarat & Felstiner, 1986). For instance, the client's agenda and sense of justice may be linked to showing that the plaintiff is lying as Lena talks about at the start of this section. This leads the client to expect and want his or her defence lawyer to be "hard," as Daniel says, on the plaintiff. The defence lawyer must thus explain the emotional order and the ceremonial order of the criminal trial in order to ensure that the client's expectations are calibrated with the actual performance.

Here, it is possible to not only see defence lawyers' presentations of their clients' expectations of justice, but also the emotional expectations the client has regarding the emotion rules: that it is permitted to be "hard" towards a plaintiff or witness, and that this "hardness" should be displayed or performed by being "a very American type of defender" as Daniel says, denoting aggressiveness.

Other emotional expectations that clients have include the assumption that the defence lawyer should display anger by using his or her voice as Vera tells me that some clients ask "aren't you going to raise your voice?" However, this is not permitted as I presented in the previous chapter. According to the observations I have conducted, the Rambo lawyer is a much subtler performance in the Swedish courtroom: the Rambo lawyer does not jump up and shout "objection!," instead he or she may give a slight frown or a quiet utterance, or indeed, not say anything at all (Flower, 2016a, 2016b) (the Rambo lawyer will be discussed in more detail in the next chapter).

The client's performance

Expectation management also entails explaining the client's role and performance in order to pre-emptively cool the client out and avoid "flood outs" (Goffman, 1961a, 1967) during the trial. This involves explaining what the client – as defendant – is supposed to do (and not do), both with regard to interactions (for instance, when they are permitted to speak and courtroom etiquette), and also pertaining to emotional displays. This also encompasses explaining how others can be expected to emotionally perform towards them.

Inappropriate emotions may be shown by the client backstage (for example, in the waiting room, outside the court or in the confines of the lawyer's office) which may help to ensure that the performances given in the courtroom remain within emotionally and socially approved limits (Goffman, 1952; see also Booth, 2012). Frontstage performances in the courtroom, however, should conform to the emotional regime of the criminal trial. For instance, the defence lawyers I interviewed tell me that they advise their clients not to get too angry as I have already described. This is a warning that defence lawyers talk about as being important for two reasons. Firstly, breaking emotion rules is considered to risk displeasing the court (Feigenson, 2016; Lerner & Tiedens, 2006), and secondly, breaking an emotion rule such as displaying aggression risks playing into the hands of the prosecutor.

The latter of these reasons relates to situations where the prosecutor has attempted to intentionally and strategically produce an emotion in the client in order to provide support for prosecution's case as I have already shown in the previous chapter. Siri tells me she prepares her client to expect "provocative" questions, that is, that her client may be the target of strategic emotion management at the hands of the prosecutor. Charles tells me that he prepares the client's performance in the courtroom beforehand by asking him or her questions during their meetings, questions that the prosecutor might pose. He explains that:

> Clients are emotional and you have to try and get past that. You know, when they come to me, the clients, then I have to ask lots of work-questions

> to them, and then, eventually, I see how they react (…) "I'm asking you these questions because you're going to get these questions from the prosecutor." It's also a way of keeping the client's feelings in check as well (…) I'm asking them for purely tactical reasons so that they know that this is what you're going get, you're going to get these questions and then I can flare up a bit towards the client, I can say, "yes, but it can't be like that!" (Charles)

Clients are presented by Charles as inherently emotional and thus in need of management. By explaining what to expect from the emotional performances of others, Charles is preparing clients for the eventuality that they may need to manage their own emotions at a future point, during the trial. All of the lawyers I spoke to say that they explain that their role is to ask uncomfortable questions to witnesses, plaintiffs, and at times, even their own client. Explaining this to the client may enable him or her to stay in face during the trial, and in particular, the cross-examination where the client has limited ability to sustain a sense of self that is in line with the basic values of society (Goffman, 1961a; Tracy & Tracy, 1998).

This is an important part of the client's performance that should be explained as the strategy of asking questions in order to produce emotions is talked about by all of the lawyers I interviewed. Lydia says that if she has evidence that she needs to bring forth, for example, showing that a witness is lying, the only tool she has at her disposal is "asking questions, I can't do much else." Questions are therefore used as an emotion management strategy by the prosecution and defence but the client should also be prepared to expect the opposite – that the prosecutor remains quiet, as George tells me:

> It's not a completely unusual technique, sometimes, being quiet, in order to try and produce a feeling in the witness that they haven't answered enough or that he has answered wrong or that he is stupid which can like, get him going. (George)

Emotions can therefore be "produced" by the prosecutor or defence lawyer in the recipient of their emotion work by ostensibly doing nothing – "an active commission" (S. Scott, 2017; cf. Scheffer, 2010, p. 184 for a discussion on avoidance when arguing cases). Not asking questions is therefore also a form of managing emotions aimed at producing or encouraging emotions such as nervousness.

Expectation management is also aimed at preventing inappropriate emotions from arising as a result of the routinised way in which a trial may be conducted. For the professional legal actors in the courtroom, a trial is part of a day's work, recumbent with specific roles and role expectations. The performance of these roles becomes mundane which risks being perceived as nonchalance as Kate says, by outsiders who are uninitiated in the display rules being performed (cf. Jacobson et al., 2016; Leidner, 1993; Schütz, 1971).

The lawyers I interviewed also talk about advising clients to focus on the facts of the case rather than the emotional content such as how they felt leading up to the crime. This separation of the client's emotional experiences from instrumental issues which highlight the legal argument ensures that the lawyer is able to focus on what is legally relevant (the facts of the case); however, it also enables the lawyer to avoid dealing with the client's emotional situation which they are not trained for (cf. Sarat & Felstiner, 1986). This separation is seen clearly in the courtroom as, on numerous occasions I observed a client becoming upset but receiving no comfort from the lawyer, no hand on the shoulder, glass of water poured, or comforting words. On one occasion, the defendant asked for a tissue to wipe his tears and was handed a pen by his lawyer.[16] I was intrigued by this and asked Martin if he comforts his client in the courtroom to which he replies "of course!," and that he gets "scared" to hear things like this (this is comparable with the avoidance of eye contact discussed previously which is also an unacknowledged aspect of performances). However, such "relational work" (Stacey, 2011) – providing comfort or companionship – is often talked about as belonging to the backstage and even in this region, the emphasis should be on legal support rather than on emotional support according to the lawyers I spoke to (which, the reader may remember, is also discussed in the section on eye contact).

I argue that this separation and promotion of the legal client whose case is fact-based, over the emotional client, the latter referring to an emotionally framed and driven version of events, also ensures adherence to the emotional regime of the criminal trial. It is not just about protecting the defence lawyer from emotional contagion (Hatfield, Cacioppo, & Rapson, 1993) – catching the other's emotions – but it is also aimed at avoiding the display of unwanted emotions and disruptions in the flow of interaction.

The worst-case scenario

Defendants often have expectations of "winning" the case, seen in terms of being found not guilty, but as we have already seen almost all trials lead to conviction; therefore, it is almost inevitable that the client will be convicted and should thus be prepared for this eventuality (Borgström, 2011; Nordén, 2015). In order to ensure that the client's expectations regarding the outcome of the trial are in line with the verdict, defence lawyers may present the "worst-case scenario" as Andrew says. In this way, the client is pre-emptively cooled out so that he or she can accept the verdict (Gasser, 1963; Goffman, 1952; Thomas, 2014).

This form of expectation management involves explaining "what is at stake" as Kate says and can be used as a guide for which future emotions can be managed. Lo explains that she tells her clients:

> What can be the worst-case scenario or, I mean, if the prosecutor's charges stick the whole way, what are you risking? So, you can give a

> prognosis, and then, for example you can discuss, in the choice between prison and probation, then probation is a milder sentence and the client is in agreement that, yes, I would rather have probation than prison and then you get a sentence with probation then the client is usually satisfied with it, if you, so to speak, have had, that the outcome could have been worse. (Lo)

By presenting such a worst-case scenario, it is possible to align the client's expectations with a less favourable outcome. If the court then finds in favour of the client or sentences to a lower than expected penalty, the actual verdict appears in a more positive light thus making the client more satisfied with the outcome – it could have been worse. The defence lawyer is thus cooling the client out – preparing him or her for the inevitable – however, unlike Goffman's (1952) use of the term, it does not involve misrepresenting events, rather presenting them in the worst possible light.

If the defence lawyer has succeeded in calibrating expectations, it is possible to prevent or at least diminish the client's feelings of disappointment or anger at the outcome of the trial, emotions which may need to be managed by the defence lawyer after the verdict (Wettergren, 2009). Lydia says that she does this, and consequently:

> I've rarely had someone get mad because of the result. I'm usually quite clear that it could go this way or that way. I don't know. And I never promise anything that I can't be sure about, I'm pretty careful. Then they don't get mad with the result if I have said to them that there is a risk that it might end up like this. (Lydia)

Preparing the client for a possible "loss" is therefore an emotion management strategy aimed at aligning "anticipatory emotions" (hope of acquittal) with "consequent emotions" (anger at conviction) (Kemper, 1978, p. 49). This differs from the emotion work conducted in many other professions where the aim is to produce a direct feeling in other: the passenger will immediately feel calmed and welcomed by the friendly air attendant. Here, the client's future emotions are being managed by the lawyer. I therefore propose a time dimension to the theory of emotion management: managing future emotions.

In cooling the client out beforehand, the lawyer is also proactively and pre-emptively defending against claims of an inadequate defence based on dissatisfaction with the outcome. This pre-emptive strategy of cooling the client can thus be seen as a form of facework performed by the lawyer in order to protect his or her own face (cf. S. Scott, 2017). Failure to cool the client out could lead to the client, as Goffman (1952, p. 459) so eloquently puts it, "raising[ing] a squawk" that is, making a complaint, either to the law firm or even to the Swedish Bar Association.

Another way in which the client can be pre-emptively cooled out is by informing them of the possibility of appealing, thus giving the client "another chance to qualify for the role at which he has failed" (Goffman, 1952, p. 458).

We therefore see that the role of defence lawyers, according to their descriptions, entails managing the client's expectations in order to create stable interactions within the defence team and between other interactants in the trial. This is done, they explain, by ensuring that there are congruent expectations regarding how the situation should be defined and the performances therein, thus reducing uncertainty regarding the emotional regime to be followed (cf. Harris, 2002, p. 563).

This section has shown that the defence lawyer is expected to emotionally prepare clients for a criminal trial and depicted how this is done and why. I will now briefly touch upon the management of others' emotions which I will build upon in the next chapter.

Managing own and others' emotions

I have already discussed how the client is initiated into the emotional regime of the criminal trial beforehand. However, during the trial, clients' emotions may need to be managed in order to ensure that their emotional display is in line with the overall impression the defence team is attempting to accomplish. This demands that the defence lawyer manages his or her own emotions contemporaneously which I will show by returning to the drink-driving excerpt. But to begin with, I will introduce the concept of "emotional readers" and the importance of this in courtroom interactions in managing one's own and others' emotions.

Emotional readers

The importance of interactional and emotional dexterity is a recurring theme in the interviews I conducted. Defence lawyers talk about being able to read the emotions of other actors in the trial as an important lawyering tool in order to understand the performance of others, how their own performances have been received, and how to adjust them accordingly. Defence lawyers therefore talk about themselves as being able to switch from the role of performer to audience, reading "emotional cues" (Clark, 1990; Waldron, 2000). For instance, Peter says sometimes he just sits back and watches the judges' faces to gauge, "are they cool? The lay judges, how do they look at this? To see, are they, how much attention are they paying, what impression do they show that they get from this?" He presents reading others as an important part of his role. This includes reading the faces of the judges in order to gauge the performance given by the prosecutor but also, as Richard previously mentioned regarding uncertain-sounding prosecutors, and as George also says, watching the prosecutor in order to look for slips of the prosecutor's mask (cf. Törnqvist, 2017). For instance, if they see the prosecutor get angry, they adjust their own performance as Lena tells me:

> You can exploit this in two ways as it can be a prosecutor, who is very, very worked up on the other side and then you yourself can stay calm and then you look like perhaps, the one that, yes, I don't need to flare up because I know that I'm right. You should try and exploit it. (Lena)

Defence lawyers thus talk about reading the emotions of others and using their own emotional display of calmness to build facts to convey to the judge, a display which arises in response to, and in interaction with, the prosecutor.

Stoneface is also used in this process which Daniel tells me he uses to avoid giving cues to others in the courtroom, for example, the prosecutor. He describes stoneface as a tactical strategy aimed at concealing disappointment to ensure that the prosecutor does not interpret his emotional expression as revealing a weakness in the defence team's case:

> If I somehow expressed it, that [the client gave] the wrong answer, then maybe you put more weight on it, then maybe the others in court, the lay judges and prosecutor also notice that this was something that the defence didn't want to happen and it has happened and then, perhaps the prosecutor tries to push it and then suddenly, then perhaps it's something that, well, benefits the prosecutor in the end, or that is, basically, to my client's disadvantage. (Daniel)

Daniel wants to ensure that he manages the social information, encompassing emotional information, that he gives and indeed, gives off (Goffman, 1956b, 1969). Lydia also talks about how, if she reacts with surprise at something, then there is a bigger chance that the judge notices it. She remarks that it "would be very interesting if the judge, I mean, how they read the prosecutor and the defender, how much they look at how we react."

There is, therefore, awareness amongst the lawyers, for the importance of interpreting the impression that others are conveying. This is akin to judges who both perceive and display (Roach Anleu & Mack, 2017, p. 169). Thus, similarly to Roach Anleu and Mack (2017), I find that many of the lawyers I interviewed rate interactional skills as important in their role, not just in terms of being "better at listening than talking" and "a good judge of character" in order to know which questions to ask the client, and which questions to leave as Vera tells me, but also at reading others' presentation of self – including emotional expressions – interpreting them and adjusting one's performance accordingly.

Producing emotions in others

The following excerpt was discussed in the previous chapter, but I will also present it here in order to highlight interactional emotion management in the courtroom by depicting how the defence lawyer manages his own emotions and those of his client. The excerpt is from the trial regarding drink-driving:

> The defence lawyer angles his chair slightly towards his client and says "of course, you regret that you drove?" to which the client replies that he does. The defence lawyer then states "you were in a spiral of drinking too much." His head is tipped slightly to one side and his voice is softer when he says this. (Fieldnote)

This production of regret in the client requires the simultaneous management of the defence lawyer's own emotions because, as we have already learned, emotions are always present, not just irritation, disgust, anger, and sadness, but also feelings such as boredom which the lawyers I interviewed said can arise in such straight-forward cases (see Cowen & Keltner, 2017; Neu, 2000 for a discussion on boredom as an emotion). All of these feelings should be managed in order to shape the appropriate emotional display of loyalty thereby communicating to the client that they are a team supporting the client's version of events, whilst simultaneously generating an emotional display of regret in the defendant.

This is the phase of the trial where the defence lawyer is supposed to be questioning his client, but as we see, the defence lawyer is asking questions as a way of managing the client in order to display regret. Indeed, the questions are more like statements: "you regret that you drove?"[17] The defence lawyer is actively directing the client's emotions in line with the emotion rule which states that a perpetrator of a crime should show regret, thus presenting the client in a positive light to the court (cf. Bandes, 2015b; Dahl et al., 2007; Goffman, 1956b; Kaufmann et al., 2003; Wessel et al., 2006). Emotion work is used here as another form of factwork (cf. Potter, 1996), in this instance, it is aimed at building up emotional facts: the client regrets that he drove.

I would like to highlight that, in this case, the defence lawyer manages both parts of the interaction into emotion *norms*: loyal lawyer and regretful defendant. This finding differs from previous research which tends to focus on either the management of one's own emotions in line with the norm, or management of other's emotions in line with the norm. Remember Thoits' (1996) study on support groups focused on bringing the participant's emotions in line with how they were expected to feel and express, but the emotion norm guiding the group leader's performance was neglected. In Hochschild's (1983) study, the emotions of the flight attendants are managed in line with the emotion norms of capitalism but less is noted regarding the normative goal of the passenger's emotions – they should be satisfied with the service and be willing to the use the company again, but a specific emotion norm is not discerned. I show here that the goal of interactional emotion management can be to ensure that the emotions of both the manager and managed are in line with an emotion norm: loyal lawyer and regretful defendant.

This excerpt thus introduces a third category of emotion management, namely interactional emotion management which includes both interactants – it does not solely focus on the management of one's own emotions (intrapersonal or individual) or the management of others' emotions (interpersonal) (Flam, 1990b; Hochschild, 1979; Lively & Weed, 2014; Morris & Feldman, 1996; Niven, 2015). I use the drink-driving excerpt here to show that there is a tendency to over-simplify emotion management and that the management of others' emotions demands the contemporaneous management of one's own emotions.

Concluding comments

In this chapter, I have shown that the accomplishment of the defence lawyer's role takes place within an interaction order that is highly ritualised and formal with clear roles to be performed and principles to be conveyed. Included in this is the ceremonial order which ensures that the performances within remain polite and courteous. Finally, the emotional order forms how these performances can be emotionally accomplished. All of these three orders are intertwined.

My focus has been firstly on defence lawyers' emotion talk and I find that it upholds the emotional regime of law, and, secondly, I have looked at how the role of defence lawyer involves preparing the client's emotional expectations of a trial. I then showed how defence lawyers ensure that their performances and those of their teammates remain interactionally and emotionally appropriate which is accomplished by a range of strategies. I have therefore shown that the performance of loyalty and teamwork entails emotion work and facework.

By showing the invisible rules of the interaction order, ceremonial order and emotion order, we see how defence lawyers accomplish their role – in particular, that the appropriate performance of emotions is associated with sustaining the ceremonial order.

All this suggests that the emotional regime of the criminal trial in Sweden is formed by social expectations that stifle the display of strong emotions as described in the introduction (Bergman Blix & Wettergren, 2015, p. 3). It also indicates societal differences in the manifestation of the emotional regime of law (cf. Bergman Blix & Wettergren, 2015; Daun, 1998).

Notes

1 However, it should be noted here that in certain instances, the social aspect of feelings is acknowledged, for example, as I show later on in this chapter, liking a client can be a more open source of motivation. This ambivalence towards acknowledging the social

construction of emotions and their presence in all interactions can be seen in terms of a tension between presenting oneself as a professional actor which traditionally involves denying the role of emotions as per the emotional regime of law, and talking about oneself from a more personal frame (Goffman, 1986). Linked to this, in a previous study, I showed how law students signal when they are switching from a professional statement to a personal statement by sniffing which I termed the "emotional sniff" as it conveys a shift in emotion norms (Flower, 2014). It also points to the social expectation that negative emotions should be controlled (Daun, 1998; P. N. Stearns, 1994).

2 Furthermore, the management of emotions is seen to be a tacit skill and is linked to high academic achievement therefore it may be assumed that the soft skills of lawyering come naturally in high achieving law students (Macdonald, 1999; Somech & Bogler, 1999).

3 This also implies that emotion management strategies used by defence lawyers are learned after the law program as prosecutors, judges and defence lawyers all study on the same law program, choosing to specialise after the education is completed.

4 The wording of a judgment is important in order for recipients to accepts its legitimacy and, I would add, can also be seen as a way of cooling the "losers" out (Graver, 2010, p. 125).

5 For an extreme example of this, Frederick Duchardt the defence lawyer in the U.S. who has had the most clients sent to death row denies that his repeated losses are related to his performance (D. Rose, 2016).

6 The term "negative emotions" is misleading as what classes as a negative emotion is contentious and often deemed to be negative in a moralistic sense (Kristjánsson, 2003).

7 However, it should be noted that on occasion it would be permitted for a defence lawyer to cry, particularly if it is the client's version of events that has been moving, or in a case where the client has confessed to the crime. Thus, as we will soon see with empathy, the trigger of the emotion is the deciding factor.

8 Empathy is thus a social construction – an interactional and interpretive process whereby the "empathizer imagines and shares the thoughts and feelings of the empathy recipient" (Ruiz-Junco, 2017, p. 6; Cooley, 1922). Empathy can be automatically activated when we perceive an emotional other; however, it is also possible to control empathy by cognitively re-framing one's perception, or by not thinking about the situation (suppression), or by avoiding emotional situations (Hodges & Biswas-Diener, 2007; Hodges & Wegner, 1997; Singer et al., 2004 cf. Maroney, 2011a). Empathy thus entails a clear division between self and other, that is, one is aware that the source of emotion is someone else (Cuff et al., 2016)

9 This suggests the need for empathy education in order for judges to be able to understand a defendant's background (cf. Bandes, 2017; see also Brunero, Lamont, & Coates, 2010).

10 An important aspect of ensuring the flow of interaction is the cost of a criminal trial (see Lindström & Malmberg, 2010).

11 This difference in expectations can also be seen in terms of insiders and outsiders: the legal professionals have insider knowledge whilst the outsiders are the lay participants who are uninitiated into the ritual of a trial (Becker, 1963; Jacobson et al., 2016; Rock, 1993).

12 I used the English word "objection" in this Swedish-speaking interview indicating that it is an immediately recognizable term which, as we see in the interview, brings with it associations of film and TV.

13 CSI is an American TV show based on crime scene investigators in the U.S.

14 The law and lawyers are often portrayed in films in unrealistic or unrepresentative way leading to unrealistic expectations of American-film-style trials in European countries (Greenfield & Osborn, 1995; Machura & Ulbrich, 2001).

15 For instance, "Södertäljemålet" as described in chapter five.

16 This also shows that the focus of the defence lawyer during the trial is on the evidence being presented with the client constituting at times a "side-involvement" (Goffman, 1957, p. 47) – a distraction to be dealt with to avoid breaking the ceremonial order of the courtroom.

17 Having presented these findings to judges, all of them have stated that they would not have allowed this type of leading question in the form of a statement.

Chapter 7

The teamwork of a criminal trial

Up until now I have focused on how the emotional regime of a criminal trial is upheld by performers following the emotional, interaction, and ceremonial order with particular focus on the defence lawyer. My central attention has been on the individual performance of the defence lawyer as well as the joint performance of the defence team. In chapter four I showed expectations regarding defence lawyers' loyalty, in chapter five I presented the ways in which they communicate and uphold their role, and in chapter six I lifted the emotions involved.

However, I would now like to widen this focus to show how the criminal trial itself is a team performance – a three-team interplay consisting of the judges, the prosecution, and the defence.[1] The goal of this team performance is to sustain the definition of the situation – a criminal trial – and to ensure the accomplishment of a fair and just trial. This means that not only should legal professionals sustain role differentiation between their private and professional role, they should also sustain role differentiation within the legal profession. All legal professionals taking part must therefore stay in character in order for justice to be accomplished. Within this interplay each role, including the defence lawyers, is constructed in interaction with others.

I will therefore begin by presenting my fieldnotes from a trial showing each of the team performances and which I use to depict the ritual expression of anger as part of a defence lawyer's appropriately loyal performance. It is also used to show how the defence lawyer's performance reveals the otherwise invisible rules. I move on to discuss how the criminal trial and professional roles can be upheld even when threatened, disrupted, or challenged. In particular, I reveal the underlying antagonistic tensions each team has regarding the other which can threaten interactional justice. Next, I show how emotional and interactional threats to the trial are managed and repaired. Loyalty and the interactional construction of the defence lawyer's role are themes that I return to in each of these sections and the chapter concludes with a closing argument summing up the main findings and future directions.

The criminal trial in (inter)action

Although all of the legal professionals in a criminal trial have loyalty to the law, they each have different legal principles to be performed – objective prosecutor, loyal lawyer, and impartial judge. This means that on the stage of the courtroom, each legal actor is guided by a different legal principle in order for justice to be interactionally accomplished. Accordingly, justice requires not only legal professionals possessing juridical knowledge (as is the focus of law programs), but it also requires the appropriate presentation and, at times, reparation of a public image of self and others, that is in line with the norms of the courtroom. This also calls for emotion work. My analysis therefore now moves to examining how the defence lawyer's role is accomplished as part of a larger courtroom cast and how these performances work together in order to construct a just criminal trial.

The following excerpt is taken from the audio recording of an assault trial that I observed which proved to be the most aggressive cross-examination of a plaintiff that I saw during my fieldwork in Sweden. The excerpt combines the transcript from the official audio recording of the trial (which I obtained from the court) and my fieldnotes written during the trial. The defendant is accused of assaulting his partner – the plaintiff – in their home. The plaintiff's version of events is central to the case as there were no other witnesses at the time of the assault. We join proceedings when the plaintiff is being questioned:

> The prosecutor and, afterwards, the counsel for the plaintiff ask the plaintiff to talk about the assaults. They ask their questions with a soft, gentle tone of voice with their bodies angled towards her. When the plaintiff says that she thought that the defendant was going to hit her when he stood behind her, the defence lawyer frowns and looks at the judge. The plaintiff continues, telling the court that the defendant said he was going to fetch an axe to which the defendant says "no, no, it wasn't like that." The defence lawyer immediately holds out his left arm diagonally, just above the desk, hand straight as if restraining the defendant, telling him forcibly, but in a low tone of voice, to be quiet. He looks at the judge at the same time and dips his head very slightly. Shortly afterwards he takes out a tub of snus [tobacco] and offers it to his client who declines but smiles.
>
> It is now the defence lawyer's turn to pose questions to the plaintiff:
>
> *Defence:* I hope that it's ok with you, I am going to ask some questions about recollections, mainly your recollections. And it's my job to do it, just so that you understand that (…) I wrote down: "in answer to the prosecutor's question, she goes towards [the defendant] and asks him to

go and lie down." Is that correct, what I wrote down? [Looks quickly at the judge].

Plaintiff: [Stares at the defence lawyer for 8 seconds. Jaw clenched. No reply].

Defence: I mean, that's what you said in answer to the prosecutor's question [looks quickly at the judge again].

Plaintiff: [Stares at the defence lawyer for 10 seconds. Jaw clenched. No reply].

Defence: Or you can change your statement if you want.

Plaintiff: [Stares at the defence lawyer for 11 seconds. Jaw clenched. No reply].

Counsel for the plaintiff: Can you tell us what you remember?

Plaintiff: I think this is just terribly unpleasant [starts to cry].

Defence: I apologise if it can feel like that but I'm trying to investigate your recollection so I have to be able to ask these questions. The judge can interrupt me if I stray from the facts of the case and I have full respect for that [looks at the judge] but, take your time.

Plaintiff: [Crying and sniffing for 5 seconds].

Defence: And if it's the case that you can't remember, then say so. That's important.

Counsel for the plaintiff: Do you want the defence lawyer to repeat the question?

Plaintiff: It's just impossible to answer the question either with "no" or without "no" if you see what I mean. I don't know.

Defence: No, ok, well then, I'll note that and leave that situation there.

The plaintiff continues to cry and blows her nose.

Defender: Do you remember that you have talked to the police?

Plaintiff: Yes.

Defence: Yes, it wasn't my intention to sound patronising at all, just.

Plaintiff: No, but now that's precisely what you were.

Defence: Yes, I apologise for that. Do you remember if you told the police about the event?

> He goes on to ask how the plaintiff can perceive the defendant was going to hit her, if he was standing behind her and where she was unable to see him.
>
> All of the defence lawyer's questions are posed in the same tone of voice, each question asked clearly and slowly. He makes eye contact with the plaintiff with only a quick look down at his papers every now and then or glances to the judge. His facial expressions are relaxed and neutral throughout, no headshaking, no frowning. The judge remains with a neutral expression throughout.
>
> At the end of the defence lawyer's questioning, both the prosecutor and the counsel for the plaintiff shake their heads. The counsel for the plaintiff does a bigger shake of the head and several shakes compared to the prosecutor who just his head once. (Audio recording and fieldnote)

Here, we see the three-team interplay at work. The prosecutor is presenting the case, using the plaintiff's testimony as support for this. The defence lawyer is defending his client by attempting to find holes in the plaintiff's version of events, questioning certain aspects that are unclear. The judge sits with a neutral expression throughout yet his central position in proceedings is seen in the defence lawyer directing an apology for his client's outburst (as seen in the defence lawyer's head dip) towards him, and from the way in which the defence lawyer glances at him throughout his cross-examination.

In this three-way interaction, there are other actors involved, namely the counsel for the plaintiff who, whilst not representing the state, is nevertheless supporting the plaintiff's version of events and can therefore be viewed as part of the prosecution's team. We also see the lay participants involved – the plaintiff belonging to the prosecutorial team, and the defendant belonging to the defence team. We see that lay participants have different display rules as reflected in the plaintiff's crying, whilst the defendant's outburst shows that lay participants are unpredictable factors in a trial, requiring management. Lastly, there are even lay judges present who also constitute lay participants but who belong to the judicial team.

These three teams – prosecution, defence, and judicial – rely on their own teammates to stay in character in order for the team impression to be conveyed in the eyes of the audience (the other teams present). There is thus an expectation that fellow teammates will have good conduct and follow the team line in order for the team performance to be upheld. For instance, the prosecution, counsel for the plaintiff, and the plaintiff should present a cohesive picture – united behind a shared reality, despite the three different roles within the team. The same is true of the defence team comprised of the defence lawyer and defendant, and of the judicial team, comprised of the judge and the lay judges.

By this point in the book, the reader is well-aware of the defence lawyer's official guidelines to be followed, but what are the guidelines pertaining to the prosecutor's and judge's principle performances? I will begin with the prosecutor. The prosecutor's objectivity is set out by the law which states that crime prevention work, including the preliminary investigation should be pursued objectively, bringing forth evidence that not only goes against the accused, but also in his or her favour (SFS, 1942:740, RB Kap. 23, 4§) This duty of objectivity should continue after the preliminary investigation and during the trial. Prosecutors should also follow ethical guidelines which state that, within the frame of their independence and official responsibilities, they should work objectively towards ensuring that all decisions are correct and that the legal process is carried out in compliance with the rule of law (Åklagarmyndighet, 2014).

The prosecutorial team performance in a criminal trial thus entails giving face to the plaintiff and building up the facts that the prosecution is presenting by conveying emotions in line with the plaintiff's version of events. This is seen in the soft, sympathetic facial expressions during questions and the head-shaking as a display of dissatisfaction or disdain at the defence lawyer's cross-examination. These teammates also sit together, a clear tie-sign of unity. This performance and execution of objectivity must be balanced with loyalty to the law – as we have just read – their work should comply with the rule of law.

The defence lawyer's client loyalty and conveyance of the defence team is seen when he frowns at weaknesses in the plaintiff's testimony, questioning her version of events, such as when she states she could see movement behind her. He is thus basing his performance on the defendant's version of events who denies the assault. We also see the performance of the defence team when he calms the defendant who is "flooding out" (Goffman, 1967). We see the tie-sign of the defence team sitting side-by-side and the defence lawyer offering his client snus (tobacco), signalling a degree of familiarity.

In adversarial systems, the judge plays a neutral role and here we see the impartiality of the judge who sits impassively throughout (as do the lay judges). The judge is thus performing his judicial role as set out by the law and the judicial code of conduct which states that judges should take an oath to treat all those before them impartially and equally (Domstolar, 2019a; SFS, 1942:740, RB Kap 4, 11–15§). Lay judges must also take this oath. In the above excerpt, the judges and lay judges are thus conveying impartiality and thus loyalty to the law. Later on in this chapter, I will more fully explore when this judicial team impression fails and the lay judges give the game away so to speak, comprising an internal threat to judicial face.

We therefore see that these principle performances: objectivity, loyalty, and impartiality, all entail subtle nuances. Now I want to hone in on one aspect of this scene in particular in order so show how the defence lawyer threatens the overall team performance by not dramaturgically co-operating – by skirting close to the edge of unacceptable conduct and impoliteness. He is thus on the cusp of breaking the rules which should be followed in order for the trial to flow smoothly. I will therefore now show the subtlety of the rules of interaction by unpicking this courtroom scene and focusing on the emotion of anger and the conveyance of loyalty.

Angry loyalty

The defence lawyer begins his cross-examination by giving an account for the intentional politeness to come: that he is going to question her recollection but that, "it's my job to do it." He is justifying the emotions he may produce in the plaintiff, emotions that, in another context, would be considered inappropriate to produce in someone. He is thus also explaining that the ensuing face threat is not intended to be malicious and therefore within the remit of his role (Archer, 2011a, p. 3222; M. B. Scott & Lyman, 1968). In this way, he is presenting the cross-examination as one of his role obligations aimed at uncovering evidence, ergo, his actions should not be seen as an intentional face attack – he even apologises when the plaintiff accuses him of being patronising (Goffman, 1956b; Lakoff, 1990). We see too that he uses eyework as a form of factwork – as I presented in chapter four – glancing at the judge when building up facts ("is that correct, what I wrote down?" and "that's what you said in answer to the prosecutor's question"). He also makes the professionally expected eye contact with the plaintiff throughout questioning and his tone of voice is in accordance with the professional expectations I outlined in previous chapters (Blomkvist, 1987; Mellqvist, 1994). He is therefore explaining his role and role obligations.

Rule reminders

However, we see from the response of the plaintiff that she perceives his actions as malicious. Indeed, we also see from the responses of the prosecutor and counsel for the plaintiff – the social community who are wise to the emotional regime of the criminal trial – that he is perceived to have conveyed disrespect (Tracy & Tracy, 1998, p. 227; Archer, 2011a).

The plaintiff's response – "I think this is just terribly unpleasant" and telling the defence lawyer that he was patronising her – shows that she has perceived him as rude (cf. Westlund & Eriksson, 2013). The plaintiff thus responds in a way similar to an explicit "rule reminder" (Barrett Cox, 2016; Hochschild, 1979, 1983; Tracy, 2000). This implies that there may be a difference between how reminders may be administered by legal professionals and lay participants as we will shortly see. However, it may also be a reflection on the plaintiff's lack of initiation into the order of the courtroom. She may not be aware of the rules and may therefore apply a different set of external rules. This indicates an alternate frame of understanding of the situation based on an emotional regime different to that of the criminal trial, leading her to interpret the situation as a malicious face threat (Adelswärd et al., 1988; Archer, 2011a).[2]

The performance also appears to have breached professional expectations for how a cross-examination should be conducted as we see in the head shaking by the prosecutor and counsel for the plaintiff which indicate that the rules of interaction have been violated. Head shaking thus acts as an implicit reminder of the normative practices that should be adhered to in the emotional regime of the criminal trial – in this case, that the cross-examination of a witness should be carried out politely and non-aggressively. It is also an acceptable way for the prosecution and counsel for the plaintiff to display anger or irritation towards the defence lawyer's deviation from his professional role obligations when his performance conveys too much loyalty to his client (which I will discuss in more detail shortly).

So, by using subtle gestures such as head shaking, the prosecutor and counsel for the plaintiff communicate to the judge that the lawyer has deviated from the emotional order and the ceremonial order and intentionally threatened the face of the plaintiff, by performing in an inappropriate way. This is not only a breach in the emotional regime of the criminal trial, but it also constitutes a breach in the defence lawyer's official guidelines which, you may remember, state that the defence lawyer should not scandalise or threaten an opposing party or make degrading comments (Association, 2008, p. 28). We see too that this reminder is administered more subtly than the open rebuke by the plaintiff.

The defence lawyer appears to be aware that his performance is balancing on the line of acceptability as he glances at the judge when there is a risk that his performance could be perceived as crossing it ("the judge can interrupt me if I stray from the facts of the case and I have full respect for that"). He is therefore looking at the judge to ensure that his performance has stayed within the boundaries of "reasonably hostility" (Tracy, 2011), a breach of which constitutes a threat to lawyer face as it can be perceived as unprofessional. He is thus emotionally reading the judge and then managing and adjusting his emotional performance based on the response of the judge to ensure that he stays in face and that the interaction flow continues unhindered (Goffman, 1956b).

His glances at the judge also show that it is the judge who is the "emotion supervisor" (Hochschild, 1983) on hand, sanctioning deviant performances with "rule reminders." These reminders are therefore a form of immediate "back-channel feedback" (Goffman, 1981, p. 14) on his performance. In this case, the judge conveys whether or not the defence lawyer's performance is acceptable to the social situation at hand by administering, for instance, a stern glance. Eyework can therefore be used as a subtle sanction – a rule reminder. This is also described by Hilda, who tells me about a situation from the start of her career when she laughed at the opposing counsel to show that they were wrong, "I remember that the judge looked at me and I noticed straight away that he didn't like it and I was so ashamed afterwards, ugh, I'm still ashamed when I talk about it [laughs]." Hilda realised that she had broken an emotion rule when she saw the judge looking at her in a sanctioning way and we can therefore assume that the defence lawyer in the above excerpt is also looking to the judge to see if he is being implicitly sanctioned.

In Hilda's example, the judge's reaction revealed an emotion rule stating that contempt (seen here as a form of anger) should not be displayed in the courtroom using laughter – a rule that she had not yet been socialised into. Rule reminders thus constitute an "interpersonal ritual" (Goffman, 1967, p. 168–169) aimed at bringing performances in line with expectations. This led to Hilda feeling shame as she perceived herself to have not lived up to the role expectations placed upon her and that she had broken the ceremonial order of the courtroom (Goffman, 1956b; Scheff, 2000). She had consequently discredited herself (Goffman, 1967, p. 51).

Hilda goes on to say that she realised that she had to try and show that the prosecutor was wrong "some other way." This is what emotion work is about: trying to show emotions in a way that is appropriate to the emotional regime – performing one's role and legal position whilst still remaining within the boundaries of acceptability. It is therefore not only judicial objectivity that is oriented by shame, but also defence lawyers' performances of loyalty and indeed, teamwork (cf. Wettergren & Bergman Blix, 2016). This indicates that the emotion work of defence lawyers is self-perpetuated – via socialisation – and externally monitored (cf. Harris, 2002, p. 575).

From the fieldnote presented at the start of this chapter and Hilda's experiences, we can see that rule reminders reveal emotion rules and that they can be used as an intentional face threat, controlling the conduct of others hence they serve to reveal the emotional regime which such sanctioning is designed to enforce (Goffman, 1956b; Hochschild, 1983; Reddy, 2001).

We see in the fieldnote that the defence lawyer performs an aggressive cross-examination, this is despite the absence of shouting, exaggerated facial expressions or gestures. His performance still breaks the rules of acceptability as visible in the responses of others. I argue therefore that he has performed an angry and aggressive "Rambo litigator" (Pierce, 1995). This leads to two questions: why is this performance deemed to be deviant and how should the appropriate performance of anger be accomplished?

Subtle anger

We have already seen that anger is talked about in the interviews as an inappropriate emotion – in the section on identity work, I showed that the lawyers in this study distanced themselves from Rambo lawyers or "Stockholm lawyers." Anger is seen as something to be handled with care or avoided (cf. Feigenson, 2016; Lerner, Goldberg, & Tetlock, 1998; Lerner & Tiedens, 2006; Litvak et al., 2010). One explanation for this is the perception of anger as an emotion that arises when one's self (or someone near) has been offended or injured (Litvak et al., 2010). This means that displays of anger by a defence lawyer could risk being viewed by the court as the defence lawyer acting on everyday emotions, or worse still, the emotions of the client (like you were his or her twin as Peter says). In showing anger one risks one's performance as being perceived as over involved, losing self-control, and thus unable to sustain the interaction (Goffman, 1957). One is unprofessional or indeed, overly loyal.

Anger is therefore talked about as an everyday, "unbecoming emotion" (Averill, 1994, p. 265) – incompatible with rational or normative action. In line with this, I find that rather than presenting themselves as becoming angry, defence lawyers talk about becoming indignant, annoyed, or worked-up in court. We have also seen this in my fieldnotes from the animal-in-the-car trial – the defence lawyer states that he became "quite annoyed." Indignation and annoyance are consequently talked about as acceptable acts of anger, sparked by a rule violation and the ensuing injustice (for example, if a prosecutor is perceived to be non-objective or a witness is suspected of perjury) but, importantly, without the defence lawyer being personally affronted (cf. Flam, 1990b, p. 232). Accordingly, for the defence lawyers I interviewed, anger is associated with personal offence, whilst annoyance and indignation are linked with injustice. Good lawyers don't get angry, they get annoyed.

Rare admissions of anger did occur during my interviews, admissions that were never made in the courtroom – not once did I hear a lawyer stating that they were angry. Those defence lawyers who did mention becoming angry described it as stemming from a perceived gross injustice. However, this anger was associated with a loss of control by many and, like disgust, in need of transformation, for instance into relevant questions, as Lydia tells me.

The reservation of defence lawyers regarding the open acknowledgement and acceptance of anger, preferring instead the perhaps milder form of annoyance as reflected in my interviews and fieldnotes, reinforces my position that defence lawyers' emotion talk upholds and reproduces the emotional regime of law. This also means that the appropriate rule for displaying anger – showing aggression (Averill, 1982) – in the Swedish courtroom demands even more subtlety than depicted in the previous excerpt, in order to uphold the illusion of rationality and unemotionality (Bergman Blix & Wettergren, 2015).

Rambo-Bambi

So how should anger – or annoyance – be shown? We now know from chapter five that the Rambo lawyer is talked about and interacted with as a deviation – displays should be subtle and in line with the emotional regime of the criminal trial (cf. Rock, 1993; Archer, 2011a). My data shows that the Rambo performance should be tailored to a softer, less threatening approach, more akin to the Disney cartoon character Bambi. However, I argue that hiding beneath the Bambi surface is the hard, aggressive Rambo, a film character known for his aggression, strength, and determination. I therefore present this performance as "Rambo-Bambi."[3] Defence lawyers' emotional displays are therefore adjusted to the emotional regime and are linked to their legal position and role obligations which also means that it is the defence team's version of events that is the basis for this performance. Rambo-Bambi is consequently a professional expectation which, as we have already seen, risks clashing with the social "Rambo" expectation of clients as I discussed in chapter five.

The Rambo-Bambi strategy is talked about by many of the lawyers I interviewed. For instance, Andrew says:

> I can declare you a complete idiot and saw you off at the kneecaps but if I do it in such a way so that everyone smiles at the same time and thinks "that was a nice lawyer," and "that was a nice question." Then I come back to it in the closing argument and say [to the court], "well you heard it yourselves didn't you?" (Andrew)

Perry also talks about the Rambo-Bambi approach telling me:

> I would say that the most stupid thing you can do is to be aggressive or mean, or "why are you saying this?" rather, yeah, I follow a very friendly line, like, no aggressive tone at all, nothing like that. I just ask questions every now and then. They answer a lot better if they like me than if they hate me. (Perry)

Like Perry, George describes some of the reasons for using this strategy:

> I think that you get a good answer from a witness who feels secure when you ask questions, and then it's better to try and formulate them in a way so that you get what you want and the witness doesn't even notice that he is saying the things I want him to say. (George)

Such an approach, preferring to kill the plaintiff or witness with kindness rather than killing them with aggression is a strategy that all the defence lawyers I interviewed talked about using – an approach found to be useful in other interrogation situations (Alison et al., 2014). I also observed it in all of the trials I attended. I saw no instances of aggression along the lines of "going for the jugular," rather the shows of anger I saw were subtle and toned down (see Bergman Blix & Wettergren, 2015; Flower, 2016a).

The Rambo-Bambi emotion management strategy thus combines Pierce's (1995) "Rambo litigator" and "strategic friendliness" and constitutes a form of strategic emotion work for instrumental purposes. It follows a Goffmanian (1967, 1972) "line" that is friendly and combines verbal emotives – for instance by saying "I was really surprised by the witness' statements today" (similar to prosecutors' use of emotives (Törnqvist, 2017)) – with subtle nonverbal displays such as shifting in one's chair. The rule appears to be: "say it more than show it," a rule that is learned during legal education in Sweden (Flower, 2014; see also Coupland et al., 2008).[4]

This form of emotion management differs to Hochschild's (1983) theory as it is a hidden form of emotion management. The emotional goal of her theory is to make the customer relaxed, whilst the intended goal is to entice the passenger to fly with the airline again. I argue the purpose of the Rambo-Bambi emotion management strategy has another emotional layer to it. There is a Janus-face aspect at play as Rambo-Bambi has a hidden emotional and ultimate goal (cf. Dellwing, 2012). This is the dark side of emotion work – where emotional displays hide an antithetical emotional intention that deviates from the emotion rule and which should therefore be shown in another way. On the surface, the emotion being conveyed by the performer is aimed at producing a certain emotion in others, for example, a defence lawyer showing niceness which has the superficial goal of encouraging the plaintiff to feel at ease so as to freely be able to give their account of events thus ensuring the interaction flow and emotion flow of the courtroom. However, this niceness may be a "strategic niceness" (Flower, 2016b) which has the fundamental emotional goal of lulling the witness or plaintiff into a false sense of security thus achieving the ultimate goal of them giving a less credible version of events, which, in turn, may help the client's defence (see also Kilduff, Chiaburu, & Menges, 2010).

I suggest that the difference between the American "Rambo litigator" (Pierce, 1995) and the Swedish Rambo-Bambi is a difference in display rules. The emotional regime in Swedish criminal trials sets the frame for how aggression may be displayed. Both are dramatic, aggressive performances and both are in line with the "societal emotional regime" (Bergman Blix & Wettergren, 2015, p. 3).

The interactional accomplishment of Rambo-Bambi requires skill in finding the right balance between Rambo and Bambi. As Lydia says:

> It's about being able to interrogate the plaintiff and if I act unpleasantly or if I am too hard on the plaintiff then it can turn, it can go against my client so it's a balance all the time between how tough you should be. (Lydia)

Lydia points out that being too Rambo on a plaintiff may inadvertently lead to the plaintiff's version of events being viewed as *more* credible. George also describes this telling me:

> You have to be careful because it can be the complete opposite. Before you know it, witnesses gather themselves and become incredibly certain about their testimony and then you've made a mistake (…) It's like walking a tightrope. (George)

Walking this emotional tightrope is described by many of the lawyers interviewed, not least with regard to ensuring that one does not displease the court. Rambo-Bambi is thus an interactional emotion management strategy used by defence lawyers in order to "read people and see which buttons to push to get a certain reaction" as Kate says. Again, we see that this is a performance that is presented as entailing emotional reading – taking the role of other and adjusting one's approach thereafter.

We therefore see that an angry performance can convey loyalty to the client by following and thus performing the team line.

In this chapter, I have also shown that there are contrasting adversarial performances which nevertheless should work together in order for a trial to run smoothly. I have already discussed how the inappropriate performance of a defence lawyer can threaten the emotional regime of a trial – breaking the emotion and interaction rules. I will now discuss how upholding these performances and thus the social situation of a criminal trial may be threatened by underlying conflicts. In previous chapters I have discussed the tensions that are inherent in an adversarial trial regarding the presentation of competing version of events; however, there are further tensions regarding how two parts of this three-team interaction talk about each other – namely the prosecution and the defence.

Potential disruptions

By this point, the reader is aware of the importance of staying in character, how these performances are accomplished and how deviations are sanctioned. The next step is to show how a criminal trial and role performances risk disruption, not only due to the inherent adversarial aspect of two sides presenting competing versions of events and not only because of lay participants' lack of initiation into the criminal trial, but also because of underlying tensions between the legal adversaries. Whilst of course this may seem obvious with regard to the lay participants involved, my analysis shows that even the legal professionals talk about each other in antagonistic, and, at times, disparaging terms. Prosecutors and defence lawyers thus socially construct and uphold antagonistic distinctions between the different legal roles, in other words, they do "boundary work" (Gieryn, 1983). Each legal professional role is therefore associated with selected characteristics and activities that distinguish symbolic boundaries between them (see also Allen, 2001; Åkerström, 2011). This indicates that legal professionals use emotion work to ensure that these tensions are not exposed during the trial.

Defence lawyers' talk about prosecutors

I begin by presenting how defence lawyers talk about prosecutors. In my interview with Daniel, he describes a clear boundary between prosecutors and defence lawyers regarding objectivity:

> *Daniel:* Prosecutors should be objective but [defence lawyers] don't need to be (...) For me, a good prosecutor keeps to the facts (*saklig*) – a rational and pragmatic prosecutor, and of course, a competent, that is, a legally competent prosecutor, keeps to the facts (*saklig*), is professional and tries to be objective as far as possible, because that's what they should be, even if you can question whether or not they always are.
>
> *Lisa:* Do you think that they are not objective?
>
> *Daniel:* This can always be discussed. They have a duty of objectivity (...) and I am under the impression that this should even be the case after they have commenced a prosecution. That is, even during the trial they should bring forth or take into consideration any circumstances that go against them and thus, for the suspect. And, I don't want to say it, but I have understood that some prosecutors have interpreted this duty as lasting up until you commence a prosecution and [not during the trial]. Perhaps it's a question of interpretation but I am convinced that certain prosecutors when they are actually sitting [in the courtroom], then they are like this [shows being blinkered], I am completely convinced about that – they don't let go – they are not as objective as you would have hoped they would be.

Daniel's division of loyal lawyer and objective prosecutor immediately becomes the basis for an attack on prosecutors' principle performances. That is, Daniel has an expectation that for some prosecutors, their objectivity is of a subjective nature – more focused on a conviction than searching for a representative or accurate version of events. As mentioned previously in this chapter, in Sweden the prosecution's duty of objectivity continues beyond preparing the case for trial – they should remain objective even during the trial, consequently, if evidence emerges that does not support a guilty conviction, they should present it to the court. Daniel's assumption finds similarities in the U.S. where the prosecution is perceived as having a loyalty to a particular version of events – following the party line – for example, to a defendant's guilt which may remain even when they are faced with overwhelming competing evidence leading them to refuse to accept that an injustice has occurred (Bandes, 2006a).

Daniel is also talking about when one's counterpart breaks role and deviates from his or her principle performance. On such occasions, sanctions are permitted as per the emotional regime of the criminal trial. For instance, defence lawyers talk about becoming irritated with prosecutors when they are perceived as losing their objectivity, as Peter says, "you can get irritated at the other lawyers if they slip out of their role – if they do something unprofessionally – you can point it out." Törnqvist (2017, p. 317) shows, however, that prosecutors consider it to be a breach of conduct rules if defence lawyers question their objectivity during a trial. Indeed, an open attack by an adversary on one's principle performance may lead to moral outrage, although performances of one's adversary may be criticised outside the courtroom (cf. Bergman Blix & Wettergren, 2018). That is, a prosecutor questioning a defence lawyer's loyalty, or a defence lawyer questioning a prosecutor's objectivity is a damning critique leading to moral outrage in the recipient. Such face threats risk disrupting rules of etiquette – the ceremonial order – and should instead be administered backstage, not on the frontstage of the courtroom, in order to uphold the social situation and the social roles within. However, there are occasions where such open-face threats are acceptable as I will show later on in this chapter.

The depiction of prosecutors as being blinkered is also used by Andrew. He describes them as having a list of tasks to be done: bringing the case to court, presenting the case, conducting the questioning, and calling witnesses. Andrew thus presents a stereotyped view of prosecutors as bureaucrats, a view which is mentioned by the majority of lawyers I interviewed. For example, when I ask Vera if she could ever work as a prosecutor, she replies, "prosecutor? No, no, I've never been the [laughs] complaining type [laughs]. No! [Laughs]." Prosecutors are thus not only jokingly presented as being complainers but are also frequently talked about as being boring, as Lena discusses here:

> This is a bit prejudiced, not everyone is like this [laughs], but you probably think, a little bit more, that prosecutors are a bit more this, civil servant type, a little bit borin [stops herself from saying 'boring'], I mean, a bit, that it's more routine. They have lots of cases and aren't as engaged in the way that us lawyers are. (Lena)

In contrast, lawyers portray themselves as having a great deal of freedom or independence. Perry tells me that defence lawyers are, "freestanding from all authorities, all judges, all prosecutors, all police, freestanding from all other companies. We are freestanding from everything." For Perry and for many of the other lawyers I interviewed, this independence is associated with defence lawyers "protecting the people" and is a valued aspect of their profession and for some, a key reason for choosing that path.[5]

Other lawyers I spoke to mention that prosecutors do not have contact with clients; therefore, they do not have as much sensitivity or awareness of the plaintiffs and defendants' life situations. Client contact is talked about by many of the lawyers I interviewed as being something that they enjoy in their role, and one of the things that they would miss if they had worked as a prosecutor.

On top of these demands of flexibility and social skills, defence lawyers also portrayed themselves in the interviews I conducted as being the underdogs – as having a harder job to do in comparison to the prosecutor – partly because the sympathies of the court are automatically with the plaintiff. For instance, Lena tells me that, "as a defender, you are already like, sitting on the wrong side, you really have to move over the sympathies to your client whereas the prosecutor has it from the start a bit more." Indeed, prosecutors also perceive the trial as tilted in their favour whilst judges view their judicial role as partly aimed at compensating for this disparity (Bergman Blix & Wettergren, 2018, p. 146; Roach Anleu & Mack, 2017). We therefore see here that each team presents or frames their participation in the interaction differently that is, they each have a clearly defined role.

Defence lawyers also talk about prosecutors as avoiding the moral suspicion that defence lawyers face. For instance, when I ask George whether he thinks that prosecutors face questions similar to the "how can you defend a rapist" question faced by defence lawyers he replies:

> Prosecutors don't have any such worries. They dodge this moral dilemma – their job is to try and make sure that someone who they think is guilty is convicted and, for a prosecutor, that means that if they think there is a predominant likelihood, I mean, a 51 per cent possibility for a conviction then they are obligated to press charges. And that obligation has nothing to do with his [or her] private opinion, instead he does an evaluation of the evidence and then he hands it over to the court for judgement but in the eyes of the general public, you, of course, appear as a joker – the murderer's watchman or you were that person who defended that terrible rapist – they don't distinguish between the person and the crime. (George)

We see then that defence lawyers draw clear divisions between the characteristics and activities inherent in their work, in contrast to prosecutors. So, how do prosecutors talk about defence lawyers?

Prosecutors' talk about defence lawyers

Prosecutors also use boundary work in order to delineate their role from defence work. For instance, whilst prosecutors talk about defence lawyers as having the "most important role in the justice system" as a prosecutor in Bergman Blix and Wettergren's (2018, p. 50) study states, prosecutors also talk about defence lawyers as greedy, dishonourable, unscrupulous, driven by money, and the desire for success (Törnqvist, 2017, p. 359).

Thus, similar to the negative stereotypes defence lawyers associated with prosecutors as being boring bureaucrats, when prosecutors are asked if they would like to work as defence lawyers, they also draw on undesirable characteristics and activities of defence work. For instance – defence lawyers don't do anything, they just lean back, criticise, and question everything (Törnqvist, 2017). Interestingly, this is also an understanding that was echoed by the business lawyers regarding criminal lawyers I interviewed indicating that boundary work is taking place within members of the Bar Association. This boundary work thus uses a form of character attack, targeting the moral character of their adversary although it should be noted, that the competency of one's antagonist is rarely challenged.

Prosecutors, on the other hand, present themselves as honest, important cogs in democratic societies who work without consideration for their own interests (Bergman Blix & Wettergren, 2018, p. 50; Törnqvist, 2017).

There are certain similarities to be drawn here between Sweden and the U.S. A study of American prosecutors found that they did not necessarily perceive other actors in the criminal justice system as sharing their prosecutorial professional goal of attaining justice, rather the police want to clear cases, judges want to throw out cases and, defence lawyers want to get more clients (Bevis, 2009). These conflicting goals thus meant that prosecutors placed even greater demands on themselves to show respect and professionalism to others which also meant maintaining objectivity in order to construct justice (Bevis, 2009).

The boundary work of defence lawyers and prosecutors can not only entail character attacks, but it can also include criticism of role performances. For instance, Törnqvist (2017, p. 314) shows that prosecutors evaluate defence lawyers based in part on their performance in the courtroom – how they are as interactants. These performances are divided into two categories: confrontational and those more willing to come to a consensus. The first of these categories is used as a positioning tool for prosecutors to present and contrast their consensus-oriented approach which they consider to be more appropriate. We see therefore that it is not only defence lawyers, but also prosecutors who position their performances away from Rambo-lawyers. Overly zealous lawyers are portrayed by prosecutors as being overly loyal to their clients, wanting to win at all costs.

Defence lawyers are thus depicted by prosecutors as their antagonist as may be seen in the oppositional ways they talk in interviews as presented here, but also in the way in which they relate to the concept of "truth." Törnqvist (2017) writes that prosecutors talk about themselves as truthful – true to yourself and to all others as one of the prosecutors in her study describes it. They thus present loyalty to their own values near the top of the loyalty hierarchy (see Arvidson & Axelsson, 2017).

This relationship to the "truth" contrasts with the way in which defence lawyers talk about it. For instance, when I ask Sandra whether defence lawyers talk and think in terms of the "truth" she replies that she never does as "the truth is quite a vague term." Many of the other criminal lawyers I interviewed supported this, stating that it is never possible to know the true version of events, for instance, their client's intentions at the time of the crime as even the client might have been unaware of his her intentions (see Jacobson et al., 2016). Defence lawyers tend instead to talk about a client's "version of events." In this way, they are again able to use their professional role to align their loyalties with their client and, consequently, avoid having to take a personal moral standpoint as to whether someone is telling the truth or not (see Bandes, 2006a). As we have already seen, in one's professional role as defence lawyer, taking such a stand is not a part of one's role obligation.

We see that prosecutors also construct defence lawyers in an antagonist position, describing them as having qualities and characteristics that prosecutors eschew. Prosecutors' objectivity is called into question in several of the interviews I conducted, just as lawyers were accused by prosecutors of being overly zealous in defending their clients. These can be seen as the source of underlying emotions in need of management in the frontstage of the courtroom yet revealed in the backstage situation of the research interview. This leads to the question – what role does the judge play in all of this?

The judge

Judges are expected to display an impartial demeanour throughout proceedings following the judicial line of innocence until proven guilty (see Bergman Blix & Wettergren, 2018) and in my interviews with defence lawyers judges are portrayed as competent performers, appropriately upholding judicial face. The importance of this impartial exterior is talked about by Kate who says:

> Of course, it's not good if the judge shows that he or she thinks one thing or another about what is happening in the courtroom, when it comes to the case. Judges who act out and are angry at the accused because he is doing this or that can probably be seen as though they have already decided [about the case]. (Kate)

Kate goes on to tell me that judges should "not be active in the [trial] process, but should sit there and listen to both sides." We see therefore that it is not only defence lawyers who use stoneface, but also judges. Indeed, such performances of impartiality, in particular, a routine, business-like demeanour used when interacting with other courtroom participants, may, on the one hand be the "least 'emotional' of the demeanors in terms of overt emotional display, though achieving it may entail the most emotion management" (Roach Anleu & Mack, 2017, p. 168). A study of judges in Sweden finds that they pride themselves on displaying an impartial demeanour (Bergman Blix & Wettergren, 2018) and my study indicates that they are indeed perceived by defence lawyers as succeeding in this emotion management goal. The judges' contribution to interactional justice is thus to convey impartiality and the legitimacy of the court as an institution (Roach Anleu & Mack, 2017).

My interviews with defence lawyers also show that judges are not talked about as robots, but rather as emotional beings who are skilled emotional readers. Portraying judges as a non-robotic, emotional being means that judges also risk losing face if they fail in their emotion management, because, as George says, "they're only human (...) they're social beings, they don't exist in a vacuum even if they think that themselves. That's not how it is." George talks about judges presenting themselves in line with the emotional regime of law but that he himself is wise to their condition – that they are only human and thus susceptible to influence (cf. Bergman Blix & Wettergren, 2015; Maroney, 2011a, 2016). George is unusual in his position, as in contrast, we have already seen that the majority of the defence lawyers I interviewed say that they do not need to "perform" because there is no jury present to be influenced thereby implying that judges are perceived as immune to it. Many of the defence lawyers I spoke with thus present judges in terms of upholding the traditional dichotomy between emotionality and rationality. Opening up the possibility that judges are "only human" and thus possible to influence as George does here, opens up questions regarding the impartiality and objectivity of judges (Bergman Blix & Wettergren, 2015).

We see then that defence lawyers' talk portrays judges as competent performers, able to uphold their professional principle and perform loyalty to law, unlike the objectivity of prosecutors which is sometimes questioned. However, the lay judges are talked about in another manner altogether as I will now show.

Lay judges

The role of lay judges in a trial is, in some regards, somewhat ambiguous according to many of the defence lawyers I interviewed, an outlook that is reflected in other parts of society. Although lay judges take the same judicial oath as judges and are talked about as constituting an important part of democracy – representing laymen and the voice of society thereby increasing confidence and transparency in the legal system – their lack of judicial training has been a source of both praise and critique. Lay judges' political appointment is another point of contention which tends to garner criticism. They are frequently talked about as either an insignificant player in a trial, or at worst, a direct hindrance for the smooth flow of justice. Lay judges are thus portrayed as a threat to judicial face by failing to convey the impartiality integral to their role – their dramaturgical loyalty falters (Goffman, 1959). This can also be seen in terms of a failure to perform loyalty to the law which, the reader may remember, is also an aspect of the lay judges' role.

When I read through my fieldnotes, I found several examples from trials where lay judges have taken out mobile phones or diaries from their pockets or bags and looked at them during a trial. Instances of lay judges openly picking their nose are not uncommon. Both of these constitute deviations from the ceremonial order – they are impolite.

Neither is it uncommon to see lay judges deviating by openly displaying emotions, for instance, note the lay judges in the following excerpt from a murder trial:

> The female defendant is giving her version of events. She is silently crying and shaking. One of the lay judges is looking at her with very soft facial expressions, mouth slightly pouting, bottom lip jutting out slightly. She looks sympathetic or upset. One of the other lay judges is looking at the defendant with a completely different expression – shaking her head, slightly frowning, head tipped to one side. (Fieldnote)

I should add that, in this trial, the judge remained with a neutral expression throughout. In another trial for assault, the plaintiff is describing how the defendant kicked her in the stomach when she was pregnant and that she feared for her baby's life:

> One of the lay judges looks at the plaintiff with an expression I interpret as sympathetic. She has a small pout with her bottom lip sticking out a little bit. Her eyes are soft. Later on, when the defendant is giving evidence, he claims that he did not attack the plaintiff. When he says this, the lay judge draws her upper lip up, as though something smells bad. It looks like a sneer. Her whole face is involved in the movement. She also shakes her head when the defendant contradicts another claim made by the plaintiff. (Fieldnote)

During my fieldwork, not once did I see a judge check a mobile phone or a diary. Nor did I see any of them picking their nose or shaking their head. Emotional expressions, if displayed at all, tended to be far more toned down than those displayed by lay judges.

Many of the lawyers I interviewed have stories of lay judges acting inappropriately. For instance, Harry tells me that he represented a defendant in a trial where one of the lay judges started to cry before the defendant's side of the case had even been heard. Of this Harry says "that vote was lost in the trial" – he interpreted the lay judge's crying as revealing that she had already decided on the case. When I then asked Harry if it is unacceptable for lay judges to cry he told me that it was ok, but as this lay judge had only heard one side of the case "she was on thin ice." I ask Andrew whether this has ever happened to him and he replies that it has not; however, when I ask if a lay judge has ever fallen asleep during one of his trials, he begins by answering my question before launching into a discussion of the lay judge system in general. He says:

> Fallen asleep? God, yes! Fallen asleep and turned away when we have looked at forensic reports which have been a bit too gross for example. Like, when it gets to be a bit too grotesque. Unfortunately, there are those kinds of lay judge who are just killing time. There has been a lot of criticism against the lay judge system and I can agree with the critique, to a certain extent. I think, for example, for me, it feels wrong that lay judges are appointed by political parties. I think that it's so damned horrible and I see so many problems that I just want to scream on the one hand [...] I don't have any support for this but I think that it can create situations where certain political parties think that certain types of crime should have a harder punishment or whatever you call it – they want to get their party politics through in the criminal case. Luckily, they are, of course, stopped by judges. But, yeah, I see problems. (Andrew)

It should be briefly noted here that sleeping lay judges are not unknown and have even caused retrials (Palmgren, 2018). Andrew is talking not only about the problems he sees regarding the political appointment of lay judges – that they may make politically based decisions in court which is echoed by many of the lawyers I interviewed – he is also implying that lay judges may not be as capable at managing their emotions as judges – unable to look at gruesome images. This latter aspect – that lay judges are not as adept at managing their own emotions – is a theme that runs through all of the interviews I conducted and is also a shared understanding with other lawyers. For instance, lay judges are often perceived as easier to emotionally read than judge who are presented as difficult to interpret, hidden behind a façade of impartiality (see Bergman Blix & Wettergren, 2015; Roach Anleu & Mack, 2017).

This indicates that impartiality is considered by defence lawyers to be a professional accomplishment that entails not only an outward façade, but also an ability to separate one's everyday emotions from professional emotions. Andrew talks about this more, telling me:

> Judges are schooled in a way so that they are more, I mean, they look more at the objective factors, less on the subjective. Of course, there are also exceptions to this, but my position is that the judges are much better at being boring lawyers and putting the other stuff to one side whilst lay judges more easily let themselves be affected by feelings and things like that. That's my position. Then there are lay judges who have been in the game a long time and who would nearly function as judges themselves so to speak and then there are those who really go all in for their work and study in their spare time and things like that so I wouldn't say, you can't

> make sweeping statements about lay judges, but I would say that there is probably a greater tendency for lay judges to let themselves be influenced by things than the judges. (Andrew)

As Andrew says here, it is not possible to generalise about lay judges, but there appear to be shared understandings regarding incompetent lay judge performances in my interviews, in stark contrast to the glowing descriptions of judges. Lena also talks about this, saying that lay judges "are much worse at hiding what they feel and think." She also tells me:

> The worst example is when they sit and nod and agree with the closing argument. And then, if you check, then you understand that you have gotten them on your side when you see the result. It's not all lay judges but some of them are bad at it – you see on them that they think a certain thing. (Lena)

Lena continues by saying that her client was acquitted in the trial where the lay judge was nodding. She therefore interpreted the lay judge's nodding as agreement with the defence's case. Lena's experience is similar to that of Harry's crying lay judge in that both of these lawyers read the lay judge's emotional displays. Lena and Harry thus portray themselves as skilled emotional readers. Likewise, George tells me about a trial regarding child pornography where an expert witness told the court that it was possible to log in to a computer in Sweden from another country; therefore, the images found on the defendant's client's computer could have been put there by anyone. George tells me that when the expert witness was talking, he thought to himself:

> Now I know that the lay judge is thinking – he was so clear in his body language (...) and then he asked [the expert witness] like this, "so you mean that I can sit [overseas] and with the right equipment, and the right skills, I can go straight into someone's computer without it being noticeable?" "Yes" said the expert witness and then the lay judge leaned back and put his hands so [shows hands laced together behind his head] and then I felt that with that question and with that answer and that attitude, I know how he is going to vote on this case. And the case was dismissed and that's not usual, it isn't [laugh]. (George)

Because of the perceived inability of lay judges to manage their own emotions and thus their associated susceptibility to emotional influence, several of the lawyers I interviewed said that they angle part of their closing argument at the lay judges. For example, Andrew says, that he uses eye contact with the lay judges and tries to present:

> Not just dry law, rather I embellish a bit more and give examples. I mean, there are more feelings but whether or not it works? No, not always but

> if it works one time out of ten then I have everything to win don't I? (Andrew)

However, there are others who state that they do not try and manipulate or "play on the court's feelings" as Daniel says, although he also remarks that it cannot hurt to try. George says that he does not appeal to the lay judges' emotions as he knows that it is the "judge who completely steers the party afterwards" meaning that it is the judge who decides the case during deliberations. Many of the other lawyers I interviewed share this understanding – that lay judges simply agree with the judge. Indeed, lay judges overrule the judge in less than one per cent of trials in Sweden (Diesen, 2005).

An example of a criminal trial where the lay judges overruled the judge and where the lay judges' deliberations were controversial led to widespread media attention in Sweden in 2018. A court in Solna, Stockholm freed a man accused of spousal assault. The written judgement states that, as the defendant came from a good family unlike the victim, and that it was not unusual for women to lie about being assaulted and threatened, the defendant should be found not guilty (Ekot, 2018). Two of the lay judges who ruled were consequently expelled from their political party and indeed from their position as lay judges. In such instances, the lay judges have constituted a face threat to judicial face, not only within the confines of the courtroom, but also outside as such incidents tend to raise a great deal of media interest.

A second way in which the lay judge can threaten judicial face can be seen in the 2019 trial of an asylum activist – Elin Ersson. After the trial in which Ersson was convicted, it was discovered that, six months prior, one of the lay judges publicly described Ersson as a criminal thus making him incompetent to sit as a lay judge on the trial (Eidenskog, 2019, RB Kap, 1, 8a§; SFS, 1942:740). The discovery of the lay judge's comments thus led to a retrial being held and the lay judge being suspended. One of the most well-known cases of a lay judge being found incompetent to sit on the bench is seen in a high-profile case regarding organised crime in 2012 (*Södertäljemålet*) which was the most expensive trial in Sweden's history costing 208 million Swedish crowns (€19,530,980) before the retrial.

All of this raises questions regarding justice and rule of law. Retrials may lead to longer waiting times for those already waiting to stand trial which hampers the principle of immediacy in Swedish law which states that a person should have their case heard as swiftly as possible. Retrials may also lead to witnesses, plaintiffs, family members and legal professionals being subject to repeating their participation in a trial which may have been emotionally demanding. There is also a risk of damaging confidence in the legal system. Judicial face, and indeed the face of justice is threatened which may then negatively impact the public's trust in the legal system (Tyler, 2003, 2006).

We now see that judicial face can be threatened from within the team – by lay judges – akin to the way in which defence team face can be threatened by the team's lay participants – the defendant. In turn, the loss of judicial face can threaten the perceived legitimacy of a criminal trial and therefore, the perception of justice. Again, these underlying tensions must be kept below the surface on the frontstage of the courtroom.

So far in this chapter, I have shown the underlying tensions between prosecutors and defence lawyers, as well as regarding preconceptions of lay judges. All of these tensions should be managed in order for each performer to stay in character and for the trial to flow smoothly. Thus interactional justice entails a non-openly-confrontational, appropriate adversarialism. Whether this stems from the non-conflictual way of presenting Swedish society, or whether it stems from the Swedish legal system's inquisitorial roots which to a certain degree remain (with regard to the prosecutor's role in gathering evidence and compiling the case) is uncertain. However, it seems accurate to conclude that emotions play a key role in this process, and that openly adversarial performances are eschewed by both sides of the courtroom. Furthermore, underlying frictions should remain hidden. In the next section I will discuss how such threats can be managed when they arise in the courtroom.

Repairs and breaks

As we have just read, underlying tensions may threaten to disrupt the interactional flow of the criminal trial. However, situations can also arise which risk breaking the flow due to interactants losing face. In such situations, the interaction must be repaired by legal professionals managing the faces of other performers. I will now focus on the protective facework done by defence lawyers, which the reader may recall from chapter three, is aimed at saving the face of others (Goffman, 1959). I begin with the strategies the defence lawyer might use for saving the face of the judge. These are, however, fairly unusual to observe.

In one of the trials I watched, the defence lawyer clearly referred the court to read a page in the preliminary investigation but the judge misheard the page number and was therefore looking in the wrong place. The judge spent a minute or so looking for the right page and then commented that he couldn't find it to which the defence lawyer apologised for being unclear and repeated the page number again. This is a form of protective facework aimed at saving the face of a higher status individual – the judge – by providing a situated account in order to contain potential embarrassment (Goffman, 1959; M. B. Scott & Lyman, 1968). The trial is therefore able to continue without conflicts or role-breaks.[6]

However, there are (rare) occasions where the judge's face is threatened. Here are my fieldnotes from a murder trial describing this:

> It is now time for the defendant to be questioned. The judge asks the defence lawyer to begin his examination (which is procedurally incorrect, the prosecution should begin, before the defence). The defence lawyer frowns and says "I think that it is *much* better if the prosecutor asks questions first" he points with his hand and arm out in front of him. (Fieldnote)

Here, the defence lawyer points out the judge's mistake, thereby threatening the face of the judge as a legal professional who is knowledgeable of the law and the procedures to be followed. In such moments, tactful inattention is not permitted (Goffman, 1956b; Rock, 1993). Rather, this role break had to be highlighted, yet, still according to the ceremonial order and emotional order of the criminal trial: politely reprimanding in an emotionally appropriate manner.

The judge's face is also threatened in the following excerpt from a trial where a mobile phone rings (mobile phones should be switched off):

> One of the lay judges starts looking through his pockets to find his phone. The ringing continues for a while before he finally finds his phone and realizes that it's not his that is ringing. He then leans over and tells the judge that it is her phone. The defence lawyer says "I'll remember that one!" with a small smile on his face. (Fieldnote)

This smile serves as a way of reducing the interactional impact of the judge's deviation from the ceremonial order. On another trial I observed the defence lawyer question whether the judge was focused:

> The judge began proceedings by saying to the public gallery "no disagreements in the form of stupid comments or gestures." He looks at certain people sitting in the public gallery when he says this. Later on in the trial the judge is looking at the public gallery whilst the defence lawyer is speaking causing the defence lawyer to ask "are they being disruptive behind my back?" to which the judge replies "no." The judge stops looking at the gallery and looks at the defence lawyer. (Fieldnote)

The defence lawyer gives the judge a mild rule reminder in the form of a question "are they being disruptive behind my back" to subtly point out that the judge is breaking the ceremonial order – impolitely not focusing on the defence lawyer when he is speaking – and also deviating from the courtroom rules of interaction by not fulfilling his role obligations.

Whilst protective facework is used to uphold the face of judges (both in the courtroom but also in the interviews), at times aggressive facework may be used in order to attack the face of the prosecutor, in particular his or her objectivity as I introduced earlier in this chapter (Tracy & Tracy, 1998). As prosecutors have a duty of objectivity, this attack is aimed at questioning whether or not the prosecutor has strayed from his or her legal role obligations – his principle performance. I observed such a face attack towards the prosecutor in the trial with Mr Yellow Tie and the colour-coded compendium which we return to now as Mr Yellow Tie's associate – Mr Slicked Back Hair – is presenting the contents of the compendium. He begins by saying that it contains evidence which the defence team has found in the "*slasken*" [a term used to describe evidence that the prosecution has decided not to use in the case],

> Mr Slicked Back Hair says this with slightly more emphasis on the word "slasken" but still uses the same tone of voice, no louder voice, just more emphasis. He goes on to say, regarding some of the evidence that they have recovered which supports his client's version of events, "I think that it is noteworthy that the prosecutor has not included it." This is also said in the same polite tone of voice. (Fieldnote)

Here, the defence lawyer is openly attacking the face of the prosecutor by claiming that the prosecutor has not followed the duty of objectivity in presenting evidence that goes in favour of the defendant. In another trial, I observed a defence lawyer pointing out to the prosecutor that he had missed stating that the weapon his client was accused of possessing was not in working order – again pointing out the mistake of the prosecutor and thus threatening his face. Rules may be intentionally broken by the defence lawyer in such situations as the defence lawyer perceives justice as being disrupted – the prosecutor is not doing what he or she is supposed to do.[7] Again, this is a description of a potential face threat stemming from a legal error: the failure of the prosecutor to raise evidence in favour of the defendant.

On one occasion I observed the defence lawyer's face threatened by the prosecutor. The defence lawyer was reading his client's statement when the prosecutor interrupted, saying "sorry" and holding up a finger before asking the defence lawyer to read the whole statement as he was only reading that part of the statement that was to his client's advantage. Although the defence lawyer's actions were in accordance with their role obligations as per the Bar Association's (2008, p. 33) code of conduct – defence lawyers do not need to introduce facts detrimental to their client's case – it was perceived as an overly loyal act by the prosecution. An openly aggressive face threat can therefore be legitimately used against one's adversary if he or she has committed a role break, deviating from their position of objectivity ("even if the prosecutor does not take this into consideration, then the court should still consider it") or being overly loyal for instance. Such a role break also permits the display of an emotion that should otherwise remain hidden, namely irritation or annoyance.

Closing argument

My aim with this book is to show how defence lawyers accomplish their role, in particular, how they perform loyalty by focusing on how this is done in an emotionally and interactionally constraining social situation, namely the criminal trial. I show that such loyalty work demands emotion work, facework, and teamwork. Loyalty is thus an interactional accomplishment, which, together with the "objectivity work" (Jacobsson, 2008) of prosecutors and judges, upholds the social situation of a criminal trial and, in turn, constructs justice. Loyalty work should be seen as an accomplishment which is of relevance, not only to the Swedish legal sphere, but also to other jurisdictions and contexts where loyalty is required, for example in politics, journalism, social work, and education. Similarly, emotional regimes guide emotions and interactions in an array of organisations and professions thus the framework depicted here is transferable.

The Swedish context is particularly interesting due to the subtlety of these performances. Indeed, when I first began gathering material for my study of defence lawyers I was struck by the mundaneness of a trial. Where was the action? Where were the fiery cross-examinations and passionate closing speeches that I had expected? This, I thought to myself, is going to be a long (and dull) four years.

But then I began to understand that my expectations of adversarialism were linked with extravagant and conspicuous performances and in their place was a far more nuanced and subtle drama. I began to see patterns and distinctions, similarities and differences. I saw appropriate adversarialism. I saw principle performances. I saw predictable unpredictability and the strategies defence lawyers use to manage crises-in-the-moment. I saw unemotional emotionality, for instance, doing nothing was far from that, it was an intricate performance conveying meaning. I saw that a professional role, often considered to be based on legal knowledge, is also grounded in interactional competencies.

In short, I began to see the unwritten rules of interaction and the emotionality of unemotionality. I found that emotions should be displayed subtly, if at all – for instance, surprise should at times be hidden behind stoneface, whilst Rambo's anger should be restrained behind a Bambi-façade. I learned that defence lawyers should not stand out or indeed, stand up. Legal principles should be performed at all times and failure to do so leaves one open to legitimate face attacks. Another rule of engagement is that actions that can be perceived as impolite, such as cross-examinations, should be explained beforehand in order to reduce the risk of inappropriate emotions. These are all rules that are learned through an implicit process of what I have termed, professional emotional socialisation.

In this book, I have therefore shown that the role of defence lawyer entails emotional and dramaturgical challenges. Defence lawyers comprise a professional group that may face moral suspicion, distressed clients, unforeseeable situations, disturbing evidence, and emotional plaintiffs – all of which should be managed in a proper and appropriate manner, suitable to the overarching regime. The emotional regime of law is aimed, not only at stifling emotions' influence but also at ensuring the flow of interaction. It consists of both an emotional order (normative emotions) and an interaction order (normative interactions) with associated ceremonial order (etiquette). This framework ensures the law's protection from emotion's influence by rationalising and subduing emotions and assisting the smooth flow of justice by providing the rules of interaction. Dramatic and courteous subtlety are thus central in the theatre of the Swedish courtroom. Order in the courtroom therefore demands interactional order, ceremonial order and emotional order. These orders simultaneously and often inseparably, sustain, shape, and enable the performances of legal professionals. This is learnt through a process of professional emotional socialisation. Defence lawyers therefore construct and perform their formal, explicitly outlined legal responsibilities by negotiating informal, implicit professional and social expectations whilst simultaneously ensuring that performances remain appropriate to the emotionally rigid and interactionally strict emotional regime. They make sense of their work by using emotional accounts in particular when faced with moral outrage or for finding motivation for continuing in a role filled with losses.

Defence lawyers' loyalty performances work together with other principle performances: objective prosecutor and impartial judge in order to uphold the definition of the situation: a criminal trial. These performances, in turn, are tailored to the stage on which they are performed but risk disruption due to underlying boundaries and tensions which should be managed.

Central to the role of defence lawyer is the construction of the defence team which is aimed at ensuring that the client receives fair representation. This teamwork is an emotional and interactional accomplishment which centres on the defence lawyer's performance of loyalty. The defence team joins behind a united front and a shared reality, an accomplishment that sees defence lawyers guiding the performance, in particular, the client's role within, and ensuring that the team performance stays on track. The defence lawyer's role thus encompasses preparing clients for the ensuing co-ordinated conflict of the criminal trial with its inherent face threats and uncertainty.

The defence team is readily recognised in the Swedish courtroom as the defence lawyer and defendant sit next to each other thereby signalling that they are a team, a symbol which is supported by other tie-signs such as making or avoiding eye contact, writing notes to each other and exchanging comments. This close proximity may, at times, make it is easier for the defence lawyer – the director – to immediately manage their client's and thus team performance; however, a considerable part of direction takes place prior to the trial, in the form of expectation management. Expectation management is a crucial part of this teamwork and involves preparing one's teammate for the ritual of a criminal trial. Many of the defence lawyers I interviewed perceived defendants as being unsure not only of what their role as defendant in a trial entails, but also, what their defence lawyer will actually do during the trial. This expectation management involves describing what the various legal professionals in the courtroom will do and, importantly, how they will do it. Expectation management is aimed at reducing the risk of the client "flooding out" (Goffman, 1967) during proceedings which may have adverse consequences – for instance, revealing something regarding the client's character that the defence team would have preferred to stay hidden. This also reduces the risk of interactions, such as cross-examinations, being perceived as face threats. It is therefore a way of managing future inappropriate or unwanted emotions. Once again, expectation management is a way of conveying loyalty to the client.

A central aspect of this expectation management entails explaining the meaning of doing nothing. As we have now seen, doing nothing – stoneface – is actually doing something, actively pulling attention towards or away from facts presented in the courtroom (S. Scott, 2017). Such factwork using dramatic productions and reductions building up or undermining facts – both legal facts and emotional facts – are accomplished using bodywork and props and are an integral part of the defence lawyer's work. Accomplishing stoneface is thus an invisible emotion rule and can be used both as a form of collective facework aimed at protecting team face, but also in order to uphold the lawyer's own professional lawyer face. However, if the client does not know the underlying meaning being conveyed, doing nothing risks being taken to be just that.

Expectation management is thus aimed at building the defence team to ensure they present a unified front and to ensure that the client is aware of the rules of interaction. Collective facework strategies used by the defence lawyer are aimed at upholding this team face. For instance, defence lawyers may use vicarious facework, saving their client's face as a form of collective facework in situations where the client – the defendant – is unable to save his or her own face.

It is the defence team which arguably includes the biggest threat to the emotional regime of the criminal trial, namely the defendant. Although a trial is inherently a face threat for the defendant, threatening his or her social standing, threats to the defence team can also come from within the defence team. Such internal face threats to the version of events and united front the defence team is attempting to portray means that a defence lawyer is always on his or her toes – should always be ready to manage their client's faux pas. The source of threat may be associated with the type of strategy used to manage the face attack, with internal face attacks often dramatically reduced. However, the manner in which external face threats arising from outside the team are managed may be more of a reflection of the team line the defence team performance is attempting to uphold.

The defence lawyer's role is therefore to protect and save the face of the defendant in a social situation which is an inherent face threat to defendant face. This is made more complex due to the criminal trial being a scene of predictable unpredictability. The defence lawyer can never know with certainty what will happen next: an expert witness may change his or her testimony, the plaintiff may come with new details or one's own client may react angrily to evidence presented. The defence lawyer can never know what "the fatal question" may be that risks unleashing a face threat. Defence lawyers are consequently expected to retain a façade of stonefaced calm in such moments of crisis, conveying an impression of control and composure in a demanding situation.

Defence lawyers provide a voice to the defendant – they constitute a teammate who can package the defendant's story into legalese and represent the client's best interests. A teammate who will loyally stand by you, irrespective who you are or what you are accused of. A teammate whose ability to stay in character is strong, but who may, on occasion, let their lawyer face slip, revealing a glimpse of the undercurrent of emotions beneath the surface, seeping forth in a blink or a sigh.

Lawyer face involves a process of professionalisation, rationalisation, and thus unemotionalisation as reflected in their emotion talk. Everyday emotions become professional emotions. Emotion rules contextualise and hierarchise the appropriateness of emotions, for instance, irritation towards a client may be shown in the backstage context of the lawyer-client meeting but should not be displayed during the frontstage criminal trial performance. Disliking a client should not interfere with one's official duties; however, liking a client is an acceptable motivation to work just that little bit harder. Emotional savviness is key. Relatedly, defence lawyers present themselves as emotional readers, as being able to interpret how performances are received and as being able to manipulate performances in order to achieve instrumental goals beneficial to the client.

Linked to this, defence lawyers should also have empathy in their emotional toolbox: relational empathy is used to build the defence team whilst preparatory empathy is used to build the case. Empathy should only be sparked by legitimate triggers and it can be strategically directed in others, such as the judges. Defence lawyers' empathy talk presents it as a useful cognitive tool with affective empathy talked about as unprofessional. Their empathy talk thus upholds the false division between rationality and emotionality.

By analysing what it is that is sanctioned by the emotional supervisor on hand – the judge – I have set out the implicit rules being enforced and shown that performances should remain subtle. This is exemplified by showing how anger should be performed in order to follow the rules of the criminal trial. Courtroom performances are, however, not only externally monitored, they are also self-monitored with deviations leading to feelings of shame. This leads to the conformity to rules and the reproduction of non-theatrical theatrical performances.

The ways in which loyalty is invoked and practically accomplished are discussed and I find that different loyalties demand different emotional performances with switches in loyalty layers visible in micro-expressions and subtle gestures. Throughout this book I have also attempted to unpack cultural preconceptions regarding defence lawyers by providing possible explanations for these assumptions.

The defence lawyers' performance is therefore a multi-faceted, emotionally nuanced task demanding management of lawyer face, defendant face, and team face along with the face, and emotions of others. Each of these faces may have different emotion rules to be followed, thereby calling for emotional dexterity and interactional deftness in the professional toolbox of defence lawyers. This is not least due to the inherent adversarial aspect of a criminal trial which brings with it uncertainty, spontaneity, face threats and the constant risk of embarrassment. The criminal trial should consequently be seen as a theatre of competing realities and performances rather than character attacks, and a scene which inherently demands the dramaturgical and emotional presentation of various faces – both legal professionals and lay participants.

This book provides further support for the argument that emotions need to be managed in many different organisations, institutions and workplaces, without there being a direct link to making profit as Hochschild (1983) has been presented as focusing upon. Emotions can therefore have an exchange value in the form of creating or contributing to justice (Addison, 2017; Callahan & McCollum, 2002; Wouters, 1989). I bring forth the interactional side of emotion work which has previously focused on either one's own emotions or the emotions of other and present it in terms of "interactional emotion management." Relatedly, I extend Hochschild's (1983) work to show how emotion work may entail managing both oneself and other not just into an emotion, but into a specific emotion norm, as Hochschild (1983) indicates but does not fully develop.

After observing many trials, I argue that it is the subtlety of the theatre therein, and the emotional and professional socialisation leading to the normalization of one's everyday role performance that leads to the denial of the use of "emotional ploys" (Thelin, 2001, p. 86) in Swedish criminal trials as I mentioned in the introduction of this book. The performances are so muted as to be almost silent, so ingrained as to be taken-for-granted.

Loyalty is a central aspect of many professional roles and of many types of teamwork. My argument is that professional loyalty guides expectations, obligations, and performances. The doctor may need to display loyalty to the patient – ensuring that the patient's best interests are upheld. The teacher should show loyalty to the student – ensuring that the student receives suitable education. Everyday emotions should be managed in order to uphold one's professional role and organisational position. The performance of professional loyalty is probably accomplished in these professions in similar ways to defence lawyers who use shared rules, expectations and obligations as a resource for the management of feelings and emotions (Smith & Kleinman, 1989). By highlighting these emotion work and facework strategies, it is possible to see that defence lawyers face similar problems both within the profession and in relation to other professions.

Whilst my focus has been on the criminal trial, I argue that these findings are most likely of relevance to many other professional settings which demand that emotions are hierarchised, rationalised, neutralised, and transformed in delicate discussions, meeting, or negotiations. If the emotional regime determines whether an individual is performing appropriately and sanctioned accordingly, then we can see equivalent mechanisms in place in many organisations and contexts: schools, hospitals and prisons, politics, academia and business. Professions such as police officers, social workers, medical professionals, and members of the clergy should all ensure that their performance of a legal, ethical, or moral principle remains emotionally and socially appropriate. Teamwork is also required in many of these professions where sensitive and crucial negotiations take place demanding competent role performances wherein subtle gestures may be pivotal. The mundaneness of this everyday work in actuality conceals a cornucopia of co-ordinated action enabling the smooth flow of interaction.

Implications

This book has several practical implications. Firstly, it indicates that many defendants have inaccurate expectations of a criminal trial. This is important as studies show that courtroom experiences influence how plaintiffs, witnesses and defendants perceive themselves to have been treated by the courts, with perceptions of fair treatment increasing their sense of justice being served (Roach Anleu & Mack, 2017; Thelin, 2001, pp. 62; Westlund & Eriksson, 2013). This gap between expectation and reality can be bridged by making not just the roles, but also the *performances* of each of the courtroom's actors clear as well as the associated guiding principles of the legal system (cf. Thelin, 2001, pp. 116–117). This can also combat lay participants perceiving a trial as insulting or offensive. Whilst a criminal trial inherently involves face threats, I suggest that explaining the "rules of the game" may help towards face threats being understood as an intrinsic aspect of the interaction, rather than a character attack.

It is therefore necessary for defendants to be better informed as to what will actually happen during a trial, not just procedurally and practically, but interactionally and emotionally. This, in turn, contributes towards "procedural justice"[8] being achieved. Procedural justice thus includes interactional justice.

Moving to the practical implications for legal education, this study supports previous research I have conducted showing that emotion management is not discussed on law programs and indicates that emotion work and facework are forms of professional and emotional socialisation that are learned informally and in action (Boon, 2005, p. 229; Cahill, 1999; Flower, 2014). My study suggests that learning these strategies as part of one's legal training in law school may ease the transition the classroom to the courtroom, thus reducing uncertainty regarding expectations of one's role performance. Indeed, in other countries, professions with close client contact as well as high demands on professionalism and social distance require training in interpersonal skills including nonverbal communication in order to be certified (Robinson, 2006). Empathy training for legal professionals is also an important aspect of this.

Not only will this reduce uncertainty, but it will provide inexperienced lawyers with information regarding their role performance. This is crucial as uncertainty regarding how one's job should be done risks leading to burnout, which is characterised by exhaustion, cynicism and inefficacy (Maslach, Schaufeli, & Leiter, 2001). Burnout is also a risk factor in jobs where there are high levels of role conflict, as may be the case with defence lawyers who face competing loyalties.

This leads to another of this book's implications for the lawyering profession – a key aspect in preventing burnout is ensuring that there are buffer groups providing social support and "fun at the office," which, as we have now seen, the defence lawyers in this study talk about as being vital for their everyday work. This book therefore highlights the importance of creating a supportive atmosphere where colleagues can talk about mistakes and ask for advice. I suggest this is particularly important in a profession associated with high levels of accomplishment.

Relatedly, studies from the U.S. have shown certain negative consequences of working in the legal profession such as depression and depressive symptoms (for example, suicidal thoughts, appetite loss, and sleeping difficulty) as well as anxiety (see Bergin & Jimmieson, 2013 for an overview). As attempting to cope with stressful situations by covering up negative emotions can have negative health consequences (Petrie, Booth, & Baumeister, 1998) and working with clients' traumatic experiences has been found to lead to symptoms of post-traumatic stress disorder, depression, and burnout (Levin et al., 2011), legal professionals are in the risk zone for a number of psychosocial and psychological problems. For instance, American attorneys have been found to experience problematic drinking at a higher rate than other professional population and have a higher occurrence of mental health distress (Krill, Johnson, & Albert, 2016). Although the health consequences of working as a legal professional are beyond the scope of this book, they may nevertheless constitute an important facet of the defence lawyer's role. The findings presented here may be a step towards understanding some of the problems faced by this profession.

Regarding my contribution to the lawyering profession, McMahon (2006) warns that the evident decline in professionalism in the American courtroom in the form of aggressive lawyering and discourteous behaviour risks leading to the public becoming sceptical of criminal trials. A similar risk could arise in Sweden if performances become more Rambo than Bambi. It is therefore important to ensure that civility is maintained. This can either be accomplished by a more active judicial role in the sanctioning process or by explicit guidelines for lawyers' performances.

The findings and conclusions of this study should therefore not be seen as context specific, rather the conceptual insights and theoretical developments might be applicable to a number of relevant contexts. Indeed, it has been my aim to indicate that the courtroom can be seen as society in miniature. The mechanisms and interactions at play in the courtroom are also taking place in society at large wherever loyalty and teamwork are on display, even though details and circumstances vary.

Where do we go from here?

I suggest that the ethical component of many professions adds an extra dimension to the emotional labour they should perform (see also Harris, 2002). Many of the status professions mentioned earlier are seen to be striving for some greater good; therefore, their emotions are exchanged for a higher cause: medical care, knowledge, inner peace, or justice. This places emotional demands on the person performing these roles as they are not just performing a role, they are performing a guiding societal principle or value (see Törnqvist, 2017). The consequence of such demands is an area of important future research.

This book can also be used as a basis for future comparative studies. Emotions can have differing levels of importance in different emotional regimes, for example, consider the importance of shame in different cultures. Or in the case at hand, consider the role of anger in the courtroom. This raises questions regarding how principle performances are accomplished both within the same legal culture but also between legal cultures (Church, 1985). In this book I show that, when it comes to courtrooms, the feeling rule may permit anger; however, there are varying display rules outlining how much anger may be shown and in what way (Hochschild, 1983). For example in the United States, anger may be shown in the form of judicial bench-slaps and other outbursts (Maroney, 2012). The Swedish courtroom sees a far more restrained display rule (Flower, 2016a, 2016b). A deeper exploration of the socio-cultural embedding of work that influence or alter the appearance of emotions and the emotion rules utilised is therefore of import (Sieben & Wettergren, 2010, p. 11).

We have seen in international research that juries might be influenced by defence lawyers, and we see in my book that there are strategies used by defence lawyers when representing their clients. This prompts the question: does the defence lawyer's performance influence the judges' deliberations?

One of the findings in this study was the preconceptions that legal professionals have regarding each other which could represent an underlying tension in need of management. I suggest that addressing these tensions by enabling communication and perhaps even co-operation between these adversaries could lead to a greater understanding as to the role obligations and performances attached.

The role of lay judges in Swedish trials has shown to be a somewhat controversial one amongst legal professionals in this study. Whilst my findings represent only a very small sample of the profession, they nevertheless indicate further tensions in need of management and indeed, suggest dissatisfaction with certain aspects of the current legal system in Sweden. Further investigation is necessary in order to explore whether this study reflects a more general attitude in the legal profession and society. It is also of interest to explore other possible options, such as a jury system or the abolishment of the political appointments of lay judges.

With the growing interest in criminal trials being live reported in the form of live updates in online newspapers and tweets, this raises questions regarding how this impacts on the performances given in the courtroom. As I noted in the introduction of this book, medialised depictions of criminal trials may provide an inaccurate picture (Barthe et al., 2013; see also Eriksson, 2016; Pollack, 2001). Again, these are areas for more exploration.

Another interesting aspect of future research is how the various layers of loyalty we have in our lives are managed and performed. Does the performance of personal loyalty differ to that of professional loyalty?

Future research should also focus on female lawyers (Epstein, 1981; Menkel-Meadow, 1985; Spencer & Podmore, 1986). In particular, the consequence of having multiple emotional roles and competing loyalties, as well as exploring the possible obstacles for female lawyers becoming partners at law firms and differences in wages are important areas in need of detailed research (Wahlberg, 2017; Wharton & Erickson, 1993).

Wherever we go from here, we can now go forth with a more detailed understanding of the role of loyalty work in interactional justice.

Notes

1 Whilst it could be argued that the judge and the prosecution belong on the same team – the state – I would counter-argue that whilst they both represent the State, they nevertheless have separate responsibilities and tasks. The prosecution gathers evidence and presents it to the judges who then decide whether the evidence presented is sufficient for a conviction.
2 Bandes (2006b, p. 45) describes how the "habitual detachment" of seasoned criminal lawyers may lead to cross-examinations being experienced as brutal by those on the receiving end.
3 Of course, sometimes Bambi is just Bambi, that is, sometimes there is no underlying instrumental gain from being kind and polite. Many of the defence lawyers discuss how difficult a trial can be for plaintiffs, defendants, and witnesses; therefore, part of the role of legal professionals is to make the process as pain-free as possible.
4 I suggest that an explanation for this unofficial rule is based on the official principle of orality – that all evidence must be orally presented at trial – therefore the emotional expression of an emotion would not be included in the official proceedings unlike a spoken expression.
5 Prosecutors also present independence as a "core professional value" (Bergman Blix & Wettergren, 2018, p. 52); however, it is presented as a double-edged sword: independence can also bring with it increased surveillance, for instance, from the media, the courts, and the victims.

6 Prosecutors can also perform facework to save the face of the judge, for example when a judge is unable to get a defendant to leave the courtroom, the prosecutor may discretely assist in this process (Bergman Blix & Wettergren, 2015).
7 Another example of this can be seen in one of the largest trials ever held in Sweden – "the trial of the lone sailor" – a drug-smuggling trial which lasted over 70 days. The prosecution and defence team accused each other of breaching their juridical positions. The defence team accused the prosecution of not being objective - of throwing a "stink bomb" by not revealing all the evidence to which the prosecution countered by stating that the defence team were throwing "smoke grenades" to detract attention from the evidence (Wahlberg, 2012; Öster, 2012). All of this should nevertheless remain in accordance with the ceremonial order of the criminal trial, maintaining politeness and courtesy.
8 "Procedural justice" states that if "people view compliance with the law as appropriate because of their attitudes about how they should behave, they will voluntarily assume the obligation to follow legal rules… [and if they] regard legal authorities as more legitimate, they are less likely to break any laws, for they will believe that they ought to follow all of them" (Tyler, 2006, pp. 5–6).

References

Abrams, K., & Keren, H. (2010). Who's Afraid of Law and the Emotions? *Minnesota Law Review*, *94*(6), 1997–2074.

Addison, M. (2017). Overcoming Arlie Hochschild's Concepts of the "Real" and "False" Self by Drawing on Pierre Bourdieu's Concept of Habitus. *Emotion, Space and Society*, *23*(1), 9–15.

Adelswärd, V. (1989). Defendents' Interpretations of Encouragements in Court: The Construction of Meaning in an Institutionalized Context. *Journal of Pragmatics*, *13*(1), 741–749.

Adelswärd, V., Aronsson, K., & Linell, P. (1988). Discourse of Blame: Courtroom Construction of Social Identity from the Perspective of the Defendant. *Semiotica*, *71*(3/4), 261–284.

Ahmed, S. (2004). *The Cultural Politics of Emotion*. New York: Routledge.

Åkerström, M. (1997). Waiting – A Source of Hostile Interaction in an Emergency Clinic. *Qualitative Health Research*, 7(4), 504–520.

Åkerström, M. (2011). Slaps, Punches, Pinches – But not Violence: Boundary-Work in Nursing Homes for the Elderly. *Symbolic Interaction*, *25*(4), 515–536.

Åklagarmyndigheten. (2014). Riksåklagarens riktlinjer: Etiska riktlinjer för anställda i åklagarväsendet. Decided 17th June 2014.

Åklagarmyndigheten. (2017). Åklagarmyndighetens Årsredovisning. Retrieved from https://www.aklagare.se/globalassets/dokument/planering-och-uppfoljning/arsredovisningar/arsredovisning-2017.pdf

Åklagarmyndigheten. (2018). The Role of the Prosecutor. Retrieved from https://www.aklagare.se/en/the-legal-process/the-role-of-the-prosecutor/preliminary-investigation/police-or-prosecutor/

Alison, L., Alison, E., Noone, G., Elntib, S., Waring, S., & Christiansen, P. (2014). The Efficacy of Rapport-Based Techniques for Minimizing Counter-Interrogation Tactics Amongst a Field Sample of Terrorists. *American Psychological Association*, *20*(4), 421–430.

Allen, D. (2001). Narrating Nursing Jurisdiction: "Atrocity Stories" and "Boundary Work". *Symbolic Interaction*, *24*(1), 75–103.

Althin, P. (1994). Om retorik i brottmålsprocessen. In M. Mellqvist & M. Persson (Eds.), *Retorik och rätt: sett genom tio författares ögon* (pp. 219–227). Uppsala: Iustus Förlag AB.

Ambos, K. (2003). International Criminal Procedure: "Adversarial," "Inquisitorial" or Mixed? *International Criminal Law Review*, *3*(1), 1–37.

American Bar Association. (2018, 31 July). Annual 2018: Why Women Leave the Law – and What We Can Do About It. Retrieved from https://www.americanbar.org/news/abanews/aba-news-archives/2018/07/annual_2018_why_wom/

American Bar Association's Criminal Justice Standards for the Defense Function. (2016). American Bar Associations Criminal Justice Standards for the Defense Function. Retrieved from https://www.americanbar.org/groups/criminal_justice/standards/DefenseFunctionFourthEdition-TableofContents/

Anderson, E. (1999). *Code of the Street: Decency, Violence and the Moral Life of the Inner City*. New York: W. W. Norton & Company Ltd.

Andersson, C. V. (2015). Svenska åklagare och advokater i storbråk. *Dagens Nyheter*. Retrievedfromhttp://www.dn.se/nyheter/sverige/svenska-aklagare-och-advokater-i-storbrak/

Archer, D. (2011a). Cross-Examining Lawyers, Facework and the Adversarial Courtroom. *Journal of Pragmatics*, *43*(1), 3216–3230.

Archer, D. (2011b). Facework and Im/Politeness Across Legal Contexts: An Introduction. *Journal of Politeness Research*, 7(1), 1–19.

Argyle, M. (1974). *Bodily Communication*. London: Methuen.

Argyle, M., Alkema, F., & Gilmour, R. (1971). The Communication of Friendly and Hostile Attitudes by Verbal and Non-Verbal Signals. *European Journal of Social Psychology*, *1*(3), 385–402.

Aronsson, K., Jönsson, L., & Linell, P. (1987). The Courtroom Hearing as a Middle Ground: Speech Accommodation by Lawyers and Defendants. *Journal of Language and Social Psychology*, *6*(2), 99–115.

Arvidson, M., & Axelsson, J. (2014). Lojalitetens sociala former – Om lojalitet och arbetsliv. *Arbetsmarknad & Arbetsliv*, *20*(1), 55–64.

Arvidson, M., & Axelsson, J. (2017). Exploring Self-Loyalty in the Contest of Social Acceleration: Theorising Loyalties as Emotions and Resistance. *Journal of Political Power*, *10*(2), 133–148.

Ashforth, B. E., & Humphrey, R. H. (1993). Emotional Labour in Service Roles: The Influence of Identity. *Academy of Management Review*, *18*(1), 88–115.

Ashforth, B. E., & Humphrey, R. H. (1995). Emotion in the Workplace: A Reappraisal. *Human Relations*, *48*(2), 97–125.

Asp, P. (2012). The Prosecutor in Swedish law. *Crime and Justice*, *41*(1), 141–165.

Association, S. B. (2008). *Code of Professional Conduct for Members of the Swedish Bar Association*. Stockholm: Swedish Bar Association.

Australian Bar Association (ABA). (2018). Barristers' Conduct Rules. Retrieved from https://www.nswbar.asn.au/circulars/2010/feb/rules.pdf

Australian Bar Association (ABA). (2019). What Is the Bar? Retrieved from https://austbar.asn.au/for-the-community/what-is-the-bar

Averill, J. (1982). *Anger and Aggression: An Essay on Emotion*. New York: Springer-Verlag.

Averill, J. (1994). Emotions Unbecoming and Becoming. In P. Ekman & R. J. Davidson (Eds.), *The Nature of Emotion: Fundamental Questions* (pp. 265–269). New York: Oxford University Press.

Baker, C. D. (2002). *Ethnomethodological Analyses of Interviews*. Thousand Oaks: SAGE Publications.

Bakken, J., & Graver, H. P. (2013). Juss og retorikk – innledning. In J. Bakken & H. P. Graver (Eds.), *Juss, Språk och Retorik* (pp. 11–18). Bergen: Fagbokforlaget.

Ball, D. (1994). *Theater Tips and Strategies for Jury Trials*. Chicago, IN: National Institute for Trial Advocacy.

Bamberg, M. (1997). Language, Concepts and Emotions: The Role of Language in the Construction of Emotions. *Language Sciences*, *19*(4), 309–340.

Bandes, S. (1996). Empathy, Narrative, and Victim Impact Statements. *University of Chicago Law Review, 63*(2), 361–412.

Bandes, S. (1999a). Introduction to The Passions of Law. In S. Bandes (Ed.), *The Passions of Law* (pp. 1–16). New York: New York University Press.

Bandes, S. (Ed.) (1999b). *The Passions of Law*. New York: New York University Press.

Bandes, S. (2006a). Loyalty to One's Convictions: The Prosecutor and Tunnel Vision. *Howard Law Journal, 49*(2), 475–494.

Bandes, S. (2006b). Repression and Denial in Criminal Lawyering. *New York Law School Clinical Research Institute Paper, 09/19*(16).

Bandes, S. (2009). Empathetic Judging and the Rule of Law. *Cardozo Law Review De Novo, 1*(1), 133–148.

Bandes, S. (2015a). Empathy and Article III: Judge Weinstein, Cases and Controversies. *DePaul Law Review, 64*(1), 317–339.

Bandes, S. (2015b). Remorse and Criminal Justice. *Emotion Review, 8*(1), 14–19. DOI: 10.1177/1754073915601222, 1–6.

Bandes, S. (2017). Compassion and the Rule of Law. *International Journal of Law in Context, 13*(2), 184–196.

Bandes, S., & Salerno, J. M. (2014). Emotion, Proof and Prejudice: The Cognitive Science of Gruesome Photos and Victim Impact Statements. *Arizona State Law Journal, 46*(4), 1003–1056.

Barbalet, J. M. (1996). Social Emotions: Confidence, Trust and Loyalty. *International Journal of Sociology and Social Policy, 16*(9/10), 75–96.

Barbalet, J. M. (2001). *Emotion, Social Theory and Social Structure: A Macrosociological Approach*. Wiltshire: Cambridge University Press.

Barbalet, J. M. (2002). Introduction: Why Emotions are Crucial. In J. Barbalet (Ed.), *Emotions and Sociology* (pp. 1–9). Oxford: Blackwell.

Barrett Cox, A. (2016). Correcting Behaviors and Policing Emotions: How Behavioral Infractions Become Feeling-Rule Violations. *Symbolic Interaction, 39*(3), 484–503.

Barthe, E. P., Leone, M. C., & Lateano, T. A. (2013). Commercializing Success: The Impact of Popular Media on the Career Decisions and Perceptual Accuracy of Criminal Justice Students. *Teaching in Higher Education, 18*(1), 13–26.

Bauman, Z. (1989). *Auschwitz och det moderna samhället*. Göteborg: Daidalos.

Becker, H. (1963). *Outsiders: Studies in the Sociology of Deviance*. New York: The Free Press.

Bentelius, L., & Agneklev, K. (1998). *God Advokatsed*. Stockholm: Advokatförlaget.

Berger, P., & Luckmann, T. (1966). *The Social Construction of Reality*. London: The Penguin Press.

Bergin, A. J., & Jimmieson, N. L. (2013). Explaining Psychological Distress in the Legal Profession: The Role of Overcommitment. *International Journal of Stress Management, 20*(2), 134–161.

Bergman Blix, S. (1996). Emotional Participation: The Use of the Observer's Emotions as a Methodological Tool When Studying Professional Stage Actors Rehearsing a Role for the Stage. *Nordic Theatre Studies, 21*, 29–38.

Bergman Blix, S. (2010). *Rehearsing Emotions: The Process of Creating a Role for the Stage*. Stockholm: Universitetsservice.

Bergman Blix, S., & Wettergren, Å. (2014). The Emotional Labour of Gaining and Maintaining Access to the Field. *Qualitative Research, 15*(6), 688–704. DOI: 10.1177/1468794114561348, 1–17.

Bergman Blix, S., & Wettergren, Å. (2015). A Sociological Perspective on Emotions in the Judiciary. *Emotion Review, 8*(1), 32–37. DOI: 10.1177/1754073915601226, 1–6.

Bergman Blix, S., & Wettergren, Å. (2018). *Professional Emotions in Court*. Abingdon: Routledge.

Bergman Blix, S., & Wettergren, Å. (2019). The Emotional Interaction of Judicial Objectivity. *Onati Socio-Legal Series*. Retreived from http://ssrn.com/abstract=3364275

Bevis, E. S. (2009). *Producing Justice: Prosecutors' Perceptions of their Work*. Paper Presented at the American Sociological Association Annual Meeting, San Francisco.

Bies, R. J., & Moag, J. S. (1986) Interactional Justice: Communication Criteria of Fairness. In B. Sheppard (Ed.), *Research on Negotiation in Organizations* (pp. 43–55). Greenwich: JAI Press.

Billig, M. (1991). *Ideology and Opinions: Studies in Rhetorical Psychology*. London: SAGE Publications Ltd.

Bitsch, A. (2018a). The Micro-Politics of Emotions in Legal Space: An Autoethnography About Sexual Violence and Displacement in Norway. *Gender Place and Culture: A Journal of Feminist Geography*, *25*(10), 1514–1532.

Bitsch, A. (2018b). *Voldtektens geografi: En studie av den rettslige forvaltningen av seksuelt medborgerskap i Norge*. (Philosophiae Doctor), Universitetet i Oslo, Oslo.

Björk, M. (2011). Känslokontroll i kritiska situationer: Mikrosociologiska perspektiv på modernt polisarbete. In B. Larsson & O. Engdahl (Eds.), *Social kontroll – övervakning, disciplinering och självreglering* (pp. 204–218). Malmö: Liber.

Blackstone, W. (1844). *Commentaries on the Laws of England* (21st ed.). London: Sweet, Maxwell, Stevens & Norton.

Bladini, M. (2013). *I objektivitetens sken: en kritisk granskning av objektivitetsideal, objektivitetsanspråk och legitimeringsstrategier i diskurser om dömande i brottmål*. Göteborg: Makadam.

Blomkvist, C. (1987). *Försvararen: Handledning med några kritiska synpunkter på brottmålsförfarandet*. Göteborg: Esselte Sudium Akademiförlaget.

Blumberg, A. (1967). The Practice of Law as a Confidence Game. *Law and Society Review*, *1*(2), 15–40.

Blumer, H. (1959). *Symbolic Interactionism*. Englewoods Cliff, NJ: Prentice-Hall.

Board, B. S. (2019). *The Bar Standards Board Handbook* (3rd ed.). Bar Standards Board.

Boon, A. (2005). From Public Service to Service Industry: The Impact of Socialisation and Work on the Motivation and Values of Lawyers. *International Journal of the Legal Profession*, *12*(2), 229–260.

Boon, A., & Levin, J. (1999). *The Ethics and Conduct of Lawyers in England and Wales*. London: Hart Publishing.

Booth, T. (2012). "Cooling Out" Victims of Crime: Managing Victim Participation in the Sentencing Process in a Superior Sentencing Court. *Australian & New Zealand Journal of Criminology*, *45*(2), 214–230.

Borgström, C. (2011). *Advokaten i Brottmålsprocessen*. Stockholm: Norstedts Juridik AB.

Bornstein, B. H., & Wiener, R. L. (2009). Emotion and the Law: A Field Whose Time Has Come. In B. H. Bornstein & R. L. Weinstein (Eds.), *Emotion and the Law. Nebraska Symposium on Motivation* (Vol. 56, pp. 1–12). New York: Springer.

Boszormenyi-Nagy, I., & Spark, G. (1984). *Invisible Loyalties, Reciprocity in Intergenerational Family Therapy*. New York: Brunner/Mazel.

Braithwaite, J. (1989). *Crime, Shame and Reintegration*. Cambridge: Cambridge University Press.

Brodherson, M., McGee, L., & Pires dos Reis, M. (2017). Women in Law Firms. Retrieved from https://www.mckinsey.com/~/media/mckinsey/featured%20insights/gender%20equality/women%20in%20law%20firms/women-in-law-firms-final-103017.ashx

Brunero, S., Lamont, S., & Coates, M. (2010). A Review of Empathy Education in Nursing. *Nursing Inquiry*, *17*(1), 65–74.

Burkitt, I. (2002). Complex Emotions: Relations, Feelings and Images in Emotional Experiences. In J. Barbalet (Ed.), *Emotions and Sociology* (pp. 151–168). Oxford: Blackwell Publishing.

Burns, T. (1992). *Erving Goffman*. London: Routledge.

Cahill, S. E. (1999). Emotional Capital and Professional Socialization: The Case of Mortuary Science Students (and Me). *Social Psychological Quarterly*, *62*(2), 101–116.

Cainaniello, M. (2011). First Decisions on the Admission of Evidence at ICC Trials. *Journal of International Criminal Justice*, *9*(2), 385–410.

Callahan, J. L., & McCollum, E. (2002). Obscured Variability: The Distinction Between Emotion Work and Emotional Labor. In N. M. Ashkanasy, W. J. Zerbe, & C. E. J. Härtel (Eds.), *Managing Emotions in the Workplace* (pp. 219–231). London: M.E. Sharpe.

Cantó-Milà, N. (2013). Gratitude: Invisibly Webbing Society Together. *Journal of Classical Sociology*, *13*(1), 8–19.

Cantwell, O. (2014, 25 April). Det stora kokainmålet är över. *Aftonbladet*.

Carlen, P. (1976). *Magistrates' Justice*. London: Martin Robertson & Company Ltd.

Church, T. W. (1985). Examining Local Legal Culture. *American Bar Foundation Research Journal*, *10*(3), 449–518.

Clark, C. (1987). Sympathy Biography and Sympathy Margin. *American Journal of Sociology*, *93*(2), 290–321.

Clark, C. (1990). Emotions and Micropolitics in Everyday Life: Some Patterns and Paradoxes of "Place". In T. D. Kemper (Ed.), *Research Agendas in the Sociology of Emotions* (pp. 305–334). Albany: State University of New York Press.

Clark, C. (1997). *Misery and Company*. Chicago, IL: The University of Chicago Press.

Clayman, S. (1992). Footing in the Achievement of Neutrality: The Case of News-Interview Discourse. In P. Drew & J. Heritage (Eds.), *Talk at Work: Interaction in Institutional Settings* (pp. 163–198). Cambridge: Cambridge University Press.

Coffey, A. (1999). *The Ethnographic Self: Fieldwork and the Representation of Identity*. London: Sage Publications.

Collings, J. A., & Murray, P. J. (1996). Predictors of Stress Amongst Social Workers: An Empirical Study. *British Journal of Social Work*, *26*(3), 375–387.

Collins, R. (2004). *Interaction Ritual Chains*. Princeton: Princeton University Press.

Collins, R. (2008). *Violence: A Micro-Sociological Theory*. Princeton: Princeton University Press.

Connor, J. (2007). *The Sociology of Loyalty*. New York: Springer.

Cooley, C. H. (1922). *Human Nature and the Social Order*. New York: Scribner.

Council, T. B. (2019). Your Career as a Barrister. Retrieved from https://www.barcouncil.org.uk/media/246249/your_career_as_a_barrister_pages.pdf

Coupland, C., Brown, A. D., Daniels, K., & Humphreys, M. (2008). Saying It with Feeling: Analysing Speakable Emotions. *Human Relations*, *6*(3), 327–353.

Court, C. o. t. (2017). Guide for Counsel in Cases to be Argued Before the Supreme Court of the United States.

Cowen, A. S., & Keltner, D. (2017). Self-Report Captures 27 Distinct Categories of Emotion Bridged by Continuous Gradients. *Proceedings of the National Academy of Sciences of the United States of America*, *114*(38), E7900–E7909.

Crawley, E. M. (2004). Emotion and Performance: Prison Officers and the Presentation of Self in Prisons. *Punishment & Society*, *6*(4), 411–427.

Cuff, B. M. P., Brown, S. J., Taylor, L., & Howat, D. J. (2016). Empathy: A Review of the Concept. *Emotion Review, 8*(2), 144–153.

Czarniawska, B. (1997). *Narrating the Organization: Dramas of Institutional Identity*. Chicago: The University of Chicago Press.

Dahl, J., Enemo, I., Drevland, G. C. B., Wessel, E., Eilertsen, D. E., & Magnussen, S. (2007). Displayed Emotions and Witness Credibility: A Comparison of Judgements by Individuals and Mock Juries. *Applied Cognitive Psychology, 21*(1), 1145–1155.

Dahlberg, L. (2008). A Modern Trial: A Study of the Use of Video-Recorded Testimonies in the Swedish Court of Appeal. In A. Sarat (Ed.), *Studies in Law, Politics and Society* (Vol. 61, pp. 81–135). London: Emerald Group Publishing.

Dahlberg, L. (2009). Emotional Tropes in the Courtroom: On Representation of Affect and Emotion in Legal Court Proceedings. *Nordic Theatre Studies, 21*, 129–152.

Dahlgren, T., Hemberg, C., Lundetag, A., Nord, C., & Pedersen, I. (2014). Kvinnor arbetar, män gör karriär. Retrieved from Stockholm https://static1.squarespace.com/static/5501a836e4b0472e6124f984/t/5bc4624f4785d3ab4d01d020/1539596884917/Kvinnor+arbetar+män+gör+karriär+2014.pdf

Damasio, A. R., Everitt, B. J., & Bishop, D. (1996). The Somatic Marker Hypothesis and the Possible Functions of the Prefrontal Cortex. *Philosophical Transactions: Biological Sciences, 351*(1346), 1413–1420.

Daun, Å. (1998). *Svensk mentalitet*. Stockholm: Rabén Prisma.

Davis, M. H. (1997). Empathy. In J. E. Stets & J. H. Turner (Eds.), *Handbook of the Sociology of Emotions* (pp. 443–466). New York: Springer.

Dehaghani, R., & Newman, D. (2017). "We're Vulnerable Too": An (Alternative) Analysis of Vulnerability within English Criminal Legal Aid. *Oñati Socio-Legal Series*, 7(6), 1199–1228.

Dellwing, M. (2012). Little Dramas of Discomposure: On Doing Face-Work with Disaligning Actions. *Symbolic Interaction, 35*(2), 146–161.

DePaulo, B. M., Lindsay, J. L., Malone, B. E., Muhlenbruck, L., Charlton, K., & Cooper, H. (2003). Cues to Deception. *Psychological Bulletin, 129*(1), 74–118.

Dershowitz, A. M. (1986). *Reversal of Fortune*. New York: Random House.

Diesen, C. (2005). *Likhet inför lagen*. Stockholm: Natur och Kultur.

Dingwall, R. (1997). Accounts, Interviews and Observations. In G. Miller & R. Dingwall (Eds.), *Context and Method in Qualitative Research* (pp. 52–65). London: SAGE Publications Ltd.

Domstolar, S. (2018). Hearing in the District Court. Retrieved from http://www.domstol.se/Funktioner/English/Legal-proceedings/Trials-in-criminal-cases/Hearing-in-the-District-Court/

Domstolar, S. (2019a). God domarsed – grundsatser och frågor. In Domstolsverket (Ed.). *God domarsed – grundsatser och frågor*. Jönköping; Sveriges Domareförbund (p. 10). Stockholm: Domstolsverket.

Domstolar, S. (2019b, December 28 2017). Om du behöver hjälp. Retrieved from http://www.domstol.se/Till-dig-som-ar/Brottsoffer/Om-du-behover-hjalp/

Domstolsverket. (2017). Årsredovisning 2017 Sveriges Domstolar. Retrieved from http://www.domstol.se/Publikationer/Arsredovisning/arsredovisning_2017_sverigesdomstolar.pdf

Durkheim, E. (1912/1995). *The Elementary Forms of Religious Life*. New York: The Free Press.

Ebervall, L. (2002). *Försvararens roll: Ideologier och gällande rätt*. Stockholm: Norstedts Juridik AB.

Ebervall, L. (2008). *Advokatetik i Brottmål: En handbok*. Stockholm: Thomson Förlag.

Eidenskog, J. (2019, 14 March). Nämndeman stängs av efter kommentar om Elin Ersson. Retrieved from https://www.svt.se/nyheter/lokalt/vast/namndeman-stangs-av-efter-kommentar-pa-natet

Ekman, P. (1992). *Telling Lies: Clues to Deceit in the Marketplace, Politics and Marriage*. New York: W. W. Norton.

Ekman, P. (2004). *Emotions Revealed: Understanding Faces and Feelings*. London: Phoenix.

Ekman, P., & Friesman, W. V. (1969). The Repertoire of Nonverbal Behavior: Categories, Origins, Usage, and Coding. *Semiotica, 1*(1), 49–98.

Ekot. (2018, 5 March). Centerpartiet utesluter två nämndemän. *Sveriges Radio*. Retrieved from https://sverigesradio.se/sida/artikel.aspx?programid=83&artikel=6899664

Emerson, J. (1970). Nothing Unusual Is Happening. In T. Shibutani (Ed.), *Human Nature and Collective Behavior: Papers in Honor of Herbert Blumer* (pp. 208–222). Englewood Cliffs, NJ: Prentice-Hall, Inc.

Emerson, R. M., Fretz, R. I., & Shaw, L. L. (2011). *Writing Ethnographic Fieldnotes* (2nd ed.). Chicago: The University of Chicago Press.

Emerson, R. M., & Pollner, M. (1975). Dirty Work Designations: Their Features and Consequences in Psychiatric Setting. *Social Problems, 23*(3), 243–254.

Epstein, C. F. (1970). *Woman's Place: Options and Limits in Professional Careers*. Los Angeles: University of California Press.

Epstein, C. F. (1981). *Women in Law*. New York: Basic Books, Inc.

Eriksson, M. (2016). *Berättelser om Breivik: Affektiva läsningar av våld och terrorism*. Göteborg: Makadam Förlag.

Europe, C. o. B. a. L. S. o. (1988). *Code of Conduct for European Lawyers*. Belgium: Council of Bars and Law Societies of Europe.

European Convention on Human Rights and Fundamental Freedoms. (1950). Article 2: Right to a fair trial. Strasbourg: Directorate of information.

Feigenson, N. R. (1997). Sympathy and Legal Judgement: A Psychological Analysis. *Tennessee Law Review, 65*(1), 1–78.

Feigenson, N. R. (2016). Jurors' Emotions and Judgements of Legal Responsibility and Blame: What Does the Experimental Research Tell Us? *Emotion Review, 8*(1), 26–31.

Fielding, N. (2006). *Courting Violence: Offences against the Person Cases in Court*. Oxford Scholarship Online.

Fielding, N. (2011). Judges and Their Work. *Social & Legal Studies, 20*(1), 97–115.

Fine, G. A. (1993). Ten Lies of Ethnography: Moral Dilemmas of Field Research. *Journal of Contemporary Ethnography, 22*(2), 267–294.

Fineman, S. (2006). Emotion and Organizing. In S. R. Clegg, C. Hardy, T. B. Lawrence, & W. R. Nord (Eds.), *The SAGE Handbook of Organization Studies* (pp. 675–700). London: SAGE Publications.

Flam, H. (1990a). Emotional "Man": I. The Emotional "Man" and the Problem of Collective Action. *International Sociology, 5*(1), 39–56.

Flam, H. (1990b). Emotional 'Man': II. Corporate Actors as Emotion-Motivated Emotion Managers. *International Sociology, 5*(2), 225–234.

Flam, H. (2000). *The Emotional "Man" and the Problem of Collective Action*. Frankfurt am Main: Lang.

Fletcher, G. (1995). *Loyalty: An Essay on The Morality of Relationships.* New York: Oxford University Press.

Fletcher, L., & Weinstein, H. (2003). When Students Lose Perspective: Clinical Supervision and the Management of Empathy. *Clinical Law Review, 9*, 135–156.

Flower, L. (2013). *Emotions and the Management of Emotions on a Law Degree Programme.* (Masters in sociology with social analytical focus), Gothenburg University, Gothenburg.

Flower, L. (2014). The (un)emotional Law Student. *International Journal of Work Organisation and Emotion, 6*(3), 295–309.

Flower, L. (2016a). Doing Loyalty: Defense Lawyers' Subtle Dramas in the Courtroom. *Journal of Contemporary Ethnography, 47*(2), 226–254. DOI: 10.1177/0891241616646826, 1–29.

Flower, L. (2016b). *Dramatic Subtlety: Exploring Anger and Strategic Niceness in the Courtroom.* Paper Presented at the Scandinavian Research Council for Criminology, Bifröst, Iceland.

Fowler, A., Phillips, J., & Westaby, C. (2019). Understanding Emotions as Effective Practice in English Probation: The Performance of Emotional Labour in Building Relationships. In P. Ugwudike, P. Raynor & J. Annison (Eds.), *Evidence-Based Skills in Community Justice: International Perspectives on Supporting Rehabilitation and Desistance* (pp. 243–262). Bristol: Policy Press.

Francis, L. (1997). Ideology and Interpersonal Emotion Management: Redefining Identity in Two Support Groups. *Social Psychological Quarterly, 60*(2), 163–171.

Freund, P. E. S. (1998). Social Performances and Their Discontents: The Biopsychosocial Aspects of Dramturgical Stress. In G. Bendelow & S. J. Williams (Eds.), *Emotions in Social Life: Critical Themes and Contemporary Issues* (pp. 268–294). London: Routledge.

Fried, C. (1976). The Lawyer as Friend: The Moral Foundations of the Lawyer-Client Relation. *Yale Law Journal, 85*(8), 1060–1089.

Friedman, L. M., & Hayden, G. M. (2017). *American Law: An Introduction.* New York: Oxford University Press.

Garfinkel, H. (1984). *Studies in Ethnomethodology.* Cambridge: Polity Press.

Gasser, R. L. (1963). The Confidence Game. *Federal Probation, 27*, 47–52.

Gathings, M. J., & Parrotta, K. (2013). The Use of Gendered Narratives in the Courtroom: Constructing an Identity Worthy of Leniency. *Journal of Contemporary Ethnography, 42*(6), 668–689.

Genty, P. M. (2000). Clients Don't Take Sabbaticals: The Indispensible In-House Clinic and The Teaching of Empathy. *Clinical Law Review,* 7(1), 273–286.

Gerarda Brown, J. (2012). New Directions in Negotiation and ADR: Deeply Contacting the Inner World of Another: Practicing Empathy in Values-Based Negotiation Role Plays. *Washington University Journal of Law and Policy, 39*(1), 189–230.

Gerhards, J. (1986). Georg Simmel's Contribution to a Theory of Emotion. *Social Science Information, 25*(4), 901–924.

Gieryn, T. F. (1983). Boundary-Work and the Demarcation of Science From Non-Science: Strains and Interests in Professional Ideologies of Scientists. *American Sociological Review, 48*(1), 781–795.

Goffman, E. (1952). On Cooling the Mark Out: Some Aspects of Adaptation to Failure. *Psychiatry: Interpersonal and Biological Processes, 15*(4), 451–463.

Goffman, E. (1956a). The Nature of Deference and Demeanor. *American Anthropologist, 58*(3), 473–502.

Goffman, E. (1956b). *The Presentation of Self in Everyday Life.* Edinburgh: University of Edinburgh Social Science Research Centre.

Goffman, E. (1957). Alienation from Interaction. *Human Relations, 10*(1), 47–60.

Goffman, E. (1959). *The Presentation of Self in Everyday Life*. Harmondsworth: Penguin Books Ltd.

Goffman, E. (1961a). *Asylums: Essays on the Social Situation of Mental Patients and Other Inmates*. Harmondsworth: Penguin.

Goffman, E. (1961b). *Encounters: Two Studies in the Sociology of Interaction*. Middlesex: Penguin University Books.

Goffman, E. (1963a). *Behavior in Public Places: Notes on the Social Organization of Gatherings*. New York: The Free Press.

Goffman, E. (1963b). *Stigma: Notes on the Management of Spoiled Identity*. Englewood Cliffs, NJ: Prentice-Hall Inc.

Goffman, E. (1967). *Interaction Ritual: Essays on Face-to-Face Behavior*. New York: Anchor Books.

Goffman, E. (1969). *Strategic Interaction*. Philadelphia: University of Pennsylvania Press.

Goffman, E. (1972). *Relations in Public: Microstudies of the Public Order*. Middlesex, England: Penguin Books.

Goffman, E. (1979). Footing. *Semiotica, 25*(1), 1–29.

Goffman, E. (1981). *Forms of Talk*. Oxford: Basil Blackwell Publisher.

Goffman, E. (1983). The Interaction Order: American Sociological Association, 1982 Presidential Address. *American Sociological Review, 48*(1), 1–17.

Goffman, E. (1986). *Frame Analysis: An Essay on the Organization of Experience*. New York: Harper & Row.

Gould, A. J. J. (2014). *What Makes an Interruption Disruptive? Understanding the Effects of Interruption Relevance and Timing on Performance*. (Doctor of Philosophy), University College London, London.

Graver, H. P. (2010). *Rett, retorikk og juridisk argumentasjon: Keiserens garderobe og andre essays*. Oslo: Universitetsförlag.

Greenfield, S., & Osborn, G. (1995). Where Cultures Collide: The Characterization of Law and Lawyers in Film. *International Journal of the Sociology of Law, 23*(2), 107–130.

Grodzins, M. (1956). *The Loyal and the Disloyal*. Chicago: The University of Chicago Press.

Haas, J., & Shaffir, W. (1982). Taking on the Role of Doctor: A Dramaturigcal Analysis of Professionalization. *Symbolic Interaction, 5*(2), 187–203.

Hägg, G. (2004). *Stora Retorikboken: Praktisk retorik och retorik idag*. Finland: WS Bookwell.

Haller, L. (2003). Dirty Linen: The Public Shaming of Lawyers. *International Journal of the Legal Profession, 10*(3), 281–313.

Harris, L. C. (2002). The Emotional Labour of Barristers: An Exploration of Emotional Labour by Status Professionals. *Journal of Management Studies, 39*, 553–584.

Harris, S. (2011a). Epilogue: Facework and im/Politeness Across Legal Contexts. *Journal of Politeness Research*, 7(1), 147–152.

Harris, S. (2011b). The Limits of Politeness Re-visited: Courtroom Discourse as a Case in Point. In L. P. R. Group (Ed.), *Discursive Approaches to Politeness* (pp. 85–108). Berlin: Mouton de Gruyter.

Hatfield, E., Cacioppo, J. T., & Rapson, R. L. (1993). Emotional Contagion. *Current Directions in Psychological Science, 2*(3), 96–100.

Heath, C. (1988). Embarrassment and Interactional Organization. In P. Drew & A. Wootton (Eds.), *Erving Goffman: Exploring the Interaction Order* (pp. 136–160). Oxford: Polity Press.

Henriksen, J.-O., & Vetlesen, A. J. (2013). *Etik i arbete med människor*. Lund: Studentlitteratur.

Hess, G. (2002). Heads and Heart: The Teaching and Learning Environment in Law School. *Journal of Legal Education, 52*(1/2), 75–111.

Heuman, L. (2013). *God Advokatsed: Rättsbildning och disciplinsnämndens motiveringar.* Stockholm: Jure AB.

Hillyard, S. (2010). Ethnography's Capacity to Contribute to the Cumulation of Theory: A Case Study of Strong's Work on Goffman. *Journal of Contemporary Ethnography, 39*(4), 421–440.

Hirschman, A. O. (1970). *Exit, Voice, and Loyalty: Reponses to Decline in Firms, Organizations, and States.* London: Harvard University Press.

Hobbs, P. (2003). "Is That What We're Here About?": A Lawyer's Use of Impression Management in a Closing Argument at Trial. *Discourse & Society, 14*(3), 273–290.

Hochschild, A. R. (1979). Emotion Work, Feeling Rules, and Social Structure. *American Journal of Sociology, 85*(3), 551–575.

Hochschild, A. R. (1983). *The Managed Heart: Commercialization of Human Feeling.* Berkeley: University of California Press.

Hochschild, A. R. (2003). *The Managed Heart: Commercialization of Human Feeling* (2nd ed.). Los Angeles: University of California Press.

Hochschild, A. R. (2013). *So How's The Family and Other Essays.* Los Angeles: University of California Press.

Hochschild, A. R. (2016). *Strangers in Their Own Land.* New York: The New Press.

Hodges, S. D., & Biswas-Diener, R. (2007). Balancing the Empathy Expense Account: Strategies for Regulating Empathic Response. In T. F. D. Farrow & P. W. R. Woodruff (Eds.), *Empathy in Mental Illness* (pp. 389–407). Cambridge: Cambridge University Press.

Hodges, S. D., & Wegner, D. M. (1997). Automatic and Controlled Empathy. In W. Ickes (Ed.), *Empathic Accuracy* (pp. 311–339). New York: Guilford Press.

Holstein, J. A. (1988). Court Ordered Incompetence: Conversational Organization in Involuntary Commitment Hearings. *Social Problems, 35*(4), 458–473.

Holstein, J. A. (1993). *Court-Ordered Insanity: Interpretive Practice and Involuntary Commitment.* New York: Aldine De Gruyter.

Hughes, E. C. (1962). Good People and Dirty Work. *Social Problems, 10*(1), 3–11.

Jacobson, J., Hunter, G., & Kirby, A. (2016). *Inside Crown Court: Personal Experiences and Questions of Legitimacy.* Bristol: Policy Press.

Jacobsson, K. (2008). "We Can't Just Do It Any Which Way": Objectivity Work among Swedish Prosecutors. *Qualitative Sociology Review, 4*(1), 46–68.

Jasper, J. M. (2011). Emotions and Social Movements: Twenty Years of Theory and Research. *Annual Review of Sociology, 37*(2), 285–303.

Justice, Department of (2018). United States Attorneys' Annual Statistical Report Fiscal Year 2017. Retrieved from https://www.justice.gov/usao/page/file/1081801/download

Justice, Ministry of (2012). Judicial and Court Statistics.

Justice, Ministry of (2019). Criminal Justice Statistics Quarterly, England and Wales, October 2017 to September 2018. Retrieved from https://assets.publishing.service.gov.uk/government/uploads/system/uploads/attachment_data/file/780612/criminal-justice-statistics-quarterly-september-2018.pdf

Kahneman, D. (1992). Reference Points, Anchors, Norms, and Mixed Feelings. *Organizational Behavior and Human Decision Processes, 51*(2), 296–312.

Karstedt, S. (2002). Emotions and Criminal Justice. *Theoretical Criminology, 6*(3), 299–317.

Karstedt, S., Loader, I., & Strang, H. (Eds.). (2011). *Emotions, Crime and Justice.* Oxford: Hart Publishing.

Katz, J. (1999). *How Emotions Work.* Chicago: The University of Chicago Press.

Kaufmann, G., Drevland, G. C. B., Wessel, E., Overskeid, G., & Magnussen, S. (2003). The Importance of Being Earnest: Displayed Emotions and Witness Credibility. *Applied Cognitive Psychology, 17*(1), 21–34.

Kay, F. M., & Gorman, E. H. (2008). Women in the Legal Profession. *Annual Review of Law and Social Science, 4*(1), 299–332.

Kemper, T. D. (1978). *A Social Interactional Theory of Emotions*. New York: John Wiley.

Kendon, A. (1967). Some Functions of Gaze-Direction in Social Interation. *Acta Psychologica, 26*(1), 22–63.

Kendon, A. (1990). *Conducting Interaction: Patterns of Behavior in Focused Encounters*. Cambridge: Cambridge University Press.

Kilduff, M., Chiaburu, D. S., & Menges, J. I. (2010). Strategic Use of Emotional Intelligence in Organizational Settings: Exploring the Dark Side. *Research in Organizational Behavior, 30*(1), 129–152.

Kinman, G., McFall, O., & Rodriguez, J. (2011). The Cost of Caring? Emotional Labour, Wellbeing and the Clergy. *Pastoral Psychology, 60*(5), 671–680.

Kirchhoff, J. W., & Karlsson, J. C. (2009). Rationales for Breaking Management Rules: The Case of Health Care Workers. *Journal of Workplace Rights, 14*(4), 457–479.

Kleinman, S., & Copp, M. A. (1993). *Emotions and Fieldwork*. Newbury Park: SAGE Publications.

Knight, C., & Phillips, J. (2016). Bringing the Feelings Back: Retuning Emotions to Criminal Justice Practice. *British Journal of Community Justice, 14*(1), 45–58.

Korczynski, M. (2003). Communities of Coping: Collective Emotional Labour in Service Work. *Organization, 10*(1), 55–79.

Krill, P., Johnson, R., & Albert, L. (2016). The Prevalence of Substance Use and Other Mental Health Concerns Among American Attorneys. *Journal of Addiction Medicine, 10*(1), 46–52.

Kristjánsson, K. (2003). On the Very Idea of "Negative Emotions". *Journal for the Theory of Social Behaviour, 33*(4), 351–364.

Lakoff, R. (1990). *Talking Power: The Politics of Language in Our Lives*. New York: Basic.

Lange, B. (2002). The Emotional Dimension of Legal Regulation. *Journal of Law and Society, 29*(1), 197–225.

Larsen, J. T., McGraw, A. P., Mellers, B. A., & Cacioppo, J. T. (2004). The Agony of Victory and Thrill of Defeat: Mixed Emotional Reactions to Disappointing Wins and Relieving Losses. *Psychological Science, 15*(3), 325–330.

Laster, K., & O'Malley, P. (1996). Sensitive New-Age Laws: The Reassertion of Emotionality in Law. *International Journal of the Sociology of Law, 24*(1), 21–40.

Lee, J. (2009). Escaping Embarrassment: Facework in the Rap Cipher. *Social Psychological Quarterly, 72*(4), 306–324.

Lehrberg, B. (2014). *Praktiskt juridisk metod*. Uppsala: Iusté Aktiebolag.

Leidner, R. (1993). *Fast Food, Fast Talk: Service Work and the Routinization of Everyday Life*. Los Angeles, CA: University of California Press.

Lerner, J. S., Goldberg, J. H., & Tetlock, P. E. (1998). Sober Second Thought: The Effects of Accountability, Anger, and Authoritarianism on Attributions of Responsibility. *Personality and Social Psychology Bulletin, 24*(6), 563–574.

Lerner, J. S., & Tiedens, L. Z. (2006). Portrait of the Angry Decision Maker: How Appraisal Tendencies Shape Anger's Influence on Cognition. *Journal of Behavioral Decision Making, 19*(2), 115–137.

LeVan, E. A. (1984). Nonverbal Communication in the Courtroom: Attorney Beware. *Law and Psychology Review, 8*(83), 83–104.

Levenson, L. L. (2007). Courtroom Demeanor: The Theater of the Courtroom. *Los Angeles Law School Legal Studies Paper, 30*, 1–56.

Levin, A. P., Albert, L., Besser, A., Smith, D., Zelenski, A., & Rosenkranz, S. (2011). Secondary Traumatic Stress in Attorneys and Their Administrative Support Staff Working with Trauma-Exposed Clients. *Journal of Nervous and Mental Disease, 199*(12), 946–955.

Lief, H. I., & Fox, R. C. (1963). *Training for 'Detached Concern' in Medical Students*. London: Harper & Row.

Lind, E. A., Thibaut, J., & Walker, L. (1973). Discovery and Presentation of Evidence in Adversary and Nonadversary Proceedings. *Michigan Law Review, 71*(6), 1129–1144.

Lindström, E., & Malmberg, T. (2010). *Inställda huvudförhandlingar i brottmål* (Vol. 7). Stockholm: Riksrevisionen.

Lippestad, G. (2013). *Det vi kan stå för*. Nørhaven: Pocketförlaget.

Lipsky, M. (1980). *Street Level Bureaucracy: Dilemmas of the Individual in Public Services*. New York: Russell Sage Foundation.

Litvak, P. M., Lerner, J. S., Tiedens, L. Z., & Shonk, K. (2010). Fuel in the Fire: How Anger Impacts Judgement and Decision-Making. In M. Potegal, G. Stemmler, & C. Spielburger (Eds.), *International Handbook of Anger: Constituent and Concomitant Biological, Psychological, and Social Processes* (pp. 287–310). New York: Springer.

Lively, K. J. (2000). Reciprocal Emotion Management: Working Together to Maintain Stratification in Private Law Firms. *Work and Occupations, 27*(1), 32–63.

Lively, K. J. (2002). Client Contact and Emotional Labor: Upsetting the Balance and Evening the Field. *Work and Occupations, 29*(5), 198–225.

Lively, K. J., & Weed, E. A. (2014). Emotion Management: Sociological Insight into What, How, Why, and to What End? *Emotion Review, 6*(3), 202–207.

Lloyd, C., King, R., & Chenoweth, L. (2002). Social Work, Stress and Burnout: A Review. *Journal of Mental Health, 11*(3), 255–265.

Lundgren, K. (2016). *Landet Lagom och Framtiden*. Stockholm: Diagolos Förlag.

Lundquist, L. (1988). *Byråkratisk etik*. Lund: Studentlitteratur.

Macdonald, K. M. (1999). *The Sociology of the Professions*. London: SAGE Publications.

Machura, S., & Ulbrich, S. (2001). Law in Film: Globalizing the Hollywood Courtroom Drama. *Journal of Law and Society, 28*(1), 117–132.

Manning, P. K. (2001). Semiotics, Semantics and Ethnography. In P. Atkinson, A. Coffey, S. Delamont, J. Lofland, & L. Lofland (Eds.), *Handbook of Ethnography* (pp. 145–159). London: Sage.

Maroney, T. A. (2006). Law and Emotion: A Proposed Taxonomy of an Emerging Field. *Law and Human Behavior, 30*(2), 119–142.

Maroney, T. A. (2011a). Emotional Regulation and Judicial Behavior. *California Law Review, 99*(6), 1485–1555.

Maroney, T. A. (2011b). The Persistent Cultural Script of Judicial Dispassion. *California Law Review, 99*, 629–681.

Maroney, T. A. (2012). Angry Judges. *Vanderbilt Law Review, 65*(5), 1207–1286.

Maroney, T. A. (2015). A Field Evolves: Introduction to the Special Section on Law and Emotion. *Emotion Review, 8*(1), 3–7. DOI: 10.1177/1754073915601356, 1–5.

Maroney, T. A. (2016). The Emotionally Intelligent Judge: A New (and Realistic) Ideal. *Revista Forumul Judecatorilor, 61*(1), 61–83.

Maroney, T. A., & Gross, J. T. (2014). The Ideal of the Dispassionate Judge: An Emotion Regulation Perspective. *Emotion Review*, *6*(2), 142–151.

Maslach, C., Schaufeli, W. B., & Leiter, M. P. (2001). Job Burnout. *Annual Review of Psychology*, *52*, 397–422.

Mather, L., & McEwen, C. A. (2001). *Divorce Lawyers at Work: Varieties of Professionalism in Practice*. Oxford: Oxford University Press.

Mattsson, E. (2014). *Rättens iscensättning: Rum, framträdanden, gränser* (Doctoratal Dissertation in Theatre Studies), Stockholm University, Stockholm.

May, A. (2005). Advocates and Truth-Seeking in the Old Bailey Courtroom. *Journal of Legal History*, *26*(1), 71–77.

McBarnet, D. (1981). Magistrates' Courts and the Ideology of Justice. *British Journal of Law and Society*, *8*(2), 181–197.

McChrystal, M. K. (1992). Lawyers and Loyalty. *William and Mary Law Review*, *33*(1), 367–427.

McConville, M., Hodgson, J., Bridges, L., & Pavlovic, A. (1994). *Standing Accused*. Clarendon: Oxford Unviersity Press.

McCormack, K. (2014). Ethos, Pathos, and Logos: The Benefits of Aristotelian Rhetoric in the Courtroom. *Washington University Jurisprudence Review*, 7(1), 131–155.

McEwan, J. (2011). From Adversarialism to Managerialism: Criminal Justice in Transition. *Legal Studies*, *31*(4), 519–546.

McKinlay, A., & Dunnett, A. (1998). How Gun Owners Accomplish Being Deadly Average. In C. Antaki & S. Widdicombe (Eds.), *Identities in Talk* (pp. 34–51). London: Sage.

McMahon, W. C. (2006). Declining Professionalism in Court: A Comparative Look at the English Barrister. *Georgetown Journal of Legal Ethics*, *19*, 845–858.

McQueen, R. (1999). Of Wigs and Gowns: A Short History of Legal and Judicial Dress in Australia. *Law in Context: A Socio-Legal Journal*, *16*(1), 1–16.

Mead, H. (1934). *Mind, Self, and Society from the Standpoint of a Social Behaviorist*. Chicago: Chicago University Press.

Mellqvist, M. (1994). First Impression Last – Om sakframställning. In M. Mellqvist & M. Persson (Eds.), *Retorik och rätt: sett genom tio författares ögon* (pp. 226–241). Uppsala: Iustus Förlag AB.

Menkel-Meadow, C. (1985). Portia in a Different Voice: Speculations on a Women's Lawyering Process. *Berkeley Women's Law Journal*, *1*(1), 39–63.

Menkel-Meadow, C. (1987). The Comparative Sociology of Women Lawyers: The "Feminization" of the Legal Profession. *Institute for Social Science Research*, *3*(4), 1–19.

Merton, R. K. (1968). *Social Theory and Social Structure*. New York: The Free Press of Glencoe.

Miller, W. I. (1997). *The Anatomy of Disgust*. Cambridge: Harvard University Press.

Misztal, B. (2001). Normality and Trust in Goffman's Theory of Interaction Order. *Sociological Theory*, *19*(1), 312–324.

Morris, J. A., & Feldman, D. C. (1996). The Dimensions, Antecedents and Consequences of Emotional Labor. *Academy of Management Review*, *21*(4), 986–1010.

Munukka, J. (2007). *Kontraktuell lojalitetsplikt*. Stockholm: Jure.

Murphy, P. W. (2002). "There's No Business Like....?" Some Thoughts on the Ethics of Acting in the Courtroom. *Texas Law Review*, *44*(1), 111–125.

Musial, K. (1998). *Tracing Roots of the Scandinavian Model. Image of Progress in the Era of Modernisation* (Vol. 17). Berlin: European University Institute.

Neu, J. (2000). *A Tear Is an Intellectual Thing: The Meanings of Emotion*. Oxford: Oxford University Press.

Newman, D. (2012). Still Standing Accused: Addressing the Gap between Work and Talk in Firms of Criminal Defence Lawyers. *International Journal of the Legal Profession, 19*(1), 3–27.

Newman, D., & Ugwudike, P. (2013). Defence Lawyers and Probation Officers: Offenders' Allies or Adversaries? *International Journal of the Legal Profession, 20*(2), 183–207.

Niven, K. (2015). Why do People Engage in Interpersonal Emotion Regulation at Work? *Organizational Psychology Review, 1*(1), 1–19.

Nordén, E. (2015). Utvecklingen av personuppklarade misstankar och bifallna åtal 2004–2014. Retrieved from Stockholm: www.bra.se/kortanalys

North, D. (1990). *Institutions, Institutional Change and Economic Performance*. Cambridge: Cambridge University Press.

Nussbaum, M. C. (2004). *Hiding from Humanity: Disgust, Shame, and the Law*. Princeton: Princeton University Press.

Nussbaum, M. C., & Kahan, D. M. (1996). Two Conceptions of Emotion in Criminal Law. *Columbia Law Review, 96*(2), 269–374.

O'Keefe, D. J. (1990). *Persuasion: Theory and Research*. Newbury Park: Sage.

Ogletree, C. J. (1993). Beyond Justifications: Seeking Motivations to Sustain Public Defenders. *Harvard Law Review, 106*(6), 1239–1294.

Ojasalo, J. (2001). Managing Customer Expectations in Professional Services. *Managing Service Quality: An International Journal, 11*(3), 200–212.

Olsson, T. (2017). Praktisk juridik. *Advokaten, 1*, 54.

Orzechowicz, D. (2008). Privileged Emotion Managers: The Case of Actors. *Social Psychological Quarterly, 71*(2), 143–156.

Öster, U. (2012). Åklagarna har förbrukat allt förtroende. *Advokaten, 78*(8), 6.

Österberg, E. (1989). Bönder och centralmakt – konflikt, kompromiss och politisk kultur. *Scandia, 55*(1), 73–95.

Oxford. (Ed.) (2015). *Oxford Dictionary of English*. Oxford University Press.

Palmgren, S. (2018). Nämndeman sov under rättegång – får hållas på nytt. *Göteborgs-Posten*. Retrieved from https://www.gp.se/nyheter/göteborg/nämndeman-sov-under-rättegång-får-hållas-på-nytt-1.8057380

Park, R. C. (2003). Adversarial Influences on the Interrogation of Trial Witnesses. In P. J. van Koppen & S. D. Penrod (Eds.), *Adversarial versus Inquisitorial Justice: Psychological Perspectives on Criminal Justice Systems* (pp. 131–166). New York: Kluwer Academic.

Parsons, T. (1954). *Essays in Sociological Theory: Revised Edition*. Glencoe: The Free Press.

Penman, R. (1990). Facework & Politeness: Multiple Goals in Courtroom Discourse. *Journal of Language and Social Psychology, 9*(12), 15–38.

Persson, L. G. W. (2009, 21 June). Stjärnadvokater glänser sällan, Chronicle. *Expressen*. Retrieved from https://www.expressen.se/kronikorer/leif-gw-persson/leif-gw-persson-stjarnadvokater-glanser-sallan/

Persson, A. (2012). Front- and Backstage in Social Media. *Language, Disourse & Society, 1*(2), 11–31.

Persson, J. (2018). Sådan är dagens advokat. *Advokaten, 1*(84), 24–26.

Petrie, K. J., Booth, R. J., & Baumeister, R. F. (1998). The Immunological Effects of Thought Suppression. *Personality Processes and Individual Differences, 75*(5), 1264–1272.

Pierce, J. L. (1995). *Gender Trials*. Berkeley: University of California Press.

Pizzi, W. T. (1999). *Trials Without Truth: Why Our System of Criminal Trials Has Become an Expensive Failure and What We Need to Do to Rebuild It*. New York: New York University Press.

Plutchik, R. (2001). The Nature of Emotions: Human Emotions Have Deep Evolutionary Roots, a Fact That May Explain Their Complexity and Provide Tools for Clinical Practice. *American Scientist*, *89*(4), 344–350.

Pogrebin, M. R., & Poole, E. D. (1991). Police and Tragic Events: The Management of Emotions. *Journal of Criminal Justice*, *19*(4), 395–403.

Pollack, E. (2001). *En Studie i Medier och Brott*. Stockholm: Stockholms Universitet.

Porter, S., & ten Brink, L. (2009). Dangerous Decisions: A Theoretical Framework for Understanding How Judges Assess Credibility in the Courtroom. *Legal and Criminal Psychology*, *14*(1), 119–134.

Potter, J. (1996). *Representing Reality: Discourse, Rhetoric and Social Construction*. London: SAGE Publications Ltd.

Rapley, T. (2011). Interviews. In C. Seale, G. Gobo, J. F. Gubrium, & D. Silverman (Eds.), *Qualitative Research Practices* (pp. 16–32). London: SAGE Publications Ltd.

Reddy, W. M. (2001). *The Navigation of Feeling: A Framework for the History of Emotions*. Cambridge: Cambridge University Press.

Reddy, W. M. (2010). The History of Emotions: An Interview with William Reddy, Barbara Rosenwein, and Peter Stearns by Jan Plamper. *History and Theory*, *49*(21), 237–265.

Rennstam, J., & Wästerfors, D. (2015). *Från Stoff Till Studie: Om Analysarbete i Kvalitativ Forskning*. Lund: Studentlitteratur.

Rhode, D. L. (2003). Gender and the Profession: An American Perspective. In U. Schultz & G. Shaw (Eds.), *Women in the World's Legal Professions* (pp. 3–22). Oxford: Hart Publishing.

Riessman, C. K. (1993). *Narrative Analysis*. London: SAGE Publications Ltd.

Roach Anleu, S., & Mack, K. (2005). Magistrates' Everyday Work and Emotional Labour. *Journal of Law and Society*, *32*, 590–614.

Roach Anleu, S., & Mack, K. (2017). *Performing Judicial Authority in the Lower Courts*. London: Palgrave.

Roach Anleu, S., Rottman, D., & Mack, K. (2016). The Emotional Dimension of Judging. *Court Review*, *52*, 60–71.

Robinson, J. D. (2006). Nonverbal Communication and Physician-Patient Interaction: Review and New Directions. In M. Manusov & M. L. Patterson (Eds.), *The SAGE Handbook of Nonverbal Communication* (pp. 437–460). London: Sage Publications.

Robinson, L., & Schulz, J. (2009). New Avenues for Sociological Enquiry: Evolving Forms of Ethnographic Practice. *Sociology*, *43*(4), 685–698.

Rock, P. (1993). *The Social World of an English Crown Court*. Oxford: Oxford University Press.

Rogers, L. J., & Erez, E. (1999). The Contextuality of Objectivity in Sentencing Among Legal Professionals in South Australia. *International Journal of the Sociology of Law*, *27*, 267–286.

Rosa, H. (2013). *Social Acceleration: A New Theory of Modernity*. New York: Columbia University Press.

Rose, D. (2016). Death Row: The Lawyer Who Keeps Losing. *The Guardian*. Retrieved from https://www.theguardian.com/world/2016/nov/24/death-row-the-lawyer-who-keeps-losing

Rose, M. R., Seidman Diamond, S., & Baker, K. M. (2010). Goffman on the Jury: Real Jurors' Attention to the "Offstage" of Trials. *Law and Human Behavior, 34*(4), 310–323.

Rosenwein, B. (2002). Worrying about Emotions in History. *American Historical Review, 107*(3), 821–845.

Rosenwein, B. (2010) *The History of Emotions: An Interview with William Reddy, Barbara Rosenwein, and Peter Stearns/Interviewer: J. Plamper.* (Vol 49), Wesleyan University, History and Theory.

Rosenwein, B. (2015). *Generations of Feeling: A History of Emotions, 600–1700.* Cambridge: Cambridge University Press.

Rossing, H., & Scott, S. (2014). Familiar Strangers: Facework Strategies in Pursuit of Non-Binding Relationships in a Workplace Exercise Group. In N. Denizen (Ed.), *Revisiting Symbolic Interaction in Music Studies and New Interpretive Works* (pp. 161–183). Online: Emerald Insight.

Rossner, M., Tait, D., McKimmie, B., & Sarre, R. (2017). The Dock on Trial: Courtroom Design and the Presumption of Innocence. *Journal of Law and Society, 44*(3), 317–344.

Royce, J. (1995/1908). *The Philosophy of Loyalty.* London: Vanderbilt University Press.

Ruiz-Junco, N. (2017). Advancing the Sociology of Empathy: A Proposal. *Symbolic Interaction, 40*(3), 414–435.

Rypi, A. (2017). "You Don't Have to Say Straight Out...": Directed Impression Management at Victim-Offender Mediation Pre-meetings. *Sociological Focus, 30*(3), 261–276.

Sacks, H., Schegloff, E. A., & Jefferson, G. (1974). A Simplest Systematics for the Organization of Turn-Taking for Conversation. *Lanugage, 50*(4), 696–735.

Sandemose, A. (1934/1968). *En flykting korsar sitt spår.* Uddevalla: Bohusläningens AB.

Sangborn, J. (2016). *Regler för advokatsverksamhet* (3 ed.). Ödeshög: Sveriges Advokatsamfund.

Sarat, A. (1999). Remorse, Responsibility, and Criminal Punishment: An Analysis of Popular Culture. In S. Bandes (Ed.), *The Passions of Law* (pp. 168–190). New York: New York University Press.

Sarat, A., & Felstiner, W. L. F. (1986). Law and Strategy in the Divorce Lawyer's Office. *Law & Social Review, 20*(1), 93–134.

Scarduzio, J. A., & Tracy, S. J. (2015). Sensegiving and Sensebreaking via Emotion Cycles and Emotional Buffering: How Collective Communication Creates Order in the Courtroom. *Management Communication Quarterly, 29*(3), 1–28.

SCB. (2017). Statistics Sweden. Retrieved from http://www.scb.se/be0001-en

Scheff, T. J. (2000). Shame and the Social Bond: A Sociological Theory. *Sociological Theory, 18*(1), 84–99.

Scheffer, T. (2010). *Adversarial Case-Making: An Ethnography of English Crown Court Procedure.* Leiden: Brill.

Schudson, M. (1984). Embarrassment and Erving Goffman's Idea of Human Nature. *Theory and Society, 13*, 633–648.

Schuster, M. L., & Propen, A. D. (2011). *Victim Advocacy in the Courtroom: Persuasive Practices in Domestic Violence and Child Protection Cases.* Boston: Northeastern University Press.

Schütz, A. (1971). The Stranger: An Essay in Social Psychology. *American Journal of Sociology, 49*(6), 499–507.

Schweingruber, D., & Berns, N. (2005). Shaping the Selves of Young Salespeople Through Emotion Management. *Journal of Contemporary Ethnography, 34*(6), 679–706.

Scott, M. B., & Lyman, S. M. (1968). Accounts. *American Sociological Review, 33*(1), 46–42.

Scott, M. B., & Lyman, S. M. (1970). *The Revolt of the Students*. Columbus, OH: Charles E. Merrill Publishing Company.

Scott, S. (2015). *Negotiating Identity: Symbolic Interactionist Approaches to Social Identity*. Cambridge: Polity Press.

Scott, S. (2017). A Sociology of Nothing: Understanding the Unmarked. *Sociology, 52*(1), 3-19.

Scott, S. (forthcoming). Politeness as Collective Facework: The Case of Swedish Jante Law. *Studies in Symbolic Interaction* (in press).

Sennett, R. (1998). *The Corrosion of Character: The Personal Consequences of Work in the New Capitalism*. New York: W. W. Norton.

SFS. (1942:740). *Rättegångsbalken*. Stockholm: Swedish Ministry of Justice.

Shapiro, S. P. (2003). If It Ain't Broke...An Empirical Perspective on Ethics 2000, Screening, and the Conflict-of-Interest Rules. *University of Illinois Law Review, 1*(5), 1299–1330.

Shilling, C. (2002). The Two Traditions in the Sociology of Emotions. In J. Barbalet (Ed.), *Emotions and Sociology* (pp. 10–32). Oxford: Blackwell Publishing.

Shilling, C. (2003). *The Body and Social Theory* (2 ed.). Nottingham: Sage Publications.

Shuy, R. (2005). *Creating Language Crimes: How Law Enforcement Uses (and Misuses) Language*. Oxford: Oxford University Press.

Sieben, B., & Wettergren, Å. (2010). Emotionalizing Organizations and Organizing Emotions: Our Research Agenda. In B. Sieben & Å. Wettergren (Eds.), *Emotionalizing Organizations and Organizing Emotions* (pp. 1–10). Basingstoke: Palgrave Macmillan.

Siemens, C. (2004). *Emotional Trials: Moral Dilemmas of Women Criminal Defense Attorneys*. Boston: Northwestern University Press.

Silbersky, L. (2014, 19 December) *Sanningen om Leif Silbersky/Interviewer: J. Wackerberg*. The Scholar.

Silbersky, L. (2018) *Leif Silbersky om varför han inte tar sig an narkotikafall*. Brottscentralen, Expressen TV.

Silverman, D. (2013). *A Very Short, Fairly Interesting and Reasonably Cheap Book about Qualitative Research* (2nd ed.). Los Angeles: Sage.

Simmel, G. (1908/2009). *Sociology: Inquiries into the Construction of Social Forms*. Boston: Brill.

Simmel, G. (1921). Sociology of the Senses: Visual Interaction. In R. E. Park (Ed.), *Introduction of the Science of Sociology* (pp. 356–375). Chicago, IL: The University of Chicago Press.

Simmel, G. (1950). *The Sociology of Georg Simmel* (W. Kurt, Trans.). New York: Glencoe.

Simmel, G. (1957). Fashion. *The American Journal of Sociology, 62*(6), 541–558.

Simon, D., & Yaras, D. (2000). *Lagom svenskt*. Stockholm: Bilda Förlag.

Singer, T., Seymour, B., O'Doherty, J., Dolan, R. J., & Frith, C. D. (2004). Empathy for Pain Involves Affective but Not Sensory Components of Pain. *Science, 303*(5661), 1157–1162.

Smith, T. (2013). The "Quiet Revolution" in Criminal Defence: How the Zealous Advocate Slipped into the Shadow. *International Journal of the Legal Profession, 20*(1), 111–137.

Smith, A. C., & Kleinman, S. (1989). Managing Emotions in Medical School: Student's Contacts with the Living and the Dead. *Social Psychological Quarterly, 52*(1), 56–69.

Snow, D., & Anderson, L. (1987). Identity Work Among Homeless: The Verbal Construction and Avowal of Personal Identities. *American Journal of Sociology, 92*(6), 1336–1372.

Sobota, K. (1994). Logos, Ethos, Pathos: A Quantitative Analysis on Arguments and Emotions in Law. In M. Mellqvist & M. Persson (Eds.), *Retorik och Rätt: sett genom tio författares ögon* (pp. 210–225). Uppsala: Iustus Förlag AB.

Solomon, R. C. (1990). *A Passion for Justice: Emotions and the Origins of the Social Contract.* New York: Addison-Wesley Publishing Company, Inc.

Solomon, R. C. (1997a). In Defense of the Emotions (and Passions too). *Journal for the Theory of Social Behaviour, 27*(4), 489–497.

Solomon, R. C. (1997b). The Moral Psychology of Business: Care and Compassion in the Corporation. *Business Ethics Quarterly, 8*(3), 515–533.

Solomon, R. C. (1999). Justice v. Vengeance: On Law and the Satisfaction of Emotion. In S. Bandes (Ed.), *The Passions of Law* (pp. 121–148). New York: New York University Press.

Solomon, R. C. (2004). Aristotle, Ethics and Business. *Organization Studies, 25*(6), 1021–1043.

Somech, A., & Bogler, R. (1999). Tacit Knowledge in Academia: Its Effects on Students Learning and Achievement. *The Journal of Psychology, 133*(6), 605–616.

Sommerlad, H., Webley, L., Duff, L., Muzio, D., & Tomlinson, J. (2010). *Diversity in the Legal Profession in England and Wales: A Qualitative Study of Barriers and Individual Choices.* London: University of Westminster.

Spencer, J. R. (2016). Adversarial vs Inquisitorial Systems: Is There Still Such a Difference? *The International Journal of Human Rights, 20*(5), 601–616.

Spencer, A., & Podmore, D. (1986). In a Man's World: Essays on Women in Male-Dominated Professions. *Communication Theory, 15*(2), 168–195.

Stacey, C. L. (2011). *The Caring Self: The Work Experiences of Home Care Aides.* Ithaca: Cornell University Press.

Staske, S. A. (1996). Talking Feelings: The Collaborative Construction of Emotion in Talk Between Close Relational Partners. *Symbolic Interaction, 19*(2), 111–135.

States, Constitution of the United States. (1791). *Amendment VI.*

Statistics, Australian Bureau of Statistics. (2019). Criminal Courts, Australia 2017–2018. Retrieved from http://www.abs.gov.au/ausstats/abs@.nsf/mf/4513.0

Stearns, P. N. (1994). *American Cool: Constructing a Twentieth-Century Emotional Style.* New York: New York University Press.

Stearns, P. N., & Stearns, C. Z. (1985). Emotionology: Clarifying the History of Emotions and Emotional Standards. *The American Historical Review, 90*(4), 813–836.

Stenross, B., & Kleinman, S. (1989). The Highs and Lows of Emotional Labor. *Journal of Contemporary Ethnography, 17*(4), 435–452.

Strong, P. M. (1988). Minor Courtesies and Macro Structures. In P. Drew & A. Wooton (Eds.), *Erving Goffman: Exploring the Interaction Order* (pp. 228–249). Cambridge: Polity.

Strong, P. M. (2001). *The Ceremonial Order of the Clinic: Parents, Doctors and Medical Bureaucracies.* Aldershot: Ashgate.

Sutton, R. I. (1991). Maintaining Norms about Expressed Emotions: The Case of Bill Collectors. *Administrative Science Quarterly, 36*(2), 245–258.

Tata, C. (2007). Sentencing as Craftwork and the Binary of Epistemologist of the Discretionary Decision Service. *Social & Legal Studies, 16*(3), 425–448.

Tata, C. (2010). A Sense of Justice: The Role of Pre-Sentence Reports in the Production (and disruption) of Guilt and Guilty Pleas. *Punishment & Society, 12*(3), 239–261.

Team, G. D. R. (2006). A World of Lies. *Journal of Cross-Cultural Psychology, 37*(1), 60–74.

Tenhouten, W. D. (1996). Introduction: Sociology of Emotions. *International Journal of Sociology and Social Policy, 16*(9/10), 1–20.

Thelin, K. (2001). *Sverige som rättsstat.* Stockholm: AB Timbro.

Thoits, P. A. (1989). The Sociology of Emotions. *Annual Review of Sociology, 15*, 317–342.

Thoits, P. A. (1996). Managing the Emotions of Others. *Symbolic Interaction, 19*(2), 85–109.

Thomas, G. M. (2014). Cooling the Mother Out: Revisiting and Revising Goffman's Account. *Symbolic Interaction, 37*(2), 283–299.

Törnqvist, N. (2017). *Att göra rätt: En studie om professionell respektabilitet, emotioner och narrativa linjer bland relationsvåldsspecialiserade åklagare.* (Doctoral Dissertation in Criminology), Stockholm University, Stockholm. (38).

Tracy, K. (2011). A Facework System of Minimal Politeness: Oral Argument in Appellate Court. *Journal of Politeness Research, 7*(1), 123–145.

Tracy, K., & Tracy, S. J. (1998). Rudeness at 911: Reconceptualizing Face Attack. *Journal of Politeness Research, 4*(2), 169–191.

Tracy, S. J. (2000). Becoming a Character for Commerce. *Management Communication Quarterly, 14*(1), 90–128.

Travers, M. (1997). *The Reality of Law: Work and Talk in a Firm of Criminal Lawyers.* Aldershot: Ashgate.

Turner, J. H. (2009). The Sociology of Emotions: Basic Theoretical Arguments. *Emotion Review, 1*(4), 340–354.

Turrow, S. (1987). Crossing the Star. *Litigation: Journal of the Section of Litigation, American Bar Association, 14*(1), 40–42.

Tyler, T. R. (1988). What Is Procedural Justice?: Criteria used by Citizens to Assess the Fairness of Legal Procedures. *Law & Society Review, 22*(1), 103–136.

Tyler, T. R. (2003). Procedural Justice, Legitimacy, and the Effective Rule of Law. *Crime and Justice, 30*(1), 283–357.

Tyler, T. R. (2006). *Why People Obey the Law.* Princeton: Princeton University Press.

van Koppen, P. J., & Penrod, S. D. (2003). Adversarial or Inquisitorial: Comparing Systems. In P. J. van Koppen & S. D. Penrod (Eds.), *Adversarial versus Inquisitorial Justice: Psychological Perspectives on Criminal Justice Systems* (pp. 1–20). New York: Kluwer Academic.

Van Stokkom, B. (2011). Dealing with Defiant Citizens: Building Emotional Intelligence into Police Work. In S. Karstedt, I. Loader, & H. Strang (Eds.), *Emotions, Crime and Justice.* Oxford: Hart Publishing.

Vince, R. (2006). Being Taken Over: Managers' Emotions and Rationalizations During a Company Takeover. *Journal of Management Studies, 43*(2), 343–364.

Vinge, K. A. (1944). *Om God Advokatsed.* Malmö: Nya Litografen.

Vrij, A. (1995). Behavioral Correlates of Deception in a Simulated Police Interview. *Journal of Psychology: Interdisciplinary and Applied, 129*(1), 15–29.

Wägeus, A. (2014). *Advokaters rådgivningsansvar – Särskilt om lojalitet och omsorg.* (Masters), Stockholm University, Stockholm.

Wagner, I., & Wodak, R. (2006). Performing Success: Identifying Strategies of Self-Presentation in Women's Biographical Narratives. *Discourse & Society, 10*, 385–411.

Wahlberg, S. (2012). "Stinkbomb", säger advokaten – "Rökgranat", kontrar åklagaren efter konflikt om hemligt material. ["Stink bomb" says the lawyer – "Smoke granade", counters the prosecutor after conflict on secret material]. *Dagens Juridik.*

Wahlberg, S. (2017). "Oförklarade" löneskillnader bland jurister – kvinnor tjänar 3 300 kronor mindre än män. *Dagens Juridik.*

Waldron, V. R. (2000). Relational Experiences and Emotion at Work. In S. Fineman (Ed.), *Emotion in Organizations* (pp. 64–82). London: SAGE Publications.

Weber, M. (1946). Politics as a Vocation. In C. Wright Mills & H. Gerth (Eds.), *From Max Weber: Essays in Sociology* (pp. 77–128). New York: Oxford University Press.

Weber, M. (1978). *Economy and Society: An Outline of Interpretive Sociology*. Berkeley: University of California Press.

Welzel, C. (2016). World Values Survey. Retrieved from http://www.worldvaluessurvey.org/wvs.jsp

Wenne, L. (1988). *God Advokatsed*. Stockholm: Norstedts Förlag.

Wessel, E., Drevland, G., Eilertsen, D., & Magnussen, S. (2006). Credibility of the Emotional Witness: At Study of Ratings by Court Judges. *Law and Human Behaviour, 30*, 221–230.

Westaby, C. (2010). "Feeling Like a Sponge": The Emotional Labour Produced by Solicitors in Their Interactions with Clients Seeking Asylum. *International Journal of the Legal Profession, 17*(2), 153–174.

Westaby, C., & Jones, E. (2017). Empathy: An Essential Element of Legal Practice or 'Never the Twain Shall Meet'? *International Journal of the Legal Profession, 25*(1): 107–124.

Westlund, O., & Eriksson, A. (2013). *Bemötande i domstol*. Stockholm: Brottsförebyggande rådet.

Wettergren, Å. (2009). Fun and Laughter: Culture Jamming and the Emotional Regime of Late Capitalism. *Social Movement Studies, 8*(1), 1–15.

Wettergren, Å. (2010). Managing Unlawful Feelings: The Emotional Regime of the Swedish Migration Board. *International Journal of Work Organisation and Emotions 3*(4), 400–419.

Wettergren, Å., & Bergman Blix, S. (2016). Empathy and Objectivity in the Legal Procedure: The Case of Swedish Prosecutors. *Journal of Scandinavian Studies in Criminology and Crime Prevention, 17*(1), 19–35.

Wettre, K. (2012, 5 October). Tingsrätten tar om hela Södertäljemålet efter jäv. Retrieved from https://sverigesradio.se/sida/artikel.aspx?programid=83&artikel=5297553

Wharton, A., & Erickson, R. J. (1993). Managing Emotions on the Job and at Home: Understanding the Consequences of Multiple Emotional Roles. *Academy of Management Review, 18*(3), 457–486.

Wiklund, H. (1973). *God Advokatsed*. Stockholm: P.A. Norstedt & Söners Förlag.

Williams, R. (2000). *Making Identity Matter*. Durham: Sociology Press.

Wolfe, J. S. (1994). The Effect of Location in the Courtroom on Jury Perception of Lawyer Performance. *Pepperdine Law Review, 21*(3), 731–776.

Wolfram, C. W. (1986). *Modern Legal Ethics: Practitioners Edition*. Minnesota: St. Paul.

Wong, C. (2012). *Sweden* (Vol. 1). London: Hart Publishing.

Wouters, C. (1989). The Sociology of Emotions and Flight Attendants: Hochschild's Managed Heart. *Theory, Culture and Society, 6*(1), 95–123.

Wright Mills, C. (1940). Situated Actions and Vocabularies of Motive. *American Sociological Review, 5*(6), 904–913.

Wright Mills, C. (1951). *White Collar*. London: Oxford University Press.

Zembylas, M. (2004). Emotion Metaphors and Emotional Labor in Science Teaching. *Science Education, 88*(3), 301–324.

Index